The Cradle of Culture
and What Children Know About Writing and Numbers Before Being Taught

Liliana Tolchinsky
University of Barcelona

Psychology Press
Taylor & Francis Group

New York London

Reprinted 2009 by Psychology Press

Library of Congress Cataloging-in-Publication Data

Tolchinsky Landsmann, Liliana
The cradle of culture and what children know about writing and numbers
before being taught / Liliana Tolchinsky.
     p. cm.
   Includes bibliographical references and index.
ISBN 0-8058-3843-0 (cloth : alk. Paper) — ISBN 0-8058-4484-8
(cloth : alk. Paper)
1. Children—Writing. 2. Child development. 3. Literacy. 4. Numeracy. I. Title.

LB1139.W7 T65   2003
302.2´244—dc21
                                        2002073214
                                           CIP

10 9 8 7 6 5 4 3 2

The Developing Mind Series

Series Editor
Philip David Zelazo
University of Toronto

Co-Editors
Dare Baldwin, *University of Oregon*
David F. Bjorklund, *Florida Atlantic University*
Judy DeLoache, *University of Virginia*
Lynn Liben, *Pennsylvania State University*
Yuko Munakata, *University of Colorado, Boulder*

The Developing Mind Series brings you readable, integrative essays on fundamental topics in cognitive development—topics with broad implications for psychology and beyond. Written by leading researchers, these essays are intended to be both indispensable to experts and relevant to a wide range of students and scholars.

The Cradle of Culture
and What Children Know About Writing and Numbers Before Being Taught

Contents

Preface

Our personal history begins with the episodes that remain etched in our memories. Similarly, the history of social communities begins with the records and traces of their deeds and beliefs. This book is about the two main recording systems in our culture: written language and numerals. I approach these two notational systems from diverse perspectives, including historical, semiotic, and psychological perspectives, but I do so with one aim: to demonstrate that children raised in a literate community have their own path to writing and numerals and that this path is worthwhile for psychologists, teachers, and parents to understand.

The view of development that constitutes my conceptual framework is deeply rooted in constructivist epistemological principles that stem from the work of Jean Piaget. Piagetian conceptions have been severely undermined by both sociocultural and nativist paradigms—the former arguing for identifying development with social internalization, and the latter arguing for hard-wired, built-in knowledge. In my view, however, Piagetian concepts still provide the most constructive, consistent, and deep view of human development.

I depart, however, from the classical Piagetian paradigm by stressing the importance of specific symbolic systems for development. My claim is that the particular features of writing and of written numeration play an important role in the learning process. I attempt to show that the acquisition of writing and numerals is characterized by a constant interaction between children's implicit knowledge and the particular formal features of the two systems. That is why learning notational systems is not just a matter of acquiring a new instrument for communicating existing knowledge; it involves cognitive change within a particular domain. The acquisition of a writing system transforms children's view of language, just as the acquisition of a written numeration system transforms children's understanding of the number domain. It is in this sense that I insist throughout the book that notational systems are not only communicative tools that serve to convey a particular content, but also epistemic tools (i.e., *objects-to-think-with*). Consequently, it is essential for developmental psychologists and teachers to understand the properties of each system.

A reflection on the particular characteristics of the object of knowledge—writing and numerals—must include a reflection on their social history. I am strongly convinced that the social history of a particular cultural artifact throws light on the development of the individual. A look at notational systems from a historical perspective helps us to understand that their features are not obvious, but took centuries to be attained. We should not be surprised then if children take some years to grasp their meaning.

Certainly, literacy and numeracy intermingle with schooling, with different forms of social organization, and with access to other goods besides notational systems. So, the effects of literacy can hardly be isolated from other sociocultural variables—they are always one facet of more general social engagement. It was with this reasoning in mind that I included in this book some of the work done on the consequences of learning to write. I address the purported changes on the perception and conceptualization of language and discuss the personal history of certain individuals for whom literacy has had far reaching consequences. Yet, I also felt it necessary to address other cases in which literacy failed to produce any cognitive change. This is only to demonstrate how complex and multifaceted the kind of object we are dealing with is.

My approach to literacy and numeracy is deeply rooted in the seminal work of Emilia Ferreiro, in whose initial research team I participated as a student a long time ago in Buenos Aires, Argentina. I must confess that, having discovered many years later what a research team is at different Universities around the world, I feel embarrassed to use the same denomination for that one. We were a group of students without any kind of financial support rushing to every school that allowed us to interview their pupils. We were fascinated by the possibilities of trying the clinical method and by the answers we got from preschoolers and first graders when we asked them to read and to write. At that time, teaching literacy was banned from preschool, and formal instruction started in first grade, word-by-word in a piecemeal fashion. None of the answers we received then from our young subjects appeared in any book on linguistic or cognitive development. Indeed, the idea of asking preschoolers and first graders to read and write so that we could learn about their concepts of writing was completely revolutionary at that time. Later on, I discovered that 50 years before

Ferreiro, Luria, and Vygotsky had done something very similar, although with a different aim and interpretation. At that time, however, I was unaware of their research.

After moving to Israel, I was able to explore whether the child's path to writing is language- and script-specific or whether it involves universal steps in its acquisition. To this end, I had the privilege to be guided by Iris Levin from Tel Aviv University. Many of the thoughts developed in this book are owed directly to her and to the stimulating discussions at the Unit for the Study of Human Development and Education. A postdoctoral Spencer fellowship helped me greatly to pursue my research in early literacy once I moved to the University of Barcelona.

Central to the main ideas of the book and its core epistemological and psychological tenets is the work of Annette Karmiloff-Smith. Annette provided a more comprehensive and detailed psychological framework for approaching and understanding not just the development of writing, but the whole domain of notational development. Annette also, in her Hampstead kitchen, asked the crucial question that placed me at my computer most weekends during the last 3 years: "Why don't you write a book about all this?"

Many people contributed to this task. Some produced illuminating works on the many facets of writing and writing systems. I am thinking here about the work of Giorgio Cardona, Armando Petrucci, and Colette Sirart. Others rethought the role of literacy in history, including Jack Goody, Eric Havelock, and Marshall McLuhan, and still others opposed their views, including Brian Street and Mary Carruthers. I was also very much influenced by the work of French thinkers such as Jean Hébrard, Anne Marie, and Roger Chartier, who have an incredible capacity to reveal the unconventional facets of the historical development of reading and writing deeply supported by their careful research. Others whose works have strongly influenced my view on historical, developmental, and semiotic issues are present in my citations, although that is probably not a complete list. I hope they will forgive me if sometimes I refrain from repetitive citations as a service to the reader.

Additionally, many friends and colleagues from near and far have influenced my views, including Maria Cristina Martinez, Jorge Ajurianea, Tulio Graciani, Ana Teberosky, Ana Maria Kaufman, Rosa Simo, Lucia Rego, Maria Eva Donato, and Neuss Roca. I also would particularly like to acknowledge my collaborative work in recent years with Ruth Berman and Dorit Ravid, who have greatly influenced my views on literacy and language. I had the privilege to participate in an International Research Project on Developing Literacy coordinated by Ruth Berman and funded by the Spencer Foundation, which provided the most stimulating environment for rethinking my previous work on literacy.

So many thanks to Sven Stromqvist, Harrier Jisa, Judy Reilly, and Ludo Verhoeven.

A number of people helped enormously by critically reading succesive drafts of parts of this volume: Ruth Berman, Rosa Gil, Jana Selzer, Ana Sandbank, and Eva Teubal. Special thanks go to Xesca Grau and Myriam Nemirosky, who were generous enough to share with me materials from their classes and research, and to Noemi Argerich who helped me with bibliographic searches. I also would like to thank Kang Lee and Mark Aronoff, who read the entire manuscript, and provided constructive suggestions, pointed out inconsistencies, and raised deep questions. Particular thanks go to Philip Zelazo, the Series Editor who combed every line for wording, spelling, and conceptual precision with infinite patience and wisdom. And many thanks to Katty Kiss—without her dedicated and clever reading this book would have been simply unreadable. Finally, thanks above all to Eduardo, my life companion, who supported this work from beginning to end in any possible sense.

A note on transcriptions, links to glossary, dating, and gender: Written forms have been transcribed using uppercase letters and oral forms using lowercase italics. In transcribing how children wrote Coca-Cola I have used COCA COLA, whereas their reading of it is rendered as *coca cola*. The same rendering is used for quoting verbal utterances. Whenever words are in a language other than English I have used the original language and translated into English using simple quotation marks. Thus, when children wrote TE and read *te* I have added 'tea.'

Technical and specific words are defined in the Glossary. An asterisk is used to indicate the first use of a word that is included in the Glossary. For dating historical events I have followed the lead taken by Geoffrey Sampson (1985), who noted: "… I was struck with a difficulty that must have occurred to other authors of works which range over many millennia, namely the inadequacy of the expressions 'AD' and 'BC.' A phrase such as 'the 5th century AD' makes no sense, and it is odd to call the thousand years preceding Christ's birth the first millennium before Christ when it was the last such millennium. Furthermore, the constant reference of events to the birth of Christ is often provincial, for instance in the context of ancient China, and may even offend some readers' religious sensibilities when Hebrew is under discussion … I therefore follow the lead of Joseph Needham and use plus and minus signs in the normal mathematical way, omitting the plus sign where no confusion is possible" (p. 24).

Concerning the explicit use of gender when no specific person is involved, whenever possible I use plural forms, otherwise I have decided to act randomly. If I imagined the subject I was writing about to be male I used "he," if female, I used "she." I trust my unconscious has not betrayed an inequitable treatment of gender.

Introduction

What Children Know and We Have Already Forgotten About Writing and Numerals

A persistent myth about literacy and numeracy among educators, parents, and researchers alike is that to know anything about written language and numerals, children must be instructed. In the pages that follow, I try to persuade you that this assumption is wrong, that children develop a great deal of knowledge about writing and numerals before they are formally taught to read or do math. I also attempt to convince those investigating human development and those in charge of teaching that they will gain a lot from acknowledging the evolving knowledge presented in this book.

Long ago, developmental psychologists discovered that children have wonderful ideas on subjects as diverse as where dreams come from, why bricks fall down but balloons fly, or what the differences are between worms and rubber bands, despite their apparent similarity. This is a book about children's ideas on writing and numerals. Some of their ideas appear highly inventive, but they are indeed right. For example, if you give a 4-year-old a set of three cards, TTTT, BOOK, TABLE, and ask him to separate those cards that can be read from those that cannot, he will set aside the card containing four repeated letters TTTT and will probably say that *it cannot be read; it always says the same thing.*

But, if you ask the same child to separate cards containing numerals, rather than letters, you will find that he is not so quick to reject a card containing four repeated numerals 4444. He will readily accept that they are *good for counting*. He is right because however much repetition a string of numerals shows (for example, 31416666666666666 …), any combination of numerals is both acceptable and meaningful. However, when it comes to letters, not every combination is acceptable or meaningful. Some strings of letters are acceptable but have no meaning (for example, "dag" and "doog"), others are neither acceptable nor meaningful (for example, "dgd," "ddd," "aaa," and "aei"), whereas only some are both acceptable and meaningful (for example, "dog" and "dig").

Sometimes, however, children's ideas are wrong. Following the example just discussed, if we add to the set of cards shown to the same 4-year-old two cards containing single letters R and S, he also will set aside the cards containing single letters and reject each one as good for reading because *it is too little to say anything*. The assumption that a single letter cannot be read because *it is too little to say anything* is wrong, but nonetheless useful.

Look back over the previous sentences and you will realize that, in each case, the shortest words (*a, it, is, in*) can be predicted from the context, whereas the longest words are those that provide the content and the context (*ideas, letter, anything, right*). The longest words are those that are indispensable for getting the message across and, at the same time, the most difficult to predict. Therefore, if you focus your reading efforts on the longest words, you also will most likely understand the shortest by a process of inference.

As subtle as these distinctions are, they seem to be grasped before the age of 5 years, that is, before children know how to read or write or have the slightest notion of the specific quantities that are represented by the numerals. Throughout the book, I hope to make sense of children's ideas so as to determine which of them are on the right track, which are mistaken but necessary steps in the learning process, and which are simply erroneous.

The examples just quoted were extracted from empirical studies examining toddlers' and preschoolers' ideas about writing and numerals. These studies show that even children of such a tender age have a sort of internal rudder, compass, or steering device that guides them when dealing with writing and numerals, even before they have acquired the knowledge of how to use writing to represent messages or numerals to represent quantities. Moreover, they treat each of the two systems as distinct from each other. That is, children's evolving knowledge about these two notational systems is domain-specific.

At the simplest level, acting in a domain-specific manner means that we attribute certain *properties* to one domain but not to the other, we know that certain *activities* can be performed in one domain but not in the other, and certain

operations can be carried out in one but not the other. Let's say we act in a domain-specific manner with the aforementioned worm and rubber band. If so, a
worm might be treated as belonging to the domain of living things and the rubber band to the domain of inanimate objects. Therefore, we will attribute to the
worm the property of self-propelled movement and the property of dying, but
will not attribute those properties to the rubber band. We may love or hate the
worm and decide to feed it, but not the rubber band, and we may decide to
stretch the rubber band, but not the worm. In so doing, we are sensitive to the
particular constraints of each domain and we act in a domain-specific manner.
We live pervaded by all sorts of visual and auditory signals, such as faces, lights,
music, pictures, speech, road signs, and noises. They usually occur simultaneously in time and space. Without the capability to differentiate among them
and to react accordingly, we would be constantly confused.

When I mentioned earlier that children treat writing and numerals as two
distinct domains, I meant that they attribute to each different *properties*, and
think they are used for different *activities*, and to perform different *operations*. So
far, I have not specified which properties, activities, and operations, but I am
sure that the reader already has begun to realize the many things we can say
about a numeral that we cannot say about written text, or the many things we
do with letters but not with numerals and vice versa. There are, however, many
things that we can do with both writing and with numerals, or indeterminately
with each. I need, therefore, to clarify the concept of the domain and in what
sense writing and numerals are both similar and distinct.

DEFINING A DOMAIN OF KNOWLEDGE

Writing is a rather ambiguous term in English. Originally, it was a term designating
the process of scoring or tracing an outline on a surface of some kind. The same
term is used not only as a verb describing the process, but also for designating the
outlined traces, the *products*. Indeed, the same process gives rise to many different
kinds of products, including signatures, hallmarks, scores, maps, graphs, writing,
and drawings. Anthropologists and philosophers are greatly challenged when
asked to explain the differences between these products and to define the functions they fulfill; I return to this point in chapter 1. Here, I jump directly to some
conclusions so as to explain in what sense writing and numerals constitute specific domains of knowledge, and to clarify the terminology being used.

I suggest considering a domain as an environment containing entities (objects or people) and norms defining their use, like a territory in which a number
of rules define certain activities. I will leave to one side, for the moment, the debate as to whether this environment is internal or external to the mind or

whether its boundaries are completely closed. However, we should not lose track of the metaphor of an environment (or a territory) when trying to understand the extent to which writing and numerals are specific domains.

When we enter the territory of writing based on an alphabetic system, we have to use a definite set of entities or graphic objects (e.g., letters, blank spaces, dots). If, for any reason, I decide to create new objects or to introduce entities from a different territory, I must justify to the territory's other inhabitants the reasons for my so doing. With time, the new objects or entities may cease to be recognized as outsiders. These days, for example, we accept the use of "&" or "@" in writing linguistic messages, or the use of letters in writing mathematical messages. However, when they were first introduced, they required justification and their use gave rise to doubts.

The use of a limited set of entities is obligatory for ensuring the transport and reproduction of the original message. This limited and distinctive set of graphic entities used to record states, statements, and processes in such a way that they can be transported and reproduced by different people at different times and in different spaces is called a *notation*. The two main notations in our culture are the alphabet and the Hindu-Arabic numerals, yet the systems of punctuation marks and musical scores are also notations. Each notational system has a prototypical function. Letters are primarily used for writing linguistic messages, although they can be used for representing order on shelves or variables in algebra. Something similar occurs with numerals. Although numerals are not used solely for representing quantities, we usually relate numerals to quantity. Therefore, as an initial indication of domain specificity, it can be seen that writing and numerals use different notations, are used to perform different activities, and are governed by different norms.

Okay, you may argue, so they are two specific notational instruments or notational tools, but why insist on their constituting domains of knowledge? Is it not more reasonable to say that it is the content or functions to which these notational forms refer (i.e., language and numbers) that are the domains of knowledge, and not the forms used in referring to them? Many psychologists adopt this line of reasoning, viewing writing and numerals as *heuristics* (e.g., Gelman, 1998), tools, or instruments. In this view, language and numbers are the domains of knowledge, whereas writing and numerals are simply tools used to represent these domains.

This line of argument frequently adopts a *derivative* view of the relation between the notational forms and the domain of knowledge. A derivative view posits that knowledge of the domain of reference is what enables the child to learn how to use the notational tools. This view suggests, for example, that children first acquire spoken language and then map this knowledge onto the writing tool. If the writing tool is alphabetic writing, in which letters roughly correspond to sounds, then it is argued that children must be aware of the sound structure of the words in order to be able to map this knowledge onto the corresponding letters.

The same holds for the relation between numbers and numerals. A derivative view holds that a child's understanding of the notion of number paves her way for the notational system of numerals. Some psychologists think that it may be even "deleterious" to promote the use of notations until children have mastered the notion of numbers and the additive structure of number systems (e.g., Kamii & De Clark, 1985). These psychologists think that children first need to learn about a particular domain, independently of the graphic instantiation of that particular domain, and then they will easily apply this knowledge when it comes time to learn how the notational system functions. At that time, what children must learn is how to map their knowledge of language onto the representational features of writing and their knowledge of numbers onto the representational features of numerals.

This, however, is not the view that permeates this book. The relation of writing to language and numerals to numbers is not conceived of as derivative. Indeed, my fourth goal is to demonstrate that notational systems are not only communicative tools that serve to convey a particular content, but they are also *epistemic tools*. In line with many others (Clark, 1997; Lee & Karmiloff-Smith, 1997; Olson, 1994; Vygotsky, 1986), I consider notations to be *objects-to-think-with*, not just graphic instantiations or the tools for representing a domain. In this view, some features of notational systems overlap with some of the features of the domain in which they are used, but add certain features of their own. More than just tools for solving problems in a particular domain, they introduce other problems. Learning a notation is not simply a matter of mapping existing knowledge onto a new representational medium; rather, there is a *constant* interaction between the features of the notational system and the entities, processes, and rules of the corresponding domain of knowledge. As a result, learning a notation is not just a matter of acquiring a new instrument or communicating existing knowledge; it involves cognitive change within both the domain of the notational system and the domain that this notational system represents. Thus, the acquisition of a writing system transforms children's view of language, just as the acquisition of a written numeration system transforms children's understanding of the number domain. I claim that there is a "boomerang effect" between a person's capacities and the properties of notations. Individuals approach notations with their own ideas about the properties and functioning of notations but these properties, in turn, have a transforming effect on the individual's initial ideas. Indeed, I argue that this is the key process in the formation of notational knowledge.

Let me illustrate this point of view by offering a few examples:

Some 7-year-olds are successful in tasks believed to evaluate their concept of numbers (e.g., conservation tasks) and yet they have problems with the positional value of the written system of numerals. When faced with numbers constituted by the same numerals but in different positions (e.g., 64 and 46), they say that both are worth the same "because they have the same numbers" (Scheuer, 1996). Having some operational notion of number does not help them to solve this problem; they have to learn the special ways in which the notational system represents units of different levels.

Some 5-year-olds have no concept of the value of large quantities. They do not know how much 2061 is, or whether it is more or less than 2031. Yet, when they are shown a series of four numerals (2600, 2601, 2602, 2603) and are asked *to write the next number in the series*, they find a way of doing so correctly. They are able to make sense of numerical written information, despite their lack of knowledge regarding the quantities. Children's understanding of quantitative concepts, such as counting and addition, is not necessarily predictive of their ability to record or decode numerical information (Wolf & Gardner, 1983).

Italian-speaking preschoolers refuse to write sentences such as "Birds are not flying" when they stand under pictures displaying flying birds (Pontecorvo & Rossi, 2001). They explain that because the birds are flying (in the picture), it is hard to write that they are not flying. The same children had no problem, however, writing "Birds are flying." In general, preschoolers find it difficult to write statements that are seen by them as false or impossible ("Cats are flying").

Spanish-speaking and Hebrew-speaking first graders find it difficult to say a word "in little bits" (Tolchinsky & Teberosky, 1997). After listening to a word and being presented with various examples, preliterate children were unable to say the sounds in a word, for example, for the word *radio*, one by one: r/a/d/i/o. Of greater interest, perhaps, is that even those children who do know how to spell the words correctly find this task difficult. Many among them tend to say the names of the letters rather than pronouncing the individual sounds that compose the word. Both when writing and when pronouncing the sounds in the words, they use the letters to handle the sounds rather than the sounds to handle the letters.

Illiterate adults are also incapable of separating the sounds in a word. Nevertheless, once they have learned to write in an alphabetic system, they are able to do so without any trouble (Bertelson, Cary, & Alegria, 1986). I believe that this is a strong evidence in favor of the effect of the notational system, in this case the alphabetic system of writing, on the perception of language.

These examples demonstrate three aspects of the relation between notations and domains of reference:

1. There are certain characteristics of the tools that are difficult to learn from the domain of reference alone. Rather, each system generates new

problems, problems that were not present in the domain of reference. The meaning of position is a problem in written numerals, not in the concept of numbers; the separate representation of sounds is a problem in spelling, not in speaking.

2. There are certain characteristics in the domain of reference that are not directly applicable to the tools. The truth-value of linguistic expressions, such as, "cats are flying," is not represented in writing, despite children's assumptions to the contrary.

3. There are certain characteristics of the tools that facilitate learning in the domain of reference. Literate people know more about spoken language than illiterate people; people who have learned to use numerals know more about numbers than do people who have not. What we know about a certain domain may be expanded and even changed as a function of the kinds of "symbolic experiences" that we have had in that particular domain (Gelman, 1998).

Up to this point in the discussion, I have focused on the potential differences between writing and numerals because my purpose was to argue in favor of a domain-specific position. There is no doubt, however, that written language and numerals share a fundamental property—both are external representations. Indeed, all the products of the process of writing are *external representations*.

External representations are a very special kind of object. They are not substances such as water or paper, although they occupy space, occur in time, and have particular shapes and sometimes color. Neither are they mental states, although we can think about drawings, letters, and numerals. Nor do they constitute procedures, although we use motor procedures to draw both letters and numerals. Unlike things that are what they are, such as a stone, external notations are *of* something, or *about* something. These special objects impose their own character on what is represented. The same message can look very different when put into a picture, a map, or writing. In some cases, we will not even recognize the same message.

Within the wide territory of external representations then, writing and numerals are sort of subdomains because they make use of a notation (i.e., the alphabet and the Hindu-Arabic system of numeration). Every notational system is an external representation but not every external representation is notational. The inclusive relation between these constructs is shown in Fig. I.1.

The outer circle represents the domain of external representations, the middle circle the domain of notational systems, and the inner circle the domains of writing and numerals. The overlapping section between writing and numerals represents the properties they share because they are means of external representation that use a notation. These shared properties are analyzed in chapter 1.

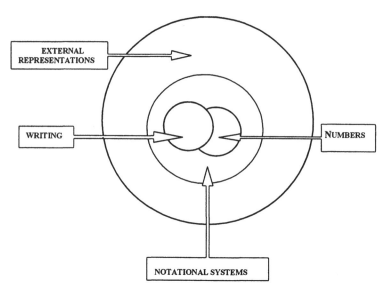

FIG. I.1. Types of external representations.

The nonoverlapping section represents the features that distinguish these two notational systems. They will be analyzed in chapters 4 and 5.

The entities in the domain of external representation are the various pictorial and scriptorial devices—drawings, pictures, schemata, photographs, models, musical scores, writing systems, numerical systems, graphs, charts, mathematical notations, road signs, computer icons—that we have created and continue to create. These devices have many features in common, as they are all external representations. Yet, at the same time, each has its own unique features. One function of these devices is to serve as communicative tools, but they also serve as aesthetic, magical, prestigious, and epistemic tools. They are epistemic tools in two related senses. On the one hand they enable more efficient thinking for handling our thoughts. On the other hand, our cognitive functioning is "in large part shaped and changed by the representational artifacts we ourselves create" (Wartofsky, 1979, cited in Wells, 1999). Furthermore, because work on our own thoughts is one of the sources of cognitive change, external representations are tools for cognitive change.

Although I have framed writing and numerals in the more general domain of external representations, my focus in this book is on the course of development toward alphabetic writing and the written system of numeration. Of course, writing texts entails much more than commanding the alphabetic system, and doing mathematics entails much more than gaining full command of the written system of numerals. Nonetheless, both processes are essential components.

Learning the writing system is just one fiber in the thread of pragmatic and grammatical knowledge that children have to master in order to become competent writers, but it is imperative, and it fosters the others. The same is true for mathematical knowledge. Mastering the written system of numeration is just one fiber in the thread of mathematical knowledge that children must learn. However, it is imperative and the others are also fostered.[1]

A DEVELOPMENTAL DOMAIN-SPECIFIC PERSPECTIVE ON WRITING AND NUMERALS

The crucial question at this point is, do children learn to act in a domain-specific manner once they are literate or numerate, or do they initiate the learning process with domain-specific "hypotheses"? (I have placed the term between single quotes to indicate that I am using it with an approximate meaning). In general terms (and here I am referring not only to notational knowledge), the question is whether domain specificity is an outcome of experience or whether it is a device to guide experience. Going back to our initial example, do we discover that worms and rubber bands are from different domains as a result of observing movement, feeding, stretching, or our feelings of hate or love toward one but not the other? Or do we somehow *know* that they belong to different domains and consequently act differently with each?

Research in infancy has shown that even newborn babies make domain-specific distinctions about the world. Babies who were once described as undifferentiated from their environments and invaded by chaotic information, lacking even the capacity to recognize that what they hold and what they see are the same thing, are now thought to make categorical language–sound discriminations, and distinguish between their mother tongue and other languages, and between faces and other patterns. That is, there are indications that we arrive in the world with a propensity to make sense of our environment, or at least with a natural sensitivity to certain environmental distinctions.

Yet, human faces, animals, and language are natural objects. A newborn's sensitivity to the features that distinguish one of these objects from another is surprising, but it is relatively understandable that natural objects become the object of a baby's cognitive curiosity from a very early age. Even those who be-

---

[1]The strength of this "weaving" metaphor, based on Wittgenstein's (1953/1958) metaphor of the notion of number, lies in the fact that it highlights the constant interaction between conceptual, procedural, and symbolic/notational components. The strength of a thread "does not reside in the fact that some one fiber runs through its whole length, but in the overlapping of many fibers" (Miller, 1996, p. 217). This interpretation is a far cry from that which relates notational knowledge as being derived from the notions constructed in a particular domain.

lieve that children learn everything from their environment, that they are not born with any kind of knowledge, will likely accept the idea that babies are born with a biologically grounded curiosity and the potential to understand living things and even language.

Here, however, I am suggesting that this natural propensity also can apply to such cultural objects as writing and numerals, the functioning of which is strictly conventional. Human beings create these representational objects, but only the "cultural pool … contains the information which defines what these object are, tells us how to construct these objects, and prescribes how the objects are to be used. Without culture, we would not have or use such things" (D'Andrade, 1981, p. 180).

The fact is that we live most of our lives in a culturally manufactured environment. Therefore, if exposure to and interaction with objects in the environment play a role in learning, there is no reason why babies should gaze at and explore only faces and dogs, when they are also surrounded by a proliferation of advertisements, calendars, clocks, labels, posters, and road signs. Cultural information impregnates our daily life even before birth, and therefore there is no reason why children should behave as active specialized learners only of the natural environment and not also of the information contained in the cultural pool.

Thus, the main purpose of this book is to show that writing and numerals, two very old cultural objects with a long social history, also have a developmental history that is domain specific. The existence of this *developmental* history can only be imagined if we believe that children are constructive learners who do not limit themselves to absorbing instruction. Rather, they are personally involved in using their own previously acquired knowledge in constant interaction with the information provided by the environment. This information is never directly absorbed, but transformed through this previous knowledge. This is why the developmental history does not overlap the history of the teaching method and may take a different path from those methods traditionally used in teaching children to read or do math. This is precisely the reason that educators should know about this developmental history. Let's call this a pragmatic reason.

A weak version of the pragmatic reason is quite straightforward. If teachers know how and what their pupils understand, they will be in a better position to teach them. A stronger version of this pragmatic basis, however, suggests that the strength of the pupils' conceptions is such that it is better to take these concepts into account because they are liable to impede any process of learning ("if you can't fight them, join them"). Children's ideas on a particular topic might be stronger than teaching efforts, so it is advisable to take their point of view into account if we want them to progress. None of this is particularly new.

So, where does the novelty of my claims lie? One of the most influential scholars in developmental psychology and pedagogy was the Swiss genetic epistemologist* Jean Piaget (1896–1978). After many years under the influence of the Piagetian paradigm, we are already well convinced that children are active and constructive learners. The novelty of my claims lies in the proposal to extend this constructivist stance to the domain of conventional notational systems, and in positing a domain-specific process of construction for writing and numbers.

A CONSTRUCTIVIST PERSPECTIVE ON WRITING AND NUMERALS

Piaget never studied the developmental course of writing or number notation. Yet, from his general position on representation and representational tools, it is possible to infer how he would have related to this topic. Besides, as a genetic epistemologist, his aim was to determine how people acquire knowledge in general. Therefore, his ideas serve to help us understand and to explain acquisition processes in any domain of knowledge. One of the core Piagetian ideas holds that, to incorporate information, even of a conventional kind, children must make that information their own through reorganization and reconstruction processes. Children gain knowledge not only from their environment and from genetic specifications, but also from their work on their own representations. Thus, he claimed that any theory of knowledge should include a theory of the development of that particular knowledge. Such a view does not put learning and development into opposition; instead, it defends the belief that constructive learning takes place even in domains that are taught at school.

The history of these constructive processes constitutes the developmental history of that information. Therefore, the developmental history of writing would be the history of the transformations children perform on the information culturally transmitted to them. This idea is at the heart of my approach to literacy and numeracy. Similar to some others (e.g., H. Sinclair, 1988), I am applying one of the main epistemological assumptions made by Piaget (Beilin, 1985) to notational systems.

Yet, by claiming a domain-specific developmental path to writing and numerals, I am departing from two central tenets of Piagetian thought. First, I am departing from the idea that figurative knowledge is subordinated to operative knowledge and does not promote cognitive change. Second, I am departing from the idea that there is a common developmental course to every external representation.

Piaget distinguishes two aspects of knowledge—the operational and the figurative. To distinguish between these two aspects of knowledge, I shall use the well-known conservation task. In this experimental task, children are shown two rows of marbles with six marbles in each set, for example. First, the children are asked to verify whether the number of marbles is the same in each row. Some children will do this by putting one marble in front of the other and verifying that there is a marble to marble correspondence; some others will do it by counting. After that, the marbles in one of the rows are spaced out more widely so that the row is now longer. The children are questioned again as to whether the number of marbles in the two rows remains the same.

According to Piaget, only when the child is able to perform a number of *mental* actions can he understand that nothing has been added or subtracted, and that if the rows were the same before, they are still the same (and, therefore, the number of marbles in each row remains the same). What the child sees in the experimental task is a series of states. Initially, he sees the two rows of marbles in front of him, then the movements performed by the experimenter when changing the placement of the marbles and, finally, the two rows with the marbles placed further apart from one another. The *figurative aspect of knowledge* provides the mental image of each of these states. However, it is the *operative aspect of knowledge* that provides an understanding. It is this operative aspect that realizes the internal reversal of the process (I can return the row to its initial length), and the internal compensation of the differences (I see more space between the marbles, but less density). Note that these operations are dynamic, they develop in time, and they are reversible (they go back and forth); these characteristics cannot be captured by images. Pictures, or any form of external representation, can provide information about static states, but not about processes. Only operational knowledge leads to a fuller understanding of the processes.

Moreover, Piaget claimed that figurative knowledge is eventually subordinated to later developing operational knowledge, such that there is a unidirectional influence of the operational on the figurative: "It has been shown that the formation of operations drives the development of figurative symbolism, which in turn provides the basis for operative thought" (Piaget & Inhelder, 1966, p. 147). There is, however, a complementarity and interdependence between the two aspects. At each point in the development, the operative aspect directs the formation of the symbols, providing them with meaning, and the figurative aspect, in turn, promotes the acquisition and fixation of the information provided by the environment, which often comes in symbolic form (e.g., through language).

However, for Piaget there is no development of the figurative aspects, per se; rather, changes in the figurative aspects occur as a function of operational development. In contrast, I am suggesting that it is important to study figurative knowledge—drawing, writing, or numbers—in its own right and not as subordinated to operational knowledge.

A second Piagetian idea that appears to be challenged by my approach is that there is a common developmental source for every kind of external representation. Piaget stressed the developmental interdependence of all the manifestations of figurative knowledge: language, symbolic play, deferred imitation, and mental imagery. They are all aspects or manifestations of what he called *the semiotic function*. This function refers to "the ability to represent something, a *signified* something (object, event, conceptual scheme, etc.) by means of a *signifier* which is differentiated and which serves only a representative purpose: language, mental image, symbolic gestures" (Piaget, 1951, as cited in Gruber & Vonechè, 1977, p. 489). Thus, writing and numerals, in common with all other representational manifestations, would arise from the semiotic function and would have a common developmental source.

I can find no fault with the idea that the development and understanding of any representational manifestation arises from the capacity we have to create representations. In this sense, all representational manifestations have a common source. However, the extent of developmental interdependence among the different representational manifestations is still open to debate. By this, I mean that the way in which the development of mental imagery, drawing, writing, numerals, and symbolic play are related or independent from each other is still unknown. In this book, I attempt to explore some interdependencies between drawing, writing, and numerals, rather than taking a developmental interdependence between them for granted.

PRIVATE AND PUBLIC ASPECTS
OF WRITING AND NUMBERS

Frequently, when I comment on examples of the sort presented at the beginning of this chapter and defend the precocity and elaboration of preschoolers' knowledge of writing and numerals, I receive reactions such as "Well this might be true for *certain* children" with a stress on *certain* to mean those raised in middle-class, highly educated environments. Indeed, this may be the case. The number of opportunities to interact with written texts or to use numbers and the kind of literacy and numeracy activities in which children are involved is socially dependent. The practice of group reading is common in some communities, but rare in others; in some families, writing and reading of scientific papers and reading dictionaries and encyclopedias are daily activities, but others limit their reading to the newspaper and their writing to Christmas cards. Nevertheless, and taking for granted the social underpinnings of literacy, my focus in this book is what happens in the child's interactions with writing and numerals, in the private aspect of the literacy link.

Because writing is at the same time a strictly individual circumstance in which a person enters into an intimate relation with a system of signs, and a set of social practices strongly linked to social, economic, and political circumstances, any literacy event can be seen from either a private or a public angle. Take the case of dyslexia, for example. We can focus on the psychological and neuropsychological characterization of dyslexia, the private aspects. We can explain in a very detailed way how dyslexic children read and write words, sentences, and texts; we can discuss different forms of diagnosis, evaluation, and treatment. An alternative possibility, however, is to focus on the social public aspects to the study of dyslexia. Note, for example, that in France, the detection and treatment of dyslexia flourished together with the democratization of secondary schools (1959–1974), when thousands of students from the lower social classes began to be integrated into the educational system after having been shut out from secondary education. This brings up the extent to which these social circumstances were a determinant in the interpretation of reading difficulties.

I will focus primarily on the private aspects of the learning process of writing. However, by focusing on the private, this does not mean that the learning process occurs in isolation. Children build up their knowledge in a web of family practices and social interactions. Yet, a full recognition of the fundamental role of the environment in developing notational knowledge does not preclude the recognition of the active role played by endogenous factors. The study of "emergent literacy" has been especially prone to view the learning process solely in terms of sociocultural practices. Studies framed in the sociocultural approach to literacy have provided detailed descriptions of these practices (e.g., Heath, 1983; Street, 1984) and invaluable insights into the importance of the context of acquisition for the developing child. However, whereas the focus of these studies is on what is going on around the learning process, my focus will be on what is going on within the learning process.

LITERATE ADULTS' IDEAS
ABOUT THE DEVELOPMENT OF WRITING

How widespread is the belief that there is a developmental history to literacy and numeracy? Is this a commonly held adult belief? Whenever I directly seek adults' ideas about preschoolers' knowledge of writing, I realize how difficult it is to imagine ways of knowing that differ from our own. Further, this occurs despite the fact that these ways of knowing were our own when we were in the process of growing.

I undertook a very simple simulation game with a group of 30 adult linguistic students attending their first class in a course in "developmental literacy" in

Bogotá, Colombia. I asked the students to write their names, three words, and one short sentence, imagining that they were children. They were asked to complete this task as if they were 4-year-olds, then 5-year-olds and, finally, 6-year-olds. The goal of the simulation game was to tap into adults' ideas about the development of preschoolers' ways of writing. The words and the sentences were some of the many used with children of these ages, so there was documentation of what "real children" would do.

The results of the simulation game showed that the students generally failed to imagine any substantial development. A small group of students sketched a different figurative drawing for each word and sentence or produced a scribble that resembled a quick writing pattern, but the large majority wrote conventionally. It is true that many wrote with a trembling hand and committed spelling mistakes that are common in Spanish (e.g., using the letter B when V should have been used or putting G instead of J), but the principles underlying their simulated writing were strictly alphabetical, with one letter for each individual sound in the words, even when simulating the way 4-year-olds write.

I had expected to see a large number of drawings, mainly as examples of the simulated writing of 4-year-olds. I had thought that most adults would assume that this is what 4-year-olds do when asked to write. I was surprised by the fact that so many students attributed conventional knowledge of writing to 4-year-olds, when they were well aware that formal schooling does not start in Colombia until age 6. I also was surprised to find such a generalized attribution of consistency to the children. The participants in the simulation game supposed that children would do the same when writing their own name, the words, and the sentence. If they drew one word, then they would draw everything else, and if they wrote one word conventionally, then they would write everything else conventionally. Thus, the participants attributed to children a sort of either/or knowledge of writing; either children knew how to write everything or they did not know how to write anything. The simulation game was repeated with a group of 42 psychology students in Barcelona, Spain. Again, no one was able to imagine ways of writing that were not regulated by alphabetic principles. According to some of those questioned, preschoolers will draw; according to most, they will write alphabetically. They could not imagine ways of writing regulated by other nonalphabetical principles. Further, they showed difficulty in imagining forms of intermediate knowledge. The participants were able to imagine total lack of knowledge or total command of it, but not degrees of knowledge.

Here, I will challenge two assumptions held by the participants: the assumption that children move from drawing to conventional writing and the assumption that children's early writing is regulated by alphabetic principles. Moreover,

I will try to overcome two epistemological barriers obstructing the participants in the simulation game: the barrier preventing the conception of evolving forms of knowledge and the barrier of decentering from the principles regulating the systems with which the participants are familiar, so as to imagine other ways of writing. Evolving forms of knowledge about the writing systems that children are exposed to constitute the focus of this book but, in order to appreciate them, it is necessary to move away from the principles that regulate the familiar notational systems. A useful way of decentering is to see how other systems function. That is the reason why I will constantly compare literacy developments in different writing systems.

OUTLINE OF THE BOOK

External representations, among which are notational systems, constitute the "subject matter" and the domain of development in question. If someone thinks that development proceeds along the same path in every domain (i.e., a domain-independent view of development), then the subject matter can be largely ignored when analyzing developmental sequences. However, if we believe that the entities, rules, and operations of a particular domain are essential to the developmental process, then we have to understand these entities, rules, and operations from the point of view of the specialists. Chapter 1 provides a description of *what* children are acquiring when learning to write or to use numerals from a semiotic perspective.

Semioticians are specialists in the study of external representations; therefore, chapter 1 presents some of the ideas that they have proposed in explaining the features shared by means of external representation and the particular ways in which writing and numerals convey meaning. The notion of notation is essential for grasping the differences between these two systems, and also the specificity of the task toddlers and preschoolers perform when learning about writing and numerals. At the same time, chapter 1 presents a first approach to the different operations that are put into play by toddlers and preschoolers in the process of learning notational systems. Finally, a reflection on the properties of external representation in general and notational systems in particular will provide crucial clues for the reasons that external representation in general and notational systems in particular are such potent cognitive tools, in addition to being useful communicative tools.

Of course, notational systems have their own history, and entities and rules change over time, as do the activities performed with these entities. Once upon a time, numerals were not used in calculations. It took hundreds of years and much struggling until numerals were adopted for use in accounting. Chapter 2 reviews some of the milestones in the history of writing and number systems, as well as the origins of the system considered the ancestor of writing and number systems. A number of historical cases are presented illustrating that significant developments in the history of writing were achieved whenever a script was borrowed and adapted to a new language, for example, when the Greeks adapted the Semitic alphabet. With the help of a script, people were able to reflect on their own linguistic representations and adapt the script to their own language. For them, writing was not only a tool for transmission and accumulation of knowledge, but also a tool for thinking about their own language.

Historical examples are helpful for illustrating in what sense writing and numerals are objects to think with, which is one of this book's main claims. These examples also serve to illuminate both the kind of problems people try to solve with a notation and the new problems that a notational solution might create. Moreover, taking a historical perspective helps *decenter* us from our own writing systems and open our minds to other organizing principles. If we can look at children's systems of writing with a *decentered* eye, we are in a better position from which to appreciate children's ideas about writing and numerals.

Chapter 3 looks at the individual's history of writing, that is, its psychogenesis. It explores the spontaneous development of writing among children raised in communities that use an alphabetic system of writing. Drawing on empirical studies conducted in different languages and scripts, the stages children go through before the acquisition of the alphabetic principle are outlined. I must clarify, however, that the term "stage" is used here with its ordinary meaning as the level or scenario in which certain phenomena strictly related to the development of writing occur; it is not meant to imply a domain-neutral, age-dependent period of general development as in the Piagetian sense.

I will show that, from very early on, writing is a problem space for the developing child. Long before children learn how to use writing for communication, they impose certain constraints on the number of signs and their internal variety that serves to organize the notational input and facilitate attribution of meaning to the individual signs. Children's attempts to interpret their own writing play a crucial role in their discovery of the links between writing and spoken language, and they eventually lead to the discovery of the alphabetic principle.

I tell only part of the individual story toward literacy, however—the part that concentrates on writing, but excludes all reference to the development of discursive forms and different text types. The acquisition of the writing system is not a precondition or prerequisite for gaining access to the different genres of written prose. Almost completely illiterate adolescents were able to identify syntactic constructions that are characteristic of the formal written mode in French (Blanche-Benveniste, 1982). Urban middle-class children are able to differentiate narratives from descriptions before they are able to write a story conventionally (Tolchinsky-Landsmann, 1990), and they produce texts in a journalistic style even though they can hardly decode a newspaper (Teberosky, 1990). Nevertheless, the focus of chapter 3 is not on the acquisition of the discursive forms, but rather on the way children grasp the functioning of the alphabetic writing system. At any rate, this process demonstrates in a nutshell what is claimed to be a constant feature of work with external representations in general and writing in particular—a dialectic process of interaction between internal and external forms of representations that transforms initial understanding of a certain phenomenon.

Chapter 4 explores the way children come to understand the written system of numeration. Looking at numerals, attending to their names, perceiving the ways in which they are commented are, for the developing child, experiences as real as sensorimotor experiences with balls, cars, sand, or people. As with alphabetic writing, children's understanding of the written system of numeration is separable, although not separate, from children's mathematical knowledge. Therefore, it is possible to explore knowledge of numerals as a domain of development and not only as derivative from mathematical knowledge. Indeed, the written system of numeration is a source, and not only an outcome, of mathematical knowledge. The information children gather from notations, as well as the information they are able to produce, is not an aggregate on top of previously acquired notions that serves to amplify these notions, but rather a permanent ingredient of developmental processes.

Chapter 5 focuses on children's view of the relation between writing and numerals. It starts by analyzing similarities and differences between alphabetic writing and numerals from the perspective of a literate adult, and then considers the extent to which these distinctions are taken into account by children before schooling. It becomes evident that toddlers and preschoolers explore each of the systems according to their own formal constraints before learning how to use them as representational tools. However, the need to communicate quantitative meanings and labels leads to representational strategies from which it may be inferred that children confuse the two systems. Nevertheless, only when children are at least minimally aware of the formal features of each system are they able to manipulate them to fulfil their representational needs.

In an attempt to address the origin of this differentiation, I will consider, on the one hand, the views of illiterate adults on the relations between writing and numerals and, on the other hand, some neuropsychological data related to the differentiation of letters and numerals in pathological states. The consideration of these three sources—development, illiteracy, and neuropsychology—supports the idea that the differentiation between systems is not an outcome of schooling;

it is facilitated (or provoked) by the contexts in which notations usually appear, the ways of talking about the notational elements, and the activities people perform with writing and numbers, but it is also grounded in human beings' biological endowment. Neurological studies with brain damaged patients suggest that there are specific neurological pathways that support handling of alphabetic materials and they differ from those that serve to handle Hindu-Arabic numerals.

Initial differentiation between systems is indeed a favorable beginning because it guides children in their processing of the mass of notational input and in the attribution of meaning to the notational elements—sounds to letters and numerosity to numerals. However, more mature uses of the systems require using letters and numerals for other functions; for example, the use of the same notational forms with multiple meanings and senses is common in advertisement and computer programs. It seems, then, that more than learn how to differentiate between the systems, children will learn, as they become literate in their communities, to blur the distinction between systems.

Chapter 6 is the only chapter about literacy as it is currently understood. This term, which originally meant the ability to read and write, has acquired a much broader sense in the specialized literature, becoming "synonymous with its hoped-for consequences" (Aronoff, 1994, p. 68). However, in the discussion of the effects of literacy, a great divide occurs. Some scholars claim that the technology of writing is responsible for the achievements of Western rational thinking (e.g., Goody, 1977; Olson, 1994). Others believe that it is in the context of its use and learning, more than in its technological features, that the possibility of influence on cognition and language lies (Street, 1984). The first view, usually termed the "technological view," defends the enormous implications of the alphabet first, and of printing later, in the development of thought, self-consciousness, reasoning, memory, perception of language, and even the difference between truth and falsity. The second view, known as the "ideological view," considers most of these assertions to be exaggerated and many to be historically false. As shown by the already classic study undertaken by Scribner and Cole (1983), the fact that the Vai people had a syllabic writing system apparently did not produce any cognitive revolution, either in their capacity to memorize, or in their capacity to classify and make logical inferences. Moreover, nonalphabetic cultures were able to produce reason scientifically, and most of the achievements attributed to the use of writing can be traced to oral discursive forms (Carruthers, 1990).

The technological view has not only been criticized for the "promises" that literacy failed to fulfill, but also for its conception of writing and of the history of writing, which concentrates almost exclusively on writing as the representation of speech. Anthropologists, philosophers, and sociologists adopting an "ideological" stance also highlight the magic status writing has acquired in some cultures, the signs of prestige underlying spelling, the social conditions of scribes, and the consequences of literacy in people's lives. Chapter 6 examines some of the purported consequences of learning to write on the perception and conceptualization of language and on the life of certain people.

The bulk of this book focuses on what children know about writing and numerals prior to being formally instructed. This is useful information for developmental psychologists and educators, and it will help them to understand crucial issues of human development. The developmental perspective is set aside for a while and the next chapter looks at the object of knowledge: the two notational systems that children will make their own in the course of development. These notational systems form part of the vast domain of external representations and constitute the subject matter of semiotics, the doctrine of signs.

1

What Philosophers Say About Representational Means That May Help Us to Understand What Makes Writing and Numerals so Special

Since earliest times, human beings have shown a strong disposition for leaving traces. The caves discovered in December 1994 by Jean Marie Chauvet at Pont d'Arc are covered with markings dating back more than 30,000 years. Newspapers were quick to describe the markings as "drawings," and the markings were immediately incorporated into the history of Western painting. But are they works of art? How do people know when something is a painting, a piece of writing, or a mathematical text? Is there something in the shape of the marks that helps them come to a decision?

Ask a literate adult how to distinguish *pictorial* paintings or drawings from *scriptorial* signs, such as written texts, musical scores, or mathematical formulae. The individual would probably find the request rather odd. If the marks on the cave resembled rhinoceroses and bears, then the person would say that they must be drawings. Such a reply responds to the generalized supposition that looking similar to something known (i.e., bearing a figurative resemblance) distinguishes pictorial from scriptorial devices.

Yet, surely the fragile nature of this claim is obvious. Although it may apply to the figurative drawings and the written texts with which people are familiar, drawings do not necessarily have to be figurative and written texts are not always like the ones with which they are familiar. If individuals rely on figurative resemblance as the feature that distinguishes pictorial from scriptorial, how are they supposed to view a painting by the Catalan artist Joan Miró, where all there is are black lines—some wavy, some straight—crossing white spaces with the sudden appearance of a large dot? Certainly, this would not be identified as a written text, but figurative resemblance does not seem a very suitable criterion for qualifying this sort of art as pictorial.

Forms or devices in which there is some figurative resemblance to known objects are called *iconic*. Iconic devices are very frequently pictorial, but not every pictorial device is iconic. Some paintings bear no resemblance to anything known, and yet people recognize them as being pictorial. Nevertheless, figurative resemblance has been known to cause confusion about what might constitute writing. When the first Persian cuneiform texts were discovered, some skeptics held that the marks had been made by birds walking across soft clay (Harris, 1986); if they looked like footprints, then it was thought that they could not be writing. To illustrate the intrinsic ambiguity of outward appearance, look at Fig. 1.1.

Is it a piece of writing or is it part of a painting? Is it scriptorial or pictorial? It is, in fact, both: Islamic calligraphers insist that the function of writing is phonetic, semantic, and esthetic at the same time.

The questions just posed (i.e., How do people know that something is a drawing? Is figurative resemblance important for distinguishing a drawing from something that it is not? What makes a shape a drawing or a piece of writing?

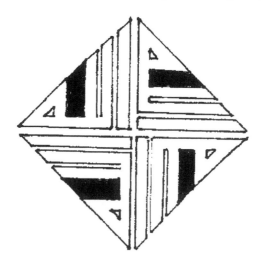

FIG. 1.1.   Ala in Kufic writing. Specially designed by the calligrapher Mohamed Ben Ali Bouaziz. Reprinted with permission.

How does a particular shape acquire meaning?) are typical of the branch of philosophy known as *semiotics*, which is a discipline also known as the "doctrine of signs." The subject matter of semiotics is what has been called external representations; some semioticians called them *signs* (Pierce, 1966; Sebeok, 1996), whereas others use the word *symbols* (Cassirer, 1944, p. 32) for referring to external representations, in general. For the present discussion, I use these terms interchangeably.

Early in history, the first semioticians were physicians, cabalists, specialists in visual arts, or diviners, but currently they are mostly philosophers (Eco, 1988). Philosophers of every stance have gone to great lengths to explain the similarities and differences between external representations and to understand how they acquire "meaning."

The term "semiotic" was used in the introduction when referring to Piagetian ideas about the relation between external representations. Piaget suggested that humans develop a semiotic function that serves to produce and to interpret different kinds of signs and symbols. According to some philosophers (e.g., Cassirer, 1923/1972), this "semiotic," or "symbolic," function makes us human. Although chimpanzees can be trained to interpret symbols (Savage-Rumbaugh, 1990; Savage-Rumbaugh, Shanker, & Taylor, 1998), the capacity to produce external representations has been attained only by Homo sapiens, as explained by Gould (1991):

> Our closest ancestors and cousins, *Homo Erectus*, the Neanderthals and others, possessed mental capacities of a high order, as is indicated by their range of tools and other artifacts. But only Homo Sapiens shows direct evidence for the kind of abstract reasoning, including numerical and aesthetics modes, that we identify as distinctively human. All indications of ice-age reckoning—the calendar sticks and counting blades—belong to *Homo Sapiens*. And all ice-age art—the cave paintings, the Venus figures, the horse-head carvings, the reindeer bas-reliefs—was done by our species. By evidence now available, Neanderthal knew nothing of representational art. (pp. 319–320)

In contrast to other species, human beings are not only able to use different kinds of signs, but they can also deliberately create signs of other signs in almost unlimited ways. Note, for example, that we have created paper currency that once used to stand for gold; we then created checks that stand for currency; and then we created plastic cards that stand for checks.

This chapter explores some of the ideas that semioticians have proposed in discussing the features shared by the different means of external representation and highlight those that are particular to writing and numerals. It also shows that the concept of notation, which is a special kind of external representation, is crucial in defining these features. Developmental psychologists need to reflect more widely on the possibilities offered by semiotics as a means to gain a better understanding of their own field. Those who are interested in the development of notational systems require a semiotic approach to these systems, just as psychologists interested in the development of numeracy require a mathematical approach to this concept. By using semiotics, psychologists will gain a more accurate description of *what* children are acquiring when learning to write or to use numerals. They will also have tools for appreciating children's reactions to the representational means and for understanding the developmental differences found in these two learning processes.

Further, a reflection on the properties of external representation and notational systems provides crucial clues for the reasons that they are such potent cognitive, as well as communicative, tools. Their potency results from the amount and variety of cognitive work we put into play when using, interpreting, and forming external representations. We perform multiple mental actions and form multiple perspectives.

Think, for example, about writing a simple list of numerals. While we are making them, we look at them, comparing what has been written with what remains to be written. At the same time, we may monitor the written numerals with oral numerals to see whether each corresponds to the one we need; at the same time, we judge the accuracy of the trace and the place in the series. We can perform the same mental actions after we have finished writing the list. We can look at the list and again compare what we have already done with what we were trying to do.

The perspectives from which these actions are performed are multiplied when the same person is both the producer and the interpreter, or when the situation is repeated at different times and spaces, individually or in groups. It is important to note here (and as emphasized throughout this book) that, in addition to the known claim that external representations increase our capacity for recording and recall, they also multiply the cognitive operations that we can perform and, by so doing, function as a motor for cognitive change. Thus, it is not only memory that is increased, but also cognitive flexibility.

Writing this chapter proved particularly difficult. Icons, symbols, and signs are very much a part of daily life and many expressions include references to these notions. People say, for example, that someone presents "clear *signs of fatigue*" or that a particular cold cream is excellent against "early *signs of aging*." As such, developing some order in this vast and speculative domain was highly taxing. In addition, it is difficult to define something that is so familiar. The effort is worthwhile if, by the end of this chapter, there is an appreciation of the enormous cognitive task underlying the apparently simple observation of a 4-year-old who says, *I have this one in my name,* while pointing at a letter in a printed word.

THE CONFINES OF SEMIOTICS

Pictures, drawings, maps, hallmarks, graphs, signatures, musical scores, mathematical equations, photographs, figures, and letters are examples of external representations and are the subject matter of a discipline known as semiotics. Everyone uses external representations; people wave their hand to mean goodbye, they draw arrows to indicate directions, and they put their signature on letters. Semioticians not only use them, but also have made external representations their field of inquiry.

Credit for creating a general "science of signs" (Harris, 1987) is shared by the Swiss linguist Ferdinad de Saussure (1857–1913), the founder of modern linguistics, and Charles S. Pierce (1839–1914), one of the United States' most original and versatile intellectuals (who was, among other professions, a mathematician, astronomer, chemist, engineer, and philosopher). Saussure called this science *sémiologie* back in 1894, and Peirce called it *semiotics* in 1897, both from the Greek *semeion,* or "sign."

However, the Greek physician Hippocrates was among the first who used the basic principles of semiotics, in reference to what today would be called *symptoms.* In trying to prevent his colleagues from misuse of symptoms for the diagnosis of illness, he asked them to consider the general condition of the patient, the place where he lived, and even his cultural habits, before interpreting any particular symptom (Danesi, 1996; Eco, 1988). Hippocrates explained that symptoms are not self-evident; they function as a sort of indication, whose meaning should be inferred *in context.* The Hippocratic conception of symptoms still persists. Physicians, clinical psychologists, and psychoanalysts work very hard to infer the meaning of symptoms *in context* rather than establish a direct equivalence between symptoms and pathological states. However, whether symptoms should be included at all in the domain of semiotics is still a matter of controversy.

What does fever have in common with drawings or signatures? Why would they be considered the subject matter of semiotics? To that question, semioticians state that the three (fever, drawings, and signatures) have a "double face" (Sebeok, 1996, p. 34); they are what they are; yet, at the same time, they evoke something beyond them. Each of the examples listed at the beginning of this section—pictures, maps, hallmarks, graphs, photographs, figures, or letters—has a double face; they are simply pigments or patterns of ink on paper; but, at the same time, they point at something beyond them.

To explain this double face, Saussure introduced the two technical terms that marked the history of semiotics and linguistics. According to Saussure, a sign is constituted by the *signifier* and the *signified* (Saussure, 1916/1987). The signifier is the formal side of the sign and the signified is the content side of the sign. In the case of spoken language, the signifier is the sound pattern and the signified the concept; in the case of sign language, the signifier is the manual gesture and the signified the concept. The two sides of the sign are, however, *inextricably* linked like the two sides of a paper page. In this view, there is no such thing as a signifier without something signified, or a signified without a signifier. Indeed, the fact that external representations are signifiers is the big difference between mere things and external representations. Mere things *are* what they are, but external representations are *about* something or *of* something. Pictures and photographs are of or about people, houses, or whatever; graphs refer to variables, letters to sounds, and so forth.

When defining *semiotics*, symptoms (e.g., fever) were among the first signs to be studied. Nevertheless, there is a long-standing debate in semiotics concerning whether symptoms should be included at all in a general theory of signs. The key issue in this controversy has to do with the confines of this discipline. Should semiotics deal with "signs in all their forms and manifestations" (Morris, 1964, p. 1), whether they be produced, deliberately, instinctively, or spontaneously, and whether they be natural or artificial? Or should semiotics be confined to the study of signs that were deliberately created by human agents and have a social use? For those in favor of the first position, symptoms are signs and should be included in semiotic studies, whereas for those in favor of the second position, they should not. Semioticians (e.g., Charles Morris or Thomas A. Sebeok) made the point that there are no special objects that are "signs"; anything can be a sign if interpreted as such. The "double face" always requires a third party, an interpreter. Something is turned into a sign whenever someone (the interpreter) views something beyond it. Signs are signs only for an interpreter; it is impossible to explain the similarities and differences between representations apart from the interpreter, that is, apart from the subject's internal representation (e.g., Cassirer, 1944; N. Goodman, 1976; Pierce, 1935/1966).

EXTERNAL AND INTERNAL REPRESENTATIONS

It is important to include the subject's representational processes in any analysis of external representation. Three consequences follow from this decision: (a) There are no representational objects, per se; any object can be turned into an external representation in the act of interpretation; however, (b) there are objects that are created as representational objects; and (c) internal representations should be considered as a special kind of representation.

A subject who decides to do so can turn any object into a representational object. Thus, it is a matter of perspective whether a stone is a stone or whether it is taken to represent something else. However, and this is crucial to this discussion, some objects are deliberately created to mean something. That is, it is necessary to distinguish between objects that are turned into a representation by an interpreter and those that are *purposely created to be interpreted*. We are particularly interested in this latter kind of representational object because the external representations that children must acquire were purposefully created as such.

This is why the following discussions are confined to external representations produced by a human agent deliberately, and exclude those that were not (e.g., symptoms). The kinds of external representation focused on here are not only double faced, but also *intentional*. They were created by someone to be interpreted by someone else or by the creator at another time.

Finally, the third consequence of including the subject as a condition for representation is that internal representations must be taken into account among different means of representation. Thus, the figure in the introduction (Fig. I.1) was incomplete because it did not include internal representations. Figure 1.2 includes *internal representations* as the most inclusive kind of representation,

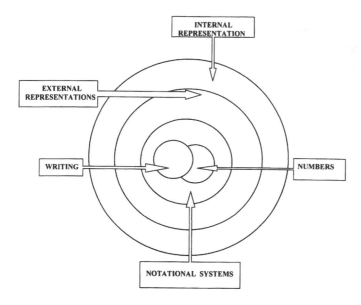

FIG. 1.2. Types of representations.

partially overlapping with external representations. An external representation is more than a translation of an internal representation onto material support. It has its own characteristics and constraints. This is why *external* and *internal* representations should be two circles that may partially overlap. Certain internal representations are not represented (or representable) by external representations.

The domain of representations is now complete and includes all types and subtypes of representation. The most inclusive circle includes internal representations, the next includes external representations, then notational forms of representation, and finally the inner ones include writing and numerals. Internal representations are the subject matter of cognitive psychologists and neurobiologists, who use the term to refer to a level of psychological functioning.[2] Not every psychological paradigm considers the notion of internal representation necessary to explain psychological functioning. However, even when a paradigm denies the causal efficacy of internal representations, it still has to define them.

These internal representations could have been called *mental* or *cognitive* representations, but the term *internal* is used to contrast with *external*. Included under this term are all types of internal representation, from neural activity to mathematical equations to poetry. At no level, however, are representations copies, either from the semiotic perspective discussed earlier or from a neurobiological perspective. As clearly explained by A. R. Damasio (1994):

> Images are not stored as facsimile pictures of things, or events, or words, or sentences. The brain does not file Polaroid pictures of people, objects, landscapes; nor does it store audiotapes of music and speech; it does not store films of scenes in our lives; nor does it hold the type of cue cards and TelePrompTer transparencies that help politicians earn their daily bread.... Given the huge amount of knowledge we acquire in a lifetime, any kind of facsimile storage would probably pose insurmountable problems of capacity. If the brain were like a conventional library, we would run out of shelves just as conventional libraries do.... We all have direct evidence that whenever we recall a given object, or face, or scene, we do not get an exact reproduction but rather an interpretation, a newly reconstructed version of the original. In addition as our age and experience change, versions of the same thing evolve. (p. 100)

---

[2]From a psychological point of view, internal representations mediate individuals' relations with other people, with objects in the world, their movements in space, and the decisions they make in time (Zelazo, 2000). Cognitive psychologists and linguists of a symbolic stance will agree with this generalized use of representational mediation except for reflexes or automatism (e.g., Bickerton, 1990). Connectionists (e.g., Churchland, 1988) will disagree because they do not think it necessary to postulate representational mediation, although there are some who defend a mixed approach (A. Clark, 1997).

TWO EXAMPLES TO CLARIFY DIFFERENT TYPES OF REPRESENTATION

First example:

Imagine yourself seated at a window, where you see a cat run in front of you. This change in the environment stimulates neural activity in your eye (inside which is your retina), and your retina undergoes certain modifications in following the cat's movements, although you are unaware of these modifications.

Second example:

Imagine a mathematician (specializing in topology) alone in her room thinking about the steps needed to transform a donut shape into another shape resembling a cup.

The modifications to your retina (provoked by the cat running) and the reflections of the topologist (while thinking in her room) are forms of internal representation.

Imagine you form a mental image of a cat and decide to find a cat and take a photograph of it.

The photo is an external representation of the animal.

Now, the mathematician is explaining to her students the different steps to transform the donut shape into a cup, using neither the blackboard nor any transparency, just describing verbally the intermediate steps to get the final shape.

The verbal explanation is an external representation of the transformations.

The mental image of the cat, the scientist reasoning silently alone in her room, the verbal explanation, and the photograph are different types of representation. The content of the first representation is *the cat as imagined* by the visual cortex, whereas the referent is the running cat. The photograph refers to the same cat, but differs in its content, which, in this case, is *the cat as it is photographed.* If the assumption is that the mathematician's verbal explanation corresponds to her reflections, then there is also the same referent in both cases, the transformation that a shape can undergo, but a different content. When speaking, the content is *the transformations as the topologist verbally states them*, whereas, when thinking, the content of the representation is *the transformation as it is thought.*

(continued)

> Despite the fact that the referent is the same, the content differs when speaking and thinking because they are subject to different constraints. When talking about the transformation of the shapes, she will have to accommodate them to the specific features of spoken language. The explanation will be constrained by the words in the lexicon, the rules of word combination, and the way spoken language is pronounced, one word after the other sequentially in time. When thinking about them, she could "see" them in her head simultaneously. The differences in representational means (mental images, *mentalesse* of any kind, special plastic paper used for photography) provoke crucial differences in the representations because each means of representation selects the features according to its own constraints and adds features of its own.

Figure 1.2 is itself an external representation created to show in a clearer way one of the messiest, although crucial, issues in psychology and semiotics—representation, types of representation, and the hierarchical relations between types. Clearly, I had some ideas about these issues before deciding to draw the figure; however, the process of externally representing these ideas, by means of a schema, forced a certain precision that was not evident to me beforehand and worked as an internal organizer. At the same time, the fact that I used a figure enabled external reviewers to point at contradictions between my claims in the text and the graphic representation. They could, as well, question certain graphic decisions. Once I received their comments, I felt compelled to better clarify my own ideas and to look for verbal and graphic means to visualize them anew. The process is a vivid (and exhausting) illustration of a constant dialectic process between internal and external forms of representations that transformed the initial understanding of a certain phenomenon (Zelazo, 2000). This process puts in a nutshell the kind of interaction I assume between external and internal representations at any phase in development.

So far, I have reoriented the semiotic discussion to include internal representations. However, I will depart here from any consideration of similarities and differences among different types of internal representation. To do so would require both a psychological and a neurobiological perspective, which I am not taking here. The aim instead is to focus on external representations and to constrain a little further the type of external representations of particular interest here—those in which the representational means require and enable deliberateness, endurance, interaction in real time, and detachment.

CONDITIONS OF EXTERNAL REPRESENTATIONS

Although some semioticians explore the features of involuntary signals created by living organisms (e.g., Sebeok, 1996), they are not discussed here. Instead, the focus is on external representations deliberately created because deliberateness implies that the creator anticipates the interpreter—indeed, not only the presence of the interpreter, but also the capacity of the interpreter to make something of the external representation. The external representations that were deliberately constructed were constructed to elicit thinking in others (Wells, 1999). Physicians convert fever into a symbol or sign of influenza, but people do not produce fever deliberately. Similarly for signals; the strong smell skunks give off can be interpreted as indicating their presence, but skunks do not produce it deliberately.

Another characteristic of external representations is that they persist in time. Representations that are ephemeral and unique, for example because they are produced in the air or by a gesture and are never again repeated, are also excluded from the discussion. Those that are *lasting* external representations are examined because they were produced on enduring surfaces or with enduring objects. This excludes spoken language and sign language because their expression is fluent and does not last for offline examination (unless, of course, it is recorded).

Deliberate and lasting external representations are particularly well suited to support *interactions in real time* between production and perception (Willats, 1985). In painting and writing, as well as in all other means of deliberate external representation, a certain motor plan is put into action. This plan leaves external traces, so that the producer can look at them *while* in the process of production, and a constant interaction is engendered between two modalities, the visual and the kinetic. The results of movements can be monitored, contemplated, and adjusted while they are still being produced, immediately after production, and much later on. No matter how different the products might be (ranging from a painting to a musical score), the process of interaction between production and perception is a universal condition shared by all means of external representation. This kind of interaction explains why a lasting and deliberate representation can be turned into a generative problem space, not only after being completed, but also while it is being produced.

Moreover, lasting and deliberately created representations become separated from the producer and from the conditions of production (Lee & Karmiloff-Smith, 1996). Once formed, the result becomes *detached* from the process and the context of production, from the time during which it was produced, and from the producer. Furthermore, all these components (process, context, time, and producer) somehow become embedded in the product. Consider Leonardo da Vinci's *Mona Lisa*. There is no doubt that while being created, there was a strong interaction between the artist and every brush stroke on the picture. Today, the creator of the *Mona Lisa* is no longer alive—the scenario in which the picture was produced has changed and time has moved on. Nonetheless, the oeuvre has become a source of information about the process of production, the context of production, the time when it was produced, and the producer. It has been converted into a detached source of information for all who contemplate it.

Clearly, Leonardo could look at his creation once it was complete, and today people can look at it in the Louvre. As Leonardo looked at it, he acted as interpreter (of his own creation) in the same way that we now act as interpreters of his creation. In general, for any lasting external representation, the creator can look at the result from the outside and act as an offline interpreter. Leonardo was able to compare his *Mona Lisa* with other paintings, just as any lasting representation enables creators to compare it with others that they have created themselves or that have been created by others.

Creators and interpreters can infer and recover information about aspects of the original process, such as the context, the time, or the referents. However, what is inferred from the external representation is never identical to the original aspects—it is just more or less accurate information about those aspects. Notice that the discussion has come back, although from a different angle, to the assertion that a representation can never be a copy. Instead, the aforementioned characteristics make external representations a special kind of object that serves many different functions, from the most mundane to the most sacred. Indeed, from buying and selling to the most holy rituals, every cultural act involves the creation and interpretation of external representations.

DIMENSIONS FOR DISTINGUISHING PICTORIAL AND SCRIPTORIAL DEVICES

Pictures, drawings, maps, hallmarks, graphs, signatures, photographs, numerals, and letters have a dual face; they enable online interaction between production and perception and, once detached from the conditions of production, they become sources of information for any interpreter. Despite these common features, they are each a different "representational product." There are three dimensions along which representational products are often distinguished: motivated/arbitrary, personal/conventional, and isolated/systematic. Let's consider whether these dimensions allow us to differentiate pictorial and scriptorial devices.

The first dimension, motivated/arbitrary, refers to the relation between the form of the signs or symbols and the content they represent. In this dimension, the line of demarcation separates *motivated* products like pictures, drawings, and photographs from *arbitrary* products like numerals and letters, leaving many products—including maps, hallmarks, graphs, and signatures—somewhere in between. A representation is said to be *motivated* if the formal features of the sign are justified in terms of the features of its content or the features of the referent. If individuals use the color red to draw a tomato because tomatoes are red, they are justifying one feature of the sign (its color) in terms of the referent. Similarly, if they say they have written the word ENVY using this particular font to show the intense power of this sentiment, again they are justifying the outward form in terms of the meaning they wish to convey. It does not matter whether a tomato also can be green or that "envy" is not such an intense sentiment from another person's point of view; it does matter that the use of certain features is justified in terms of the content or the referent of the representation.

A representation is said to be *arbitrary* if the features of its content (or referent) do not explain its formal features. Individuals do not explain the outward shape of the symbol $ in terms of the particular shape of dollar bills, nor do they explain the letters included in the word DOLLAR in terms of wealth or poverty. In arbitrary representations, the link between forms and content is not expressed in terms of similarity, causality, part–whole relations, or logical or natural links. If this motivated/arbitrary dimension is taken as a basis for distinction, scriptorial signs are on the arbitrary extreme, whereas pictorial signs can be either. Realistic painting appeals to motivated representation, whereas abstract painting does not.

The second dimension of differentiation, personal/conventional, refers to the relation between the creator of the representation and the created representation. This dimension opposes *personal* to *conventional* signs. Personal signs are idiosyncratic and are created for personal use, interpretation, and identification, whereas conventional signs are those sustained by social agreement. Sometimes a group of people agrees on the meaning of one or a group of motivated or arbitrary representations, and they learn to react in a uniform manner. Then a convention is created. *Conventional* links are neither weaker nor less obligatory than natural links, but they are supposed to require specific social inculcation. Only convention warrants uniformity of interpretation for arbitrary signs, but many natural links can be interpreted without having established any convention. Piaget, following Saussure, used the term *signs* for the external representations that are conventional and *symbols* for the personal ones, whereas Pierce used these terms the other way around.

These two dimensions, motivated/arbitrary and personal/conventional, can appear in different combinations. A sign can be motivated and conventional or motivated and personal. There is no impediment to reaching a convention for either motivated or arbitrary sign. Large groups of people have been trained to react in a largely uniform manner to the dove of peace or to Justice holding the scales of equity; yet, this does not turn them into arbitrary signs. In comparison, many people believe that some gestures are so motivated and nonarbitrary that they can be interpreted directly, without the need to arrive at any convention. However, those who have once tried to use gestures in foreign places would probably agree that a direct understanding is not always possible. Evidently, even motivated signs may require some degree of teaching.

On these and related grounds, some philosophers (e.g., Gombrich, 1960; N. Goodman, 1976) are called "conventionalists" because they suggest that the amount of social agreement required for interpreting gestures or paintings does not differ from that required for interpreting numerals or letters. A similar claim is made in psychology. Since the work done by Bruner (1957), it has been shown that the viewer's previous knowledge strongly determines the interpretation of an external representation. According to "conventionalists," interpreting representations is always a matter of convention. Therefore, the dimensions motivated/arbitrary and personal/conventional are not sufficient for distinguishing pictorial from scriptorial devices.

The third dimension, isolated/systematic, refers to the relation among signs—whether or not they are part of a system of signs. Isolated signs, regardless of the strength of the social agreement supporting them, do not constitute scriptorial devices; there is no way of deciding whether an isolated shape is pictorial or scriptorial by simply looking at it. However, as soon as someone sees, for example, a "drawn hand" *together* with a "drawn curve," each stops being pictorial. The HAND is understood to mean "stop," easily replaceable by STOP, and different from "curve," which is understood to mean "be careful." Scriptorial signs form a system; pictorial ones do not. Thus, the only dimension by which the two kinds of signs can be reliably distinguished is whether or not they are part of a system. It is not important whether each element within the system is motivated or arbitrary, or personal or conventional, on its own. Once an element is recognized as belonging to a system, its meaning is established by the system.

Let's consider the game, "scissors, paper, rock." The participants, usually two or three, can draw each of these elements, can invent a gesture for each, or use real objects. Whatever they decide to use for representing the elements is not relevant for playing the game; what counts are the rules of the game. The rules are that "scissors" wins over "paper," but loses to "rock"; "paper" wins over "rock," but loses to "scissors"; and "rock" wins over "scissors," but loses to "paper." The game is played in turns. At each turn, each participant, *at the same time*, selects and plays one of the three elements. The winner of each turn is decided according to the rules. If one of the participants plays "paper" and the other "rock," the winner is the one who played "paper." Once the game starts, the meaning of each element determines the game winner according to the rules. It does not matter whether the game is played with drawings, objects, or marks on a piece of paper. Further, the game does not always have to be played with the same objects. The objects, their shape, or their representation can be changed as long as the rule of a hierarchical order of winner and loser(s) is preserved. This is the fundamental issue, and the materiality of the elements is of little importance. Obviously, the more efficient way to preserve the game is to produce a permanent record; the use of permanent marks will guarantee the reproduction of the rules and the operation of the game independently of place, players, scenario, and materiality of the elements. It is at this point that the notion of notation comes in.

THE NOTION OF NOTATION

A notation is an artifact that enables a state, process, or activity to be encoded, recorded, transported, and reproduced in a systematic way. Let's consider a musical score, which is a prototypical example of a notation. According to N. Goodman (1976), the use of notation enables "authoritative identification of a work from performance to performance" (p. 142). It is possible to go from the score to the performance and from the performance to the score, and it is possible to identify the piece despite the changes that might be introduced by interpreters or instruments from performance to performance.

There are many other artifacts, besides musical scores, that perform these same functions: calendars, clocks, and thermometers. By exploring the features of these artifacts, semioticians have suggested a list of conditions that a set of marks or objects must satisfy to be considered a notation.

A notation is a limited set of elements; each element has a distinctive form, a name, and a given position in the set (Harris, 1992). Consequently, people can name the elements and can recognize them as belonging to the particular set, even if they do not know how to use them, or what function each of them performs, or how the set works. For example, I know the notes on a musical score, I am able to recognize their shape, and I think I could handle their position on the staff, but unfortunately, I am unable to use them to play music. Similarly, a young child may be able to recite the alphabet, yet not know how to read, or may be familiar with the name of the digits, without knowing how to use them for calculation. This demonstrates a particular feature of notations: "They are structured systems of which the members may be defined by their internal relationships to one another, *independently* of any function each may acquire when integrated into (used for) some specific set of communicational practices" (Harris, 1995, p. 169).

The fact that notation has a limited number of clearly distinct elements facilitates learning and further establishes the generalization of the notation. These elements can, in turn, be "re-signified" for different functions, thus increasing their efficiency in the recording, transporting, and reproduction of states, processes, and activities.

Note that in this approach to notations, the notational entities or elements are separated from the situations in which they are used and thus see that the same elements may have different meanings or contents in a different context. Numerals, for example, have mainly geographical meaning in the zip code and qualitative meaning in other contexts.

The discussion thus far makes it clear that the existence of a notation as a means of recording a representational system is what makes the crucial difference between pictorial and scriptorial devices. In simple terms, writing and numerals differ from drawing most conspicuously because they are based on notation. In this view, notations act as a subclass of external representations, and notational processes are those particular representational processes expressed by way of notational systems. Drawing is not, therefore, a notational process because it does not make use of a notation, although some authors do defend the possibility of defining graphic units in drawing. It is at this point that the opinion professed here differs from that held by other authors, who hold that notations and external representations are synonymous.

The next section examines some of the proposals put forward by Harris (1992, 1995) and N. Goodman (1976) to explain what makes a set of marks, or any collection of objects, a notation. Among other issues, these two authors differ in that Harris thought that it is possible to describe the notational elements of a notational system independently from the situations in which they are used and thus see that the same elements may have different meaning or content in a different context. In comparison, Goodman considered notations as symbol-meaning systems that necessarily include both form and content. That is, he included in the description of a notational system the relation that the notational marks have with the classes of objects or events onto which they are mapped.

Conditions Met by Notational Elements

In order for notations to accomplish their function, different people must use them at different times, which highlights the fact that the purposeful marks in a notation are *copiable* (N. Goodman, 1976; Harris, 1995). Moreover, notations must be recognizable despite the alterations different users may introduce in their appearance. When standing in front of a piece of art, individuals may have the feeling that the marks used to create it are unique; in front of a piece of writing, they feel the opposite—they recognize that it uses the same letters they have always known. By the way, this is the reason why "signatures" constitute a sort of hybrid sign, neither drawing nor writing. They must be recognized as being unique; otherwise, they do not serve their identificatory function. At the same time, however, on each occasion they are used, they must be recognized as being the same (Fraenkel, 1992).

If marks are copiable, no matter who produces them or when they are produced, then they are also replaceable; one can substitute other equivalent marks. All the marks that can be used interchangeably form an equivalence class or a category. Recalling the "scissors, paper, rock" game, any mark, object, or drawing attributed to each element can be used interchangeably, no matter how different they might appear. One person's way of drawing the letter "A" may be completely different from another's way of drawing it; nevertheless, because the marks are interchangeable in every context, they function as an equivalence class. In other words, the specific marks or drawings may be very different, but they belong to a *category* of marks.

N. Goodman (1976) distinguished between actual marks, which he called "inscriptions," and the underlying category, which he called "characters." This distinction between *inscriptions* and *characters** is similar to the distinction between sounds and phonemes in language. People have different voices, and in normal speech the sounds blend. Nevertheless, speakers have a categorical perception of speech, meaning that despite the physical differences, they recognize categories of sounds called phonemes. The same holds true for a notation. Despite the physical differences in the inscriptions, the user recognizes categories of inscriptions corresponding to characters.

Think about the way two physicians draw letters. How could anyone possibly know if what they have written is the same or different without a theoretical measuring stick for comparative purposes? Printing has produced an illusion of uniformity in written displays. Yet, the degree of variability of shapes, sizes, and styles in the notational environment is still so enormous that without an internal category to help in recognizing the letter "a," nobody would ever be able to move from one font to another or from one style to another. So when children say, *"This one is in my name,"* while pointing at a letter in a printed word, they are somehow inferring an equivalence class. In a way, they implicitly recognize the basic condition of a notation; if each time we saw the inscriptions we considered them unique, we could never use them for the recording and transporting of information.

In addition to this basic condition, N. Goodman (1976) described four other conditions that characters (not inscriptions) must satisfy in order to be copiable. First, characters must have clear boundaries; they must be *syntactically differentiated* so that for each inscription it is theoretically possible to say to which class they belong. Second, they must be *syntactically disjointed*; it must be clear that each mark belongs to one and only one class of characters. Disjointedness is violated if any inscription belongs to two classes, whether simultaneously or consecutively.

It should be emphasized that it is the characters—the categories underlying classes of inscriptions—and not the inscriptions that are disjointed. For example, the notation for the game "scissors, paper, rock" may involve circles, triangles, and rectangles as characters. When a player draws a shape resembling a rhombus, it is theoretically possible to say either to which character it belongs or to reject it as not being part of the notation. Further, the rhombus can be treated as an example of any one of the classes, but not of more than one. Otherwise, it is impossible to play the game.

The fact that notational elements are copiable means it is possible to determine whether they constitute a closed or an open inventory; that is, it is possible to determine how limited the number of characters is. Notations do not necessarily form a closed inventory; new elements can be added. This happens, for example, when musical scores incorporate new notational elements under the influence of rock music. However, newcomers must be recognized as such. The more closed the system is, the less explicit are the rules required for the recognition of members; nobody needs to have an explicit reason why the letter "C" belongs to the alphabet or the number "7" belongs to the system of numerals. In contrast, mathematical notation is an example of a very open inventory, in which the invention of new notational elements or the change of meaning, order, and positioning is common (Cajori, 1928/1993).

Being copiable, distinguishable, having a name, and forming part of a sequence are features of notations as such, irrespective of the meaning of the elements or the way they are used to convey meaning. Goodman's two final conditions concern the relations between classes of characters and referents. In the *semantic disjointedness* condition, two character classes cannot have a class of referent objects or events in common. Finally, his *semantic differentiation* condition posits that for every event or object it must be theoretically possible to determine its "compliance class," or the class of events or objects to which the particular event or object belongs. Given these four conditions, well-formed notational characters will be unambiguous, that is, each character will map onto one and only one class of referents.

Context Sensitivity Revisited

Notations can be described as such, their elements and composites can be analyzed and compared, and their formal features can be appreciated separately from the function they perform. Indeed, this is what we have being doing so far in this chapter: We have been discussing the formal features of notational systems and the conditions met by notational characters from different notational systems. Notice, however, that we were using mainly one of them (the alphabet) to convey this message. As suggested by Harris (1995), characters can resignify themselves when they are used in different functional contexts in order to serve different communicative functions. In this case, alphabetic characters conveyed a message (about notation) and, from a different perspective, they served to exemplify that message.

In N. Goodman's (1976) view, the whole symbol–meaning system is redefined with shifts in context. Within a certain context, it is possible to go from the notation to the referents and from the referents to the notation; that is, there is a formal mapping in both directions. For example, when alphabetic writing is used to create a text like this one, certain marks refer to a limited range of phonological segments and, conversely, given the pronunciation of a phonological segment, its written notation falls within a limited number of alternatives. The same alphabet, however, can be used in the context of other practices, as in algebra, and the formal mapping from notation to referents and from referents to notation will change accordingly.

The distinction of formal and functional features is important because it allows for the differentiation of what children know about the formal features of notations, as well as their functions and way of operating. It is one thing to recognize the elements of a notation, their names, and their internal order; it is another to process and interpret them. In processing and interpreting, the context in which they appear is determinant. The same letters will be processed differently if they are used in the context of an algebraic equation, the table of contents of a book, or a poem. These two characteristics of notational elements— that they are copiable and may be subject to more than one interpretation according to their context—are quite complex.

Each time we are confronted with notational elements, we recognize them as being the same (disregarding variations) and, at the same time, as being subject to different interpretations. When reasoning about notations, and also when using them, we implicitly perform different operations. On the one hand, we perform a categorical attribution, without which it would be impossible to recognize a certain shape as a letter and another as a numeral. On the other hand, we infer the signified from the signifier. Toddlers and preschoolers in the process of learning notational systems put all these operations into play.

Some key points in this chapter are the following:

- External representations become such only when someone interprets them. Consequently, they are dependent on internal representations.
- External representations can be subjected to multiple interpretations.
- Nonetheless, external representations have their own characteristics and constraints.
- The creation and interpretation of external representations entails an interaction between internal and external representations that makes the external representations powerful cognitive tools. Their potency results from the amount and variety of cognitive work that is put into play when using, interpreting, and forming them.
- The main dimension that distinguishes pictorial from scriptorial devices is that the latter belong to a system. People recognize pictorial devices as unique and interpret scriptorial devices in terms of a notational system.
- The basic condition of a notation is that it is copiable. This condition is based on the psychological capacities of inference and categorical perception and it enables the reproduction of content with a defined set of elements.
- Context is necessary for defining the meaning of notational elements. The same notational elements may have different meanings in different contexts.
- The distinction of formal and functional features is crucial for evaluating notational knowledge. One should be able to name, describe, and order notational elements without having to use them in any operative way. Further, one should be able to use them in one context but not in another.

In this chapter, we have looked at external notational systems from the most abstract perspective, irrespective of social use, and ahistorically. It has been assumed that this view on notation will increase our understanding of the subject matter that children make their own when they learn to write. Nevertheless, this is only a partial view on notations, as notational systems have a long social history and many features are the result of this history. In the next chapter, we will approach notational systems through their historical origins. The purpose of this historical review is not to claim that there is a recapitulation of social history in the individual process of acquisition. Rather, this approach will hopefully illuminate many problems that children face in the process of making these social objects their own.

2

What Historians Say About the Origin and History of Writing and Numerals

Primitive man was happy, except when hungry, Rudyard Kipling assures us. In the beginning, man could neither read nor write, but then events conspired to bring about the invention of the alphabet. Just what happened exactly? In his *Just So Stories*, Kipling (1902/1989) told of a fishing expedition that a young girl, Taffimai, makes with her father. During the expedition, her father's spear breaks so they are unable to catch carp in the river. Taffimai thinks to herself that it is such a pity that she does not know how to write. She then sees a stranger approaching, which gives her an idea. She scratches a drawing on a piece of bark from a birch tree asking her mother to send a new spear. Taffimai gives the bark to the stranger and tells him to deliver the message to her mother. The drawing is misunderstood and the stranger is unable to explain its meaning because he does not speak the same language as Taffimai's tribe. The mother thinks that her husband is in danger and summons the whole tribe to help him. Confusion reigns, but when it has died down the chief of the tribe congratulates young Taffimai for her idea of transmitting messages. He predicts that the day will come when this great invention will be known as writing. He claims that although the system now consists only of drawings, one day they will be replaced by letters, "twenty six to be exact," which would not be misinterpreted as the drawing had been. The chief of the tribe then warns Taffimai that the next time she wants to communicate by means of drawings she should make sure that someone speaking her language can interpret the drawing.

I have chosen to start this chapter, which examines the historical perspective of writing and numbers, with a popular tale, a nonhistorical story, because popular tales usually reflect deep-rooted beliefs; and these beliefs sometimes, as in this case, are refuted by historical evidence. Certainly, the chief of the tribe was correct in his belief that writing would be invented, and he was also correct in observing that writing helps to record language and to overcome distance. But, he was only partially correct in his prediction about the number of letters forming the alphabet. In the Spanish alphabet, for example, there are more than 26 letters. In common with certain historians of writing, the chief of the tribe was using the English alphabet as his measuring stick. This chapter aims to show that his other claims were mistaken as well.

Writing does not derive from drawing. Although it is frequently argued that arbitrary writing systems were derived from picture writing, there is evidence to suggest an alternative development. Similarly, although there can be no doubt that one of the main functions of writing is to represent language, other human needs seem to have conspired in its genesis. Finally, contrary to what Kipling's tribal chief suggested, it was actually outsiders, unable to speak the language in which an original message was encoded, who were to play a vital role in the development of writing. As a matter of fact, most writing systems evolved from people's attempt to translate messages written in a language different from their own.

Before proceeding any further, consider the reasons for including a chapter on historical developments in a book about child development. It is tempting to suggest that "ontogeny recapitulates phylogeny," that a child's individual history recapitulates the social history of writing and numerals, as some have suggested on previous occasions (Tolchinsky-Landsmann, 1989; Tversky, Kugelmass, & Winter, 1991). Indeed, as we shall see in the following chapter, some of the ways in which children write before learning conventional writing are strikingly similar to the ways their predecessors were writing 2000 years ago. Yet, today, the environment in which a child setting out on the path to becoming literate is immersed differs so much from that of illiterate communities as they moved toward the development of writing that it is unrealistic to make any kind of claim for recapitulation. Their respective points of departure are poles apart. Nowadays, no matter the poverty one has to suffer, writing has permeated our culture to the extent that it forms part of the mental space of even the illiterate. Most children growing up in Western communities are exposed to printed materials almost from birth, and their first attempts at writing might even be electronic. Today children might learn to manipulate a computer mouse before learning how to grasp a pencil, and they might learn to interact with a computer screen before interacting with a book. It is nonsense to ignore this qualitative difference. There is something intrinsically different between inventing new tools and appropriating existing tools, as Scribner (1985) pointed out. So, if not to defend an assumption of recapitulation, what is the purpose of dwelling on historical accounts?

Psychologists and educators have much to learn from analyzing *the reasons* that led to the emergence and subsequent evolution of certain systems of writing and noting numbers. They can also learn from *the principles* underlying the different systems of number notation and writing and from *the processes* that enabled different cultures to progress from one system to another. It might sound overly scholastic—*Thou shalt learn from history*—but you will hopefully see its utility for yourself. Learning about the importance of the principle of term-to-term correspondence in the historical unfolding of number notation will make it much easier to understand its role in a child's development of number notation. A discussion of the different operations that may link elements in other notational systems will contain useful criteria for analyzing children's ways of combining numerals. An understanding of why proper names had such an impact on the history of writing will help to explain why recognizing and learning to write their own names plays such an important role in a child's acquisition of notions of writing. Finally, discovering why attempts to adapt a script created for another language led to an evolution in the scripts and in their users will help with appreciation of the role of notations in a child's development.

Let's consider this last point a bit more fully. Most writing systems and our own system of numeration did not emerge out of the blue, isolated from other forms of notation. Rather, they resulted from the adaptation or readaptation of previously existing systems. Frequently, this process of adaptation occurred when foreign conquerors or travelers encountered written signs that were used by other people. Confronted with signs written on certain objects (scrolls, tablets, and stones) or in certain places, conquerors and travelers attempted to interpret these signs. Sometimes, but not always, they were helped by local users who could act as informants. In any case, the attempt to interpret the signs triggered a number of operations. People attempting to interpret the signs had to look closely at them and search for similarities and differences. They had to infer possible meanings and attempt to map what other people said might be written there, or what they themselves believed might be written. This would be even more marked if those conquerors or travelers decided that it might be useful for them to have something similar for their own use and tried to adapt what they had found to their own needs, meanings, and languages. Then the same operations were again put into play (e.g., comparison, inferences, and mapping of possible meanings). These operations affected both the system of representation and the users. The introduction to this book, when describing the features of external representations, argued that one such feature was to enable online interaction between production and perception. When foreigners are adapting a script to their writing needs, there is an interaction between the message they want to convey and the features of the script. They may need signs that are not in the script, so they have to change the meaning of existing letters, adapting them to their needs. This occurred when the Greeks adopted the Phoenician alphabet and had to introduce signs for representing vowels. These are the occasions when learning occurs because in searching for the signs, they analyzed the message and in analyzing the message, they found a better way to represent it. In many respects, this process resembles the process undertaken by preschoolers when they are attempting to assemble a word and look for the right letter. They perform an increasing analysis of the word, which in turn facilitates a more careful representation of its components. The discontinuous characteristic of writing—the fact that there are separate graphic elements—then facilitates the analysis of a stream of speech in which sounds are blended. It is easier to monitor the analysis of speech with the help of the graphic signs of writing than by merely reflecting on the stream of speech without the support of the written signs. Once the words are analyzed into components, children can attempt more carefully to represent each component.

Incidentally, an awareness of the role of "foreigners" in the historical development of writing also helps us to appreciate how useful it is to have children speaking different languages in their classrooms. These children will be attempting to read the same written message, and each child will apply the knowledge they have of their own respective languages. It helps to imagine how useful it would be to work in class with the conflicts that may emerge when there are many ways of reading the same letters, or when the letters are not appropriate for representing a particular word in another language. The conflicts between what is said and what is written, the need to search for a particular sign to represent a sound, or the opportunity to compare different readings of the same graphic elements are excellent opportunities for raising awareness about the relation between sounds and letters.

Indeed, by addressing historical issues it is possible to move away from the familiar principles and imagine other ways of writing. The only way to appreciate children's ideas about writing and numbers is to discover the logic underlying their conceptions, and the only way to understand their logic is to break away from our own way of reasoning. If we believe that the only way to interpret 12 is as "twelve," then we will never be able to understand why some children may read the figures as "three." An awareness of the historical existence of additive systems, that is, systems in which juxtaposed signs must be added to get the value they represent, helps to explain the logic underlying some behavior that may initially appear to be simply erroneous.

However, an understanding of unconventional ways of writing requires an awareness of the difference between the principles underlying a notational system and the notational forms or elements that are used in the system, because the same forms or elements can be regulated by different principles. In chapter 1 we saw that what defines something as a drawing, writing, or a number is not its outward appearance but the fact that it belongs to a system. We also insisted that the rules of the system—what we have termed the organizing principles—determine the meaning of the elements because the same elements might be used with different principles. As an example, the elements used in cuneiform writing were used both as a syllabic system and as an alphabetic system. Similarly, for numerical notation, many times letters were used to represent numbers. For example, the chapters in the Old Testament are numbered with Hebrew letters. The Hebrew system included the beginning of the utilization of place value even though it used the letters of the alphabet. With children's evolving notations, there might be cases in which conventional English letters are used with different underlying principles—for representing parts of words instead of phonemes. And, numerals can be used under additive or multiplicative principles. Therefore, differentiating between notational shapes and notational principles is a must for understanding notational development. Finally, an additional motive for examining other systems of writing and number notations is to gain familiarity with the terms and processes that will be used later when analyzing children's productions.

But, why spend time speculating about the *origin* of writing? Here, once again, this takes advantage of the main feature of external representations, their permanence. The fact that writing is permanent, in contrast to the ephemeral nature of speech, makes it possible to trace the origin of certain early scripts and perhaps even the oldest of all. Moreover, in one of the cases examined, namely those societies that read Latin in their vernacular languages (apparently without being aware of it), there is the opportunity to trace certain aspects of the history of a spoken language through a written language. Unlike spoken language, therefore, in the case of writing there is evidence of the conditions under which a language emerged because there are actual material traces to look at. So, writing systems often emerged from a previous system or, in those cases in which no other writing system existed, there were other notational systems from which writing might have evolved.

In Kipling's tale, Taffimai resorts to drawing quite out of the blue. Notational systems, in contrast, did not emerge in a notational vacuum. As Coulmas (1990) explained about preliterate communities:

> There would be no books, no newspapers, no letters, no tax reports, no pay checks, no identity cards, no lecture notes, no street signs, no labels on commercial products, no advertisements, no medical prescriptions, no systematic education, no dictionaries or encyclopedias, no instruction manuals for radios, cars, and computers, a very different

kind of religion, a very different kind of law, and no science in the proper sense of the word; there would be no linguistics either. (p. 4)

Nevertheless, human beings have been involved in notational activities for the last 30,000 years—from daubs on a cave wall to clicking a mouse to produce a mark on a screen, every imaginable surface and instrument has been exploited in leaving traces. Even then, only a tiny part of the diversity of materials used will have stood the test of time.

In Western Asia, Europe, and pre-Columbian America, traces have been found on rocks, tortoiseshells, ox and sheep scapulae, the bark of the birch tree, papyrus, parchment, clay, wax, and stones. These marks depict figures of men and women, animals, and geometrical forms—lines, dots, circles. There were many tallying devices and a variety of markings like the brands on livestock, a craftsman's hallmarks, tattoos and totems, notches on bones and notches on sticks, and *wampum* beaded belts (Barton, 1994). Doubtless, any attempt to classify the vast number of traces left by human beings in terms of shape or function would be subverted by a literate bias concerning the uses and functions of these objects and traces. It is still a matter of discussion as to whether certain groups of objects or traces were used to fulfil specific purposes or whether the same objects or shapes might have served multiple functions in different communicative contexts (Harris, 1986). In any case, however, these diverse objects and traces were likely used to reckon time, to record events, to register people, to symbolize ownership, to represent the divine, to delimit territorial boundaries, to express danger, and to identify places, people, and merchandise.

The main purpose of this chapter is to present historical evidence in support of the argument that permeates the book: External representation in general and notational systems in particular are a source of knowledge and further development. In essence, this argument is little more than that old claim, made by more than one teacher, that "the best way to learn how to write is to write" both at an individual and at a social level.

PROTOTYPICAL ACCOUNTS
OF THE HISTORY OF WRITING

Prototypical means the most widely known, that is, what appears in almost every textbook. This account of the history of writing systems[3] describes them as having a monogenetic source (a single evolutionary line) and a history that can

---

[3]My source of information regarding the history of writing and number is somewhat limited to what is available in the West, and I would like to advise readers, in particular students of literacy research, not to take this story of the history of writing and numbers from the Western perspective as *the* history. Thanks are due to Kang Lee for the previous observation.

be characterized as "a development from embryo-writing through pictography through ideography, and then to phonetic writing, first syllabic and finally alphabetic" (Diringer, 1962, p. 23). Within this account, all forms of external representation up to phonetic writing are not considered true writing but "embryo-writing," "forerunners" (Gelb, 1963), or "protowriting" (Métraux, 1971) because they lack signs of pronunciation.

Three assumptions, which have been highly influential until very recently, underscore this account. First is the idea that writing has a pictorial origin. The second suggests that there is one path of historical development, a sort of single evolutionary line in the internal development of scripts. The third assumption is the idea that the aim of writing is to move toward a fully explicit representation of the sounds of speech. I am critical of this account for many reasons, basically for its ethnocentric bias. In this account, every system that differs from the alphabetic system is treated as inferior, less efficient, and less abstract. And the whole history of writing is as though the alphabet was always the final objective.

These assumptions, particularly the suggestion that there is a single history for all the writing systems in the world, have been very much criticized by current historians of writing (Coulmas, 1990; Harris, 1986; Sampson, 1985). They claim that such an account is simply a flashback interpretation of the history of writing, an interpretation by which any writing system is evaluated by "projecting" the features of the Greek/Roman alphabet instead of seeking to understand the system as it is. (See the aside on the Projection Principle.)

There is no doubt that phonographic (or glottographic) systems* in which individual signs refer to sounds were preceded by semasiographic systems* in which icons represent ideas. But precedence does not necessarily imply derivation or relative immaturity. Certainly, "when we transfer attention from primitive to a more highly civilized society, we invariably find that semasiographic systems are replaced by glottographic writing of one type or another though whether glottographic writing historically has always grown out of earlier semasiographic systems is an open question" (Sampson, 1985, p. 30). However, if current uses of writing are considered, then it is possible to say that writing could evolve toward semasiography. Indeed, there is an increasing tendency in this direction. Just look at the instructions of your washing machine!

Another problem with the prototypical account is that developments not directly related to speech are put to one side. In most historical accounts of writing, there is almost no mention of systems for notating numbers or mathematical operations because they are unrelated to spoken language. And yet, no set of graphic forms ever developed into a writing system without also developing a notation of number (Sampson, 1985). And more important, as discussed later, the ancestors of Sumerian writing, which is regarded as the oldest true writing system, were not born for representing spoken language. Unlike

THE PROJECTION PRINCIPLE

Projection is very common when psychologists or teachers are interpreting children's productions. Two examples, one related to the interpretation of the regulating principles of a writing system and the second related to the interpretation of children's writing, serve to clarify what is meant by projection.

India has more than 200 scripts derived from the oldest Brahami script. If the rules of English are projected onto Brahami script, it might be said that each letter stands for two elements C + V (one consonant and one vowel), so the Brahami letter (+) *ka* would be interpreted as representing /k/ + /a/. For Hindu grammarians, however, consonants are not separable elements but rather articulatory points of contact. So, each letter represents just one element; there can be no further analysis into "smaller" units. Viewed only via its alphabet, there is the risk of evaluating this script as being less exhaustive than it actually is (Filliozat, 1971).

Now consider an example of the projection principle as applied to the interpretation of children's writing. Many 4-year-olds have been observed to spell *Coca-Cola* with four letters (e.g., CAOA) instead of eight. If the rules of our way of writing are projected onto this word, then it might be said that some letters are missing. But, if attempts are made to understand the child's way of writing as it is, then the discovery is made that the child is using another unit of correspondence; instead of writing one letter for each phone, the child is writing one letter for each syllable. Thus, the child writes the word *salami* with three letters (e. g., SLI) and the word *mandarina* with four letters (e.g., MAIA).

Kipling's supposition, the seed of writing lies in the need to fulfil a very mundane necessity: that of knowing *how much of this commodity* or *how many of these items I have*. Our ancestors responded to this necessity by applying their ability to create term-to-term correspondences—a most suitable way of answering the question: *How much do I have?* But, when more than one kind of merchandise was forwarded, our ancestors had to indicate not only quantity but also kind: They had to indicate how many of each type of merchandise were delivered. At first, however, quantity was undetached from kind. That is, there were different groups of tokens for different commodities. When trading started to increase in times of economic growth, this became a problem because there was a need to look for an ever-increasing variety of tokens for the different things traded. Besides, for some quantities, it is not very practical to resort to one-to-one correspondence. Imagine getting 212 sheep and 89 cows! Gradually, from these limitations emerged the notation of number and words.

THE SEED(S) OF WRITING

The earliest findings concerning the most direct antecendent of our writing system consist of a system of artifacts used by ancient Sumerians living from the –9th millennium onward in what is now southern Iraq (Schmandt-Besserat, 1978, 1990, but see also Gelb, 1980). Artifacts have been found in abundance at archaeological sites over an area extending from southwest Turkey to Pakistan, where the economy was based on livestock and crops. They are clay tokens or counters of various geometrical forms: spheres, discs, cones, and tetrahedrons. It seems that ritual images were also used, although they did not always represent the divine. That is, the same figures served both very sacred and very mundane purposes. Through this use, the figures were "demythologized" (Crump, 1990); they lost part of their sacred value and could therefore be subject to different interpretations. Hence, the ritual images could undergo the formal changes necessary for adapting them to the keeping of records of flocks, herds, and agricultural produce to be delivered to other places. The same objects gained new meaning in the context of different activities, which is true for most notational objects.

As explained by Schmandt-Besserat (1996), "The tokens lacked the capacity for dissociating the numbers from the items counted: one sphere stood for 'one bushel of grain' and three spheres stood for 'one bushel of grain, one bushel of grain, one bushel of grain' … Thus, tokens for counting sheep were supplemented by special tokens for counting rams, ewes, and lambs" (p. 96). The forms representing the animals or products were not figurative, but it is difficult to evaluate which were motivated and which were fully abstract. (See Fig. 2.1.)

Some are visibly arbitrary, like the cylinders and lenticular disks that represented one or a group of animals, but others were probably iconic. For example, the cone and ovoid, which represented a measure of grain and a unit of oil, may stand for a small cup and a pointed jar (Schmandt-Besserat, 1996, p. 94). The organizing principles of the system were very simple. There was a *one-to-one correspondence*—between forms and animals, that is, one form for one animal. There was also the principle of *iteration*—similar forms were repeatedly used until they depicted the desired quantity. Another principle was *prototype distinction*—each kind of product had a distinctive form. This principle served to decide which animals should be included under a certain form and which ought to be included elsewhere.

FIG. 2.1.   Clay tokens from Susa, Iran. Départment des Antiquités Orientales, Musée du Lou-vre Photo R. M. N.-Jerome Galland. Reprinted with permission.

This system was created to know how many sheep or how many crops were for sale. In order to know *how many* items of something we have, we count. We can per-form the action of counting on any collection of objects whatsoever, using any list of words, but the action of counting is regulated by a number of universal principles. When counting order is not necessary, we can start with any one object; we must only take care that a different word is available for every object and that none is left without being counted. Also, the final word must include all the objects that have been counted (Gelman & Gallistel, 1978). The system from which writing stems was born to fulfill a very utilitarian function in the context of a fixed pattern of behavior[4] (counting) that could be performed with any kind of label or object, even ritual images. This use enabled the same objects to be seen with different meanings, according to the rules of use, similar to the case of the game "rock, paper, scissors," in chapter 1. Harris (1986) reflected on this process in very precise terms:

> In a pre-literate culture ... emblems (whether of the sun, the moon, the animals) pro-vide a set of graphically isomorphic archetypes which form a natural basis for any po-tential development in the direction of literacy. The seed of writing will lie in the possibility of opening up a gap between the pictorial and the scriptorial function of the

---

[4]Before the discovery of the Susa tokens, there were historians who assumed that other ritualized sit-uations, which existed in every culture, may have functioned similarly as fixed patterns of behavior from which notational systems might have arisen (Hodge, 1975).

emblematic sign. Its germination will be the process which then leads to development of a distinct set of graphic signs, which are used solely in association with the scriptorial function.

The obvious social path which such a development might follow would involve the gradually extended use of emblematic signs for purely "utilitarian" purposes. One such cultural breeding ground—and arguably the most ancient—lies in the various practices, beliefs and methods associated with counting. (p. 132)

Contrary to prototypical accounts (e.g., Gelb, 1963), a picture is not at the basis of every writing system; an accounting system lies at the basis of our own writing systems. This system used preexisting images or objects that changed their original meaning, probably sacred or magic, in the context of the new more mundane functions. This system in turn furnished some of its elements (and some of its representational strategies) to the first known writing system. The process by which this may have occurred is outlined later.

In the −4th millennium there was a major evolution in cities, trade, and crafts. Sumerian trade enjoyed a period of economic boom, which had an effect on the complexity of the representational system (in the history of writing, economic abundance and development of writing were always related). Whenever a new product had to be commercialized, a new class of token was created by means of internal differentiation of existing tokens. For example, if a cone represented a sheep and people needed to represent a cow, an animal not previously traded, they might make a hole in the cone to create a subtype of the original token. The flourishing of this economy multiplied the items and classes of items to be traded and to be inventoried. The number of forms and subtypes of forms increased, creating a truly notational system. And so a new, different operation was needed for this system.

In systems based on *one-to-one correspondence* and *iteration*—called token-iterative systems (Harris, 1986)—the checking of amounts always requires recounting. As the amount increases, so does the burden, the time, and the recording space needed. It was at this point that "bullae" (singular "bull"), clay containers to hold the tokens, appeared. The counting tokens sealed inside the bullae, perhaps for security reasons, provide a record of the transaction (Harris, 1986, p. 72). The system was very secure, but each time recounting or checking of merchandise had to be undertaken, the bullae had to be broken.

The solution to this problem can be considered "the great invention:" People started *to mark* the outside of the clay bull, when still wet, so as to indicate what was inside. They started recording the *number* and *type* of tokens inside the bull. It may be the case that the external appearance of the two signs was very similar or that each sign, one for quantity and one for quality, had different meanings in other contexts. The point is not whether they were specially created signs, or whether they had the same or different form, but rather the new semiotic relation that was established. The impressions on the bullae were signs of the tokens inside them, which in turn were signs of the counted items. They were "second-order signs," or signs of signs. When tokens were used for recording, they could be directly manipulated to control the transaction. But the impressions on the bullae could not be manipulated for checking the amount of merchandise; they had to be interpreted. Thus, these second-order signs enabled (and indeed obliged) a new activity: interpretation by thinking or by saying something. It is in *the interpretation* of the impressions where the link to language was established (Coulmas, 1990).

This is a very different explanation from that offered by the Chief of the tribe in the opening story. The Chief suggested that the need for recording a verbal message geared the invention of writing, whereas in the historical account just reconstructed the link to language is an outcome of *interpreting traces* rather than an outcome of a *reflection on spoken language*. Notice that the link to language is from the external representation to the linguistic expression rather than from the need to produce a verbal message to the external representation. It is not that people *reflect on* language and decide what should be represented; this was a later development. Initially, people recorded objects and activities, and then used language for interpreting.

METALINGUISTIC REFLECTION AND WRITING

The ability to reflect on language as opposed to the ability to use language is called metalinguistic ability. When someone says, "This word is very long," that person is reflecting on the length of the word *as such;* the word is not being used for communicative purposes. Therefore, this person produces a metalinguistic statement. People may reflect on the syntactic, lexical, phonological, or phonetic characteristics of language. In normal use, people scarcely reflect on the language they are using. It is transparent; people speak through it but do not reflect on it. In metalinguistic reflection language becomes opaque.

Some psychologists and linguists think that it is difficult to reflect on language as such without the help of a writing system that somehow fixes the flow of speech for further inspection (e.g., Olson, 1994; Scholes, 1993). With the help of writing, people can go back to what they have said and reflect on it. To think that writing emerges from the need to transmit a linguistic message assumes that people are able to reflect on what they want to say *as such,* in order to look for some means of expression (but without the help of writing because it did not exist).

The impressions on the bullae did not encode linguistic expressions, they simply denoted a group of tokens. However, they could be linguistically described; they could be named and asked for. Some were probably interpreted using words for quantity and some were interpreted with the words the language had for animals or whatever product was represented in the tokens. This might have provoked the emergence of two types of signs: one to depict the total of counted items, meaning the *number-word* used in the language as the last label of the counting procedure, and another to depict the *name of the animal or object* counted. This again speculates on a possible psychological explanation for the reasons of differentiation of the two types of signs.

Every language has count-words that are used to count objects ('one,' 'two,' 'three'), as distinct from labeling-words that are used to name objects ('apple,' 'tree,' 'sheep'), although some languages have words that serve both for counting purposes and to name parts of the body (Hurford, 1987; Ifrah, 1997). Two psychologists, Gelman (1990) and Gelman and Meck (1986), showed that very young children keep the set of count-words separate from the set of labeling-words, using them correctly in their corresponding contexts. The two psychologists suggested very convincingly that human beings have a natural tendency to separate these two kinds of terms and to apply them in different situations. In general, by 2½ years of age, American children differentiate number-words from labeling-words. Therefore, it is not unreasonable to speculate that the two kinds of signs were separated as a consequence of people being uncomfortable using two different procedures counting and naming on the same sign. Again, it is not the form of the sign that counts, but the differentiating function.

According to Denisse Schmandt-Besserat (1996), with time the tokens became less and less important, until they were substituted by impressions that could be interpreted linguistically. Sumerian script evolved from these impressions. As sound as this account might be, it has been criticized by Michalowski (1996), who provided a less "evolutionary" view, claiming that the Sumerian script did not evolve gradually but was invented as a whole. According to Michalowski (1996), some elements were taken from preexisting systems, and the signs they used for numbers may have been adapted from the clay counters, but "the quantum leap to the conceptualization of the earliest writing system was without precedent" (p. 35). In any case, however, either by gradual development or by invention, the Sumerian script was phonographic. The majority of individual signs represent whole words because Sumerian was predominately monosyllabic, but they could be used as syllables in other contexts. And the script had special signs for numerals. In fact, one of the strongest pieces of evidence demonstrating that a script is phonographic is the presence of special signs for numbers (Sampson, 1985).

So far, the discussion has identified a number of processes that seem to be at the basis of number notation and writing. An external representation was created to satisfy the necessity of recording quantity and quality, amount and kind, by applying two basic operations: term-to-term correspondence and iteration. The marks used for recording were linguistically interpreted and, from the interpretation, the recording marks became differentiated for different functions. An initial state of affairs (counting of merchandise) was modified by the use of an external means of representation (clay tokens) that was created to handle the initial situation. The initial means of representation was then modified for handling the situation more efficiently (impressions came to substitute for the tokens), but then a crucial change occurred in the way in which the means of representation was handled (from manipulation to interpretation). This in turn led to a dramatic change in the representational system (differentiation between types of signs), corresponding to the emergence of writing and number notation. Note that the purported processes trace a path of development that goes from external representation to interpretation and back to external representation recursively as new representational problems arise. The solutions to these problems resulted in a reorganization of the representational system through the introduction of new principles. The whole process illustrates anew the dialectical interaction between users and representational means (Zelazo, 2000). This path is 'packed' around the origin of notational systems. The next section tackles how it unfolds through the historical development of number notation.

PRINCIPLES IN HISTORICAL NOTATION OF NUMBER

In prehistoric wars, the winner could exact a reward from the defeated party—a certain amount paid in jewelry or cowries (shells used for money) for each warrior that had been killed. How did the winner know exactly how many men had been lost? This was accomplished by simple *concrete* numerical notations (Ifrah, 1981, 1997). Before leaving for war, each warrior would leave his own identifying stone on a pile, and after the war the survivors took back their stones. The stones that were left were used in determining the reward. By specific term-to-term correspondence, the number of lives lost could be determined. Indeed, the same procedure was employed in more pacific situations as well. If livestock had to be moved from one place to another, then the owner marked tallies on a stick. Once the *counting by marking* was finished, the tally stick could be split lengthwise, each half being the "split and image" of the other (Skemp, 1986, p. 140). These so-called token-iterative devices could then be used to perform a direct mapping to record quantity without the marker or the interpreter actually knowing how many items there were in total. Even cultures with a small vocabulary of number-words, such as the Botocudos of Brazil, who only had one word for 'unit' and another for 'pair,' could use these devices. Cultures created a similar marking of different kinds—knots, notches, or tallies—in one-to-one correspondence with the enumerated set. Ifrah (1997) was right in suggesting that numerical notation "started with this artifact called term-to-term correspondence" (p. 54). However, with increasing use and increases in the complexity of the situations to be encoded, a new operation was needed if concrete systems were to remain useful.

The Grouping Principle

Token iterative devices were a tremendous burden both for marking and for interpreting. A direct mapping had to be performed each time merchandise had to be counted. Perhaps if people had the capacity to compare a long line of tallies with a group of sheep, they may have continued to use token-iterative devices for a long time. But, fortunately for the development of numerical notations, human beings have limitations when it comes to recognizing quantities. Thus, although people are capable of rapid recognition up to three or four items (an ability called *subitizing* or *subitization*, from the Latin *subitus*, which means sudden), above four it becomes difficult to know "how many there are" or to compare two sets and decide where there are more (or fewer) items if the difference is very small (Dehaene, 1992, 1997; Mandler & Shebo, 1982). To avoid the constant toil of counting, *grouping* marks were developed as a good solution. Even today, when people have to count items of any kind, they find ways to group marks. Instead of writing IIIIII, what we usually do is write IIII-II. People can also indicate grouping by creating a space III IIII IIII, or by creating a special sign that denotes a group of marks rather than one mark. For the Romans, the letter V represented five marks.

Most societies in the world have developed this sort of grouping at a certain point in their history. For example, in the Archaic Sumerian system (at the beginning of the −3rd millennium), 'four' was written with four semicircular marks on one line but 'five' was written on two lines (Ifrah, 1997, p. 5). See Fig. 2.2.

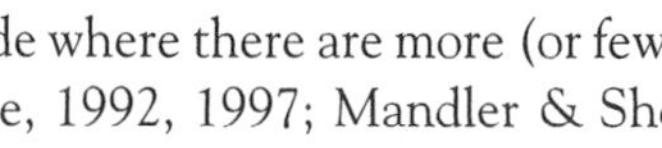

FIG. 2.2.   Digits in archaic Sumerian.

It is highly revealing that "grouping" starts, in general, above four, at the limit at which adults (and infants) are able to subitize. This suggests the universality of subitizing. Initially, grouping was accomplished by creating spaces between the same marks, but afterward it was extended by creating new notational elements *for a group of marks*. By so doing, the notation became much more economical and efficient; with fewer elements, bigger quantities could be marked without the burden of mapping once and again. However, the notation became more obscure. In notations where signs stood for groups of marks, the one-to-one correspondence that was explicit in ungrouped notations became embedded, and therefore implicit. On the other hand, in the notations where signs for groups had not been invented, the notation became more ambiguous because the elements in the notation attained different meanings, one for explicitly representing units, the other to represent groups of units.

The creation of these notational elements gave rise to three new "notational problems": First, the meaning of the elements for groups of marks had to be known; it could not been seen directly anymore. Second, direct counting was no longer possible. Third, the relation between elements of different meaning, one for units and another for groups, now had to be defined. Take, for example, the Archaic Sumerian notation where there was a graphic sign for units and a more circular sign for tens—shown in Fig. 2.3. In this case, direct counting was no longer possible.

So, in order to determine how much is represented, users had to know that the circular sign meant ten unseen elements. Then, if users knew this, in order to count, they would have to decompose (internally or externally) the notational elements—they could not count directly.

Finally, users needed to know the relation between the written elements and the operational meaning of these relations, that is, under what operation the elements are linked. According to Sumerian rules, the two elements in Fig. 2.3 had to be interpreted as 'eleven' because the Sumerian system was additive; to arrive at the total, the two adjacent elements had to be added. But had the system been multiplicative instead of additive, then the two elements would have

FIG. 2.3.   Units and tens in archaic Sumerian.

meant ten, the result of multiplying (10) × (1), therefore 10. Clearly, children in the process of becoming numerate have to deal with a very efficient but rather hermetic system. Chapters 4 and 5 show how they undo this hermetism in order to understand its functioning.

Operational Principles

Written elements can be related by addition, subtraction, or multiplication. In *additive* systems, the notational elements for units and for groups of units are juxtaposed and the total amount is obtained by addition. As seen earlier, Archaic Sumerian is an additive system. Therefore, 22 is expressed by repeating the symbol for 10 twice and the symbol for 1 twice. If elements are related by multiplication, then two elements standing one beside the other must be multiplied instead of added. And, if they are related by subtraction, then one element must be subtracted from the other. Note that the operational principles are not necessarily linked to particular grouping criteria. For any given grouping criterion (e.g., where elements may correspond to each ten, two, or twenty), the operation by which the elements are related can be addition, multiplication, subtraction, or a combination of these.

Consider the Babylonian notation, which was dominant by the end of the −2nd millennium. They used the same Sumerian signs, but had a different grouping criterion: 60. The operations relating the notational elements were addition, multiplication, and subtraction. The late Egyptian hieroglyphic system was a base 10, but the elements were related under addition and multiplication, with a strict notational constraint: No more than four repeated elements were allowed. The Roman system is based on addition, but a subtraction principle is applied as well to overcome a notational constraint. Because no element could be repeated more than three times, 'four' is written IV.

The Positional Principle

Even with marks for units and marks for groups, the number of marks needed for representing large quantities can be very big. Thus, to make the system more efficient and use a limited set of marks, another principle regulating notations is that of *place* or *position*. It was used almost from the inception of numerical notations, even before the full use of the principle of place value in the Hindu-Arabic system. This principle holds that the value of an element varies according to its position in a string of elements.

The Babylonian sexagesimal system marks the earliest appearance (−1900 to −1800) of the *principle of position* in representing number. The Roman system also makes use of position; IV is read 'four,' whereas VI is read 'six.' Thanks to this principle, the same forms can be used for different meanings. That is, forms have a face value that is evident even when they appear in isolation, and a positional value that is relevant when they are integrated in combinations. In general, the more efficient the system, the more specific the knowledge required for understanding its functioning.

NOTATIONAL PRINCIPLES AND NOTATIONAL FORMS

The principles of grouping, operation, and position can be applied to any form. The Hebrew system, for example, began to use place value, but with the letters of the alphabet. The Hebrews used all the letters of the alphabet on base 10, including the allographs (i.e., the letters that are used with a different form at the end of words), for representing the numbers up to 900. Additional symbols were then added to differentiate higher level units, for example, two dots on top of a letter symbolized a thousand. In this way, any number less than a million could be represented. Because Hebrew was written from right to left, the number with the highest value appeared on the right. Therefore, if the inscription contained *dalet* (the fourth letter) with two dots on top to the extreme right, and then *aleph* (the first letter), then it would have been read as *four thousand one*; if, on the other hand, it appeared the other way round, that is *aleph* with two dots on top to the extreme right and afterward *dalet*, then it would have been interpreted as *one thousand four.* (See Fig. 2.4.)

Almost every writing system included special notational elements for numbers, but many people besides the Hebrew used the letters of their respective writing systems for this purpose. To mention just a few, this included the Syrians, the Greeks, and the Romans who, having first developed strictly numerical symbols, later moved on to using the letters of their alphabet.

FIG. 2.4. The positional principle using Hebrew letters.

Apart from letters, there was a huge diversity of elements that were tempo-rarily structured to function as number notation. In the development of Hindu-Arabic numerals in Europe, for example, there are more than 1,000 clas-sified examples (Hill, 1915, in Cajori, 1928/1993, p. 45). Besides the notational systems used by a community, mathematicians invented and created their own marks for computational purposes or to solve mathematical problems.[5]

The Use of Notational Elements for Representing Absence

When the principle of positional value is systematically applied, the need to have a special notational element for representing the absence of units becomes evi-dent. Imagine for a moment our written system without a zero: How would it be possible to determine whether 1 was "one" or "ten"? As this system is positional, the answer is clear: The 1 must be put in the first position, and the zero in second position, thereby indicating that there is nothing in the second position. The situ-ation becomes even worse when it is necessary to indicate the absence of different orders of units, as when writing 600, where two empty spaces must be indicated.

The first attempts to solve this notational problem consisted in leaving empty spaces, as is apparent from early Babylonian tablets (Ifrah, 1997, p. 370). Obviously, this solution created much confusion when scribes, frequently igno-rant of what they were copying, deleted or modified the spacing. A special graphic element for denoting *empty space* was needed and it was first to appear in Babylonian lunar tables and numerical texts in the form of a double peg during the −3rd century.[6] This special notational element was devised to indicate an in-tentional lack of a recording and, when so needed, to denote the absence of units of a certain order. Interestingly, its use was strictly notational; it was used to ensure the correct interpretation of the empty space but not necessarily to denote "nothing." When Babylonians had to indicate that the result of a trans-action was null, they did not use this special sign, they stated in words that the result was null (Ifrah, 1997, p. 377).

The Mayas of Central America systematically used a symbol for zero in a po-sitional system of numeration over 1,900 years ago, centuries before the West-ern world adopted a symbol for zero. The few manuscripts that survive from the

---

[5]This situation still prevails even for the notation of digits. For example, 7 is notated with a crossed stroke in South America and Europe. The comma indicates a decimal place in South America but marks off thousands in North America and the United Kingdom. Thus, 6,280 will be read as *six thousand two hundred eighty* in Chicago and *six, coma, two, eight, zero* in Spain—meaning: six integers twenty eight decimals.

[6]Remember that these processes took thousands of years to develop. For a more thorough discussion of documentation, specialized references should be consulted. A very useful guide and a vivid account of the "History of Ciphers" appears in Ifrah (1997).

Mayan system[7] demonstrate the existence of a positional additive system on base 20, including zero. Numbers greater than 20 were written in a vertical column containing as many levels as units of order. Lower levels corresponded to units, then units twenty times bigger. The third level, however, was an exception because it indicated 182 instead of 20². The reason is that the Mayan system of numeration was born in the context of the construction of Mayan calendars, which included the representation of units of different orders (equivalent to current uses of days, months, decades, and millennia). The third order unit in the Mayan system of numeration corresponded to months, of which there were 18 in the Mayan calendar.

SOME CONCLUSIONS ABOUT THE HISTORICAL PRINCIPLES OF NUMBER NOTATION

In the 5,000 years since the emergence of Sumerian notation, people have invented many different systems for the notation of numerosities. On the basis of the principles just presented, it is possible to view them historically in "logical-chronological" terms from the most rudimentary to the most advanced:

1.   *Additive notations,* including systems based on the principle of addition in which each notational element has a face value independent of position and the total amount is obtained by addition. These systems of notations are no more than a simple way to represent systems of accounting graphically, although one example—the Armenian system—is quite recent, dating from +400. Other examples of this notation type are Egyptian hieroglyphs, and the Cretan, Hitite, Aztec, Sumerian, and Roman systems.

2.   *Hybrid notations,* including those systems in which the combinations of elements are determined by two operations: product and addition. Examples of these are the Assyrian Babylonian, the earliest Chinese system, and Tamil numeration.

3.   *Positional notations,* including systems that are based on positional value and require the use of zero—although the principle of position was operational before a special sign for zero was developed. Only four cultures have developed positional systems of this kind: Babylonian, Chinese, Mayan, and Hindu.

Hindu mathematicians and astronomers should be credited with the invention of the notational elements and the principles on which the Hindu-Arabic system is based. The nine digits and the zero—the ciphers (or numerals) of the

---

[7]These hypotheses about the Mayan numeration and writing system are based on the few manuscripts that survived destruction during the Spanish conquest and on the analyses of currently available documentation belonging to the Aztecs and related groups.

system—were brought West by the Arabs at the end of the 10th century.[8] However, the adaptation of the Hindu-Arabic system of numeration for calculation was a slow, painstaking process. Both the use of the abacus for accounting and other calculations and the Roman system for writing numbers were complicated and required an extraordinary ability. Nevertheless, for more than two centuries, Christian Europe refused to use numerals and considered them to be "diabolic signs" created by the children of Satan. In the meantime, the Calculators, mostly Christian priests, were considered, not without reason, supernatural magicians. Finally, in the 12th century, at the very beginning of the Renaissance, the numerals in their original Arabic form were reintroduced into our culture. During the Crusades (c. 1101–1291), Europeans more widely learned the Hindu-Arabic art of written calculation, including the use of zero. Their present-day form became fixed during the 15th century as a result of the invention of printing (Ifrah, 1997).

Our system of numeration has a consistent decimal structure involving units of different orders, each being a power of ten: 10^0 = one, 10^1 = ten, 10^2 = hundred, 10^3 = thousand, and so on. The notational elements are the nine digits (1–9) that are smaller than the base. It is a hybrid multiplicative-additive system and it is positional. The position of each digit in the numeral determines the power of the base by which it must be multiplied (e.g., $45 = 4 \times 10 + 5$; $453 = 4 \times 100 + 5 \times 10 + 3$). It also contains a zero element, which shows the absence of a given power of the base in the decomposition of a numeral.

This is the system that children have to make their own. It is efficient, economical, universally used, and rather hermetic. To master it, children must discover the meaning of the elements of its groups of marks; the meaning of position, including the fact that the same elements mean something different if they are isolated or if they appear in a string; the additive and mutiplicative relation between elements; and the zero element.

PRINCIPLES IN THE HISTORY OF WRITING

Genuine creations of writing occurred in at least three separate geographical regions: Mesopotamia and Egypt, China, and pre-Columbian America. They probably also occurred among the Harappa civilization of the Indus Valley (Pakistan). The writing systems developed in these regions were independent developments.[9]

---

[8]The first mention and illustration of the nine digits appears in a manuscript from Northern Spain dated 976 (Ifrah, 1997, p. 1,337).
[9]Early scholars sought to establish connections between the Chinese script and that of Mesopotamia. Some postulated a direct derivation of the former from the latter (Coulmas, 1990, p. 93), but these claims have never been corroborated.

The fact that there were at least three independent developments of writing, but certainly no more than six, is the strongest argument against the supposition of a "monogenetic hypothesis," for all the writing systems of the world. And, considering all the possible independent developments, it has a crucial implication: Most communities have adopted writing systems used previously by peoples who spoke other languages. Some of these situations created what might be described as diglossic situations. There were small groups of people who knew how to write in the adopted language and used it for very specific purposes (e.g., administrative matters), whereas the local language was used in most situations. However, at some point, the notation became detached from the original language and people adapted it to their own language. Recent developments in the history of writing have documented some of these adaptations that occurred in different times and places. The following case analyses refer to just four of them. The idea is to illustrate, by way of these cases, the extent to which *borrowing* affects both the development of the writing system and the user's conceptualization of it. An analysis of these cases shows that the process of interaction with a notation for *translation* into a different language is a mechanism of far-reaching consequences for the historical development of writing systems and also for the users of the systems.

The Case of Proper Names

The demand for writing and interpreting proper names is one of the main reasons that made possible and indeed necessary the phonetization of writing (Coulmas, 1990; Gelb, 1963). *Phonetization* is the process by which writing systems become phonographic, that is, systems in which written marks represent the sound aspect of words rather than their content or meaning. Any debate concerning whether phonographic systems are better or more efficient than semasiographic systems is certain to be very drawn out. For the manufacturers of dishwashers, for example, it is cheaper and more efficient to use a semasiographic system for the instruction manual than to have these instructions translated in the 20 or 30 different languages spoken by potential buyers. But, there is little doubt that children becoming literate in alphabetic systems need to develop an awareness of its phonographic quality. For this reason, it is very revealing and useful to learn how—in the history of writing—graphic marks came to be used for the phonic aspect of a word rather than for its meaning. Among the main factors that caused systems to undergo a *process of phonetization* and users to adopt phonographic interpretations was the use of signs for representing proper names.

Proper names constitute a special category of words. They are not always meaningful beyond designating persons or places, and even those that are meaningful are generally used strictly for designating person or places. In English, *Rose* is a proper name, and *rose* is also the name of a flower. But there is no confusion when I buy a red rose for my Aunt Rose, because the referent of Rose is just my Aunt Rose. Only in very particular circumstances do individuals realize that some names may have meaning as words or may have an interesting etymological history. When used as proper names, their meaning is typically disregarded and the focus is on their form and reference.

Historically, in some cultures, names were attributed sacred and magical powers. Names were considered as an integral part of the person so that knowing the name of a person was to have some power over that person. In ancient Egypt, names were written to warrant survival in the next life, and written names might be erased to destroy its owner. Indeed, the Pharaohs' names were written within a special frame with the form of a cartouche or cartridge to protect them and to assure their eternal life (L. Adkins & R. Adkins, 2000). Besides their magic powers, or perhaps related to this magic power, the need to write and to interpret proper names lead to important changes in the way that the signs of writing were used.

In Sumeria and Egypt, as well as in China and Mexico (with the Aztec writing system), societies adopted a very clever strategy. They used word signs that sounded like the name they wanted to convey, but lacked its meaning. So, people looked at the word signs and had to focus on how they *sounded*, not on what they meant in order to determine the name being conveyed.

Nowadays, people do something similar each time they read a written name, even without being aware of it. When they see written, for example, GRACE or SALLY, they focus on how these words sound and recognize them as proper names; basically, they disregard the meaning of these words and treat them just as names. This strategy might be even easier for those who do not know other meanings of these words. Indeed, people who read graphic marks knowing that it was the inscription of the name of this or that king, but were unaware *of its original meaning in the original language*, initiated the process directly associated with the name-as-it-sounds. This process likely led to an increasing phonetization of writing.

Archaic Sumerian writing, whose precursor has been analyzed extensively, eventually developed into what is known as cuneiform script. But even during its archaic stage, the script included not only logographs, but also phonographs that represented syllables, and determinative and phonetic complements, although it had fewer of these than other systems (Michalowski, 1996). According to both early and more recent historical accounts (Gelb, 1963; Sampson,

1985), it was the need to represent proper names and patronymics (names indicating genealogy), which were fundamental for administrative and commercial transactions, that led to this development. For Sumerians, place names were meaningless strings of sounds because they were inherited from previous inhabitants of their land who spoke a different language (just as in North America many place names were inherited from Native Americas; e.g., the Massachuset Indians). These names were recognized by their sound and not by their meaning. This explains why even the most archaic forms of Sumerian writing had phonographs for these categories. The same principle led to an increasing phonetization in other adaptations of cuneiform script to other languages.

Proper names, patronymics, foreign words, and nonsense also constituted subjects of phonetic analysis in the development of Korean writing. When Koreans began to compile historical records in the 7th century, they were using Chinese characters. As they wanted to write about Korean heroes and places, they started representing the Korean names using Chinese characters to represent each syllable in the name, irrespective of the meaning of the characters.

A further instance showing the role of proper names in phonetization is in the development of the writing of Hebrew. As in all the Semitic scripts, Hebrew letters represent only consonants: They are an abjad. For Hebrew words, this seems sufficient because they indicate the root of the word, and the full word can be deduced from context. Clearly, this form of representation could have easily led to mistakes, especially with foreign words and proper names. Hence, a principle was established by which some consonants (e.g., the letters *Yodh* and *Waw*) acquired a dual function (consonant or vowel) depending on context. Those were given the name of *matres lectionis* 'mothers of reading.' The use of this principle was only timidly applied initially, but its use expanded during the Hellenization period, when precise reading of Greek names and loan words became a practical necessity. Hebrew adopted the solution offered by Greek writing and started to insert a vowel sound between consonants so that proper names could be read *properly*.

The fact that proper names were represented phonetically facilitated the deciphering of many writing systems. The names of Ptolemy, Cleopatra, and Alexander the Great provided the key for deciphering hieroglyphs. From the perspective of the writing system, proper names enhance phonetization, but from the perspective of the reader or writer, they facilitate the discovery and application of phonographic possibilities; and from the perspective of the scientist, proper names are a tool for discovering the rules of a system.

The Case of Multilingual Cuneiform

The saga of cuneiform writing is another case that illustrates how "translation" acted as an impetus in the development of writing. The most archaic stage of

TYPES OF LANGUAGE

The following three examples are meant to illustrate different types of languages:

(1) *Tree, chair, good*
(2) *Trees, chairs, goodness*
(3) *Appletree, chairperson, goodwill*

The first example is made up of three separate words, and each carries independent meaning. In technical terms, each word contains one morpheme. In the second example, something has been added to the words that adds information: the plural in the first two cases, and state, quality, or degree in the third case. Each word has two morphemes in this example. The third example also shows words that include two morphemes. The difference between the words in Examples 2 and 3 is that the words in Example 2 contain what are called "bound" morphemes, that is, morphemes that cannot be used in isolation. The words in Example 3, on the other hand, include "free" morphemes, which can be used in isolation.

Now look at the following example:

(4) *Salta*

This is a Spanish word containing two morphemes that means 'x jumps now.' The first morpheme (salt) reveals that it is about jumping, but the second (a single vowel *a)* provides three pieces of information: that the word means (a) *one* (b) *something or someone* that (c) *now* jumps. No doubt the information provided by this single morpheme is much more synthetic (it is impossible to segment; it comes packed together) than the information provided by the first part or by isolated words.

The final example is even more synthetic:

(5) *Acimlúda*

This is a word in Chinook that means roughly 'he will give it to me' (it is like a sentence included in one word): *A* (future), *c* (he), *i* (it) *m* (you) *l* (the previous element *m* is the beneficiary) *ú* (moving *l* from *c*) *d* (give) *a* (future).

Languages vary according to the extent to which their words are more or less synthetic or analytical, and they are usually classified into two main types with different subtypes:

(*continued*)

Analytic   Synthetic

Isolating   Agglutinating

Inflecting

An isolating, or analytic, language is one in which all the words are invariable. Chinese is often cited as an example of an isolating language. An agglutinating language (a subtype of synthetic) is one in which words are typically composed of a sequence of morphemes. Turkish may be taken as an example of an agglutinating language. Inflecting languages (a subtype of synthetic) are those in which it is hard to segment words into morphemes because each morpheme carries various kinds of grammatical information simultaneously (as in the example of the Spanish word *salta*). Latin is an example of inflecting language.

Note the word is inflecting, not inflexional. Inflexional qualifies processes internal to words, whereas inflecting qualifies languages. Inflexional processes occur in both agglutinating and inflecting languages.

Finally, it should be noted that it being agglutinating or isolating is a matter of degree. English is fairly analytic; it has many words of one morpheme but also has many synthetic words, some of which are agglutinative (e.g., chairs) and others of which are semi-agglutinative (e.g., swung). See Lyon (1971, pp. 191–192) and Tusón (1999).

fully developed Sumerian writing is represented by the tablets of Uruk and Jemdet Nasr. At this stage, writing comprised 1,200 graphs, which were used mainly for administrative purposes. Most graphs represented numerals or units of measurement, but despite the "extreme austerity of these early inscriptions it appears to be a genuine writing system of the logographic type: graphs stand for morphemes of spoken Sumerian" (Sampson, 1985, p. 57). Sumerian is a language without inflections that belongs to the agglutinative type; grammatical relations are expressed by means of affixes. Nouns and verbs were morphologically indistinguishable and mostly monosyllabic (Coulmas, 1990, p. 79). Logographs adapt themselves very well to this type of language because there is a correspondence between full words and individual signs.

In the −3rd millennium, cuneiform graphs were in widespread use. Most were still logographic, but there were also some phonographs and some determinative graphs being used to disambiguate graphs that had multiple readings.[10] When the Sumerians were absorbed by Akkadian invaders, in −1900 at the latest, invaders were conquered by the script and language of the invaded. Although Akkadian was widely spoken, Sumerian survived as the language of the learned and served other literary functions for more than 1,000 years. Script and language were so tied together that the language remained despite the disappearance of the original speakers, and this created a situation of marked diglossia. That is, there was a huge difference between daily use of language and formal or literary uses.

A qualitative shift occurred when, around the middle of the −3rd millennium, Akkadians tried to adapt the script they had received from the Sumerians to their own language. Akkadian was a very different language from Sumerian. It was an inflecting language and its syllabic structure was also different. The adaptation of Sumerian script to Akkadian resulted in a great increase in the frequency and proportion of signs for representing syllables (syllabograms) relative to the signs for representing words (logograms). This was due to the creation of new syllabograms and the introduction of phonetic complements to indicate inflectional endings.[11] "Having been forced by the nature of their language" (Sampson, 1985, p. 56), Akkadian greatly extended the use of the phonographic principle in writing.

During its 3,000-year history, cuneiform script came to be used by some 15 different languages besides Sumerian: Akkadian, Assyrian, Babylonian, Eblaite, Elamite, Hittite, Hurian, Ugaritic, Old Persian, and others. With each language that adopted the Sumerian script, it underwent a similar process. The script became detached from the original language that had created it and far-reaching consequences ensued. Under the influence of Elamite, for example, cuneiform writing was turned into a completely sound-based system. Yet, cuneiform texts written in Hittite present many more signs related directly to meaning.

Let's speculate for a moment on how this process of adaptation might have occurred. One possibility is that the people who were to adopt the script reflected carefully on their language and decided what modifications should be made to the script to adapt it for their purposes. This would imply that the users

---

[10]More than 75% of the 150,000 cuneiform inscriptions excavated in Mesopotamia are administrative and economic documents, including legal documents, deeds for sale and purchase, contracts concerning loans, adoptions and marriages, wills, ledgers and memoranda of merchants, as well as census and tax returns (Coulmas, 1990, p. 73). Recently, cookbooks have been added as a new genre of cuneiform literature (Bottéro, 1987).

[11]The ratio between the three kinds of sign shifted dramatically. In Sumerian, logograms range from 43% to 60%, whereas in Akkadian, they range from 4% to 7%. As for syllabograms, they increased from a range of 36% to 54% in Sumerian to a range of 86% to 96% in Akkadian (Coulmas, 1990, p. 81).

had a high level of awareness of their own language and also that there were a number of specialists who decided on the modifications to be made to the script. Writing, however, was a very select activity; only a very limited circle of scribes was involved in learning and using the art of writing.

It is more plausible then, that the adaptation occurred as a natural process from the interpretation of the foreign script through the target language. The situation envisioned is that of the literate elite interpreting the script orally in accordance with their needs and while they were interpreting, looking for a better correspondence between their language and the features of the script. This is not just a planned decision to adapt the script to their language, but a gradual process of adaptation. Although the two alternatives are pure specula-tion, the second sounds more plausible.

The Case of the Phoenician Letters

Three thousand years ago, the Greeks discovered the Phoenicians' consonantal writing.[12] From this encounter, the Greek alphabet, the immediate precursor to our own alphabet, was born. The "invention" of the Greek alphabet is another clear case of an adaptation process across linguistic boundaries. It was the same consonantal inventory originally used by the Canaanites, an ancient civiliza-tion that inhabited a territory roughly equivalent to the modern states of Israel, Palestine, coastal Syria (including Lebanon), and southern inland Syria (Tubb, 1998). The Canaanites spoke a Semitic language that, like any other language, could be written in any system. There is evidence that the Canaanites used cu-neiform writing during the –3rd millennium. They used it as a syllabary in which each individual syllable required its own sign. At a certain point, probably at the very start of the –2nd millennium, they took the "wonderfully logical step" (Tubb, 1998, p. 14) of removing the vowels from the syllables, leaving the initial consonant. The consonants were then represented by signs that evoked the words having the consonant in question as the initial letter. For example, the letter 'r' was represented by a sign supposed to evoke a human head, or _ras_ in the Canaanite language. The use of consonants only was more efficient—they only had to remember 24 signs where before they need to remember some 800—and vowels could be deduced from context.

---

[12]The dating of the origin of alphabetic writing in Greece is a matter of considerable dispute (Coulmas, 1990, p. 159). It is also a matter of dispute whether the encounter with Phoenician consonan-tal writing was preceded by a period of "illiteracy" (Goody & Watt, 1968). Coulmas suggested the need to emphasize the continuity of the path of development, appreciating the contribution of both Phoenicians and Greek writing.

As mentioned earlier, any language can be written in any system and con-sonants are highly informative in many languages. It is understandable that consonantal alphabets were developed for Semitic languages in which iden-tifying the consonants was of great help in deducing the rest of the word. Consonants are the roots from which words are derived and they provide the semantic basis of words. On the other hand, vowels in Semitic languages have mostly grammatical meaning and can be deduced from the context of the word.

This Canaanite inventory was propagated by the Phoenicians as a result of Mediterranean colonization, and it came into contact with the Greek people who spoke a non-Semitic language in which the vowels are as important as the consonants when deducing the words. If the Greeks had taken the Semitic al-phabet without adding any letters (or without changing the values of some of the letters), it would have been very difficult for them to recover the words writ-ten with consonants alone. The Greek language required a more exhaustive representation of the word, consonants alone were not enough to recuperate the meaning of words while reading. Harris (1986) summarized very clearly the process and the mutual influence of the system and the user:

> As it happens, there is every reason to believe that the alphabet was devised in a poly-glot cultural situation which made translation necessary and this situation reverted on the system and on the user. The user becomes increasingly aware of the component parts of her/his language through the external representation provided by the script and the script becomes transformed in consonance with the specific characteristics of the language. (p. 117)

What the Greeks did was to use the names of the Phoenician letters and adapt them to represent the sounds of their own language. That is, they applied a notation to the analysis of words in their language and looked for one-to-one correspondences. They kept some letters with their consonant value (e.g., the Phoenician letter *kaph* was turned into the Greek letter *kappa*), and other letters acquired a different value (e.g., the Phoenician letter *aleph*, which has the value of a glottal stop in the Phoenician language, was turned into a full vowel *alpha*). They deleted letters they did not need.

In the initial uses of alphabetic writing, the principle of sound writing was so faithfully followed that even dialectical differences were marked (Coulmas, 1990). The initial adaptation underwent some changes from the first docu-ments until the Classical Greek alphabet was standardized (–500). The "inven-tion" of the alphabet by the Greeks is another illustration of interaction between the features of an original notation and the representational needs of the user that provoked a change in the original notation.

The Case of Romance Latin

Some current theories maintain that there were just two spoken languages in use at any one place in Western Europe between the end of the Roman Empire and the 12th century: Latin and the Early Romance languages. The "savants" knew how to speak and write Latin; the noneducated spoke the Romance languages without knowing how to write them until the beginning of the 9th century. Contrary to these theories, Wright (1982) demonstrated that throughout this period of the Middle Ages, people used Latin to write their own Romance languages. It turns out that in France, Spain, Italy, and Portugal, Latin texts were indeed read, but with the vernacular pronunciation.

For example, in 4th-century Spanish, the form "they come" was pronounced *'vienen'* as in Modern Spanish, but it was written in the Latin form *veniunt*. And, when the Latin form *veniunt* was read aloud, it was pronounced *'vienen.'* Similarly, the Latin form *mensibus* was read *'mezes,'* and *'mezes'* was written *mensibus*. As the grammarians of the time had it, there was no requirement to pronounce words as they were written.[13] Written Latin functioned by *indicating*, suggesting how words should be pronounced (or thought, if people were not reading aloud), but the interpretation of written Latin was carried out in the language of the reader.

It was only with Charlemagne's reform during the 9th century that a standard pronunciation for Latin was established, and, simultaneously, a clear distinction among the Romance languages was made, providing new written forms. This means that the first written documents in Spanish, French, Portuguese, and so on, do not indicate the birth of those languages, but rather their new written form. Following Wright (1982), this means that during the 12th and 13th centuries, Western Europe lived in a state of ideal diglossia, with people thinking that they were speaking and reading the same language. This is a strong example of unification of language through the written word or, as suggested by Blanche-Benveniste (1997), through the writing of words. If Wright was not mistaken, reading their own vernacular languages in written Latin helped to consolidate the Romance languages.

SOME CONCLUSIONS FROM THE HISTORICAL CASE ANALYSES

My goal in discussing the different cases of adaptation of a script was to show that, despite the fact that languages can be written in any script, many significant developments in the history of writing were achieved whenever a script

---

[13]To quote a grammarian of the 5th century (Pompeius), "Non debemus dicere ita, quem ad modum scribitur" (Wright, 1982, p. 57).

was borrowed and adapted to a new language across linguistic types. This process was evident when the Greeks adapted the Semitic abjad or when the Akkadians adapted the Sumerian script. Sometimes the inadequacy of the existing elements in representing certain categories or certain objects led to the creation of new elements. This was the case in the need to represent proper names, which led to an increase in phonographic principles, or the case in Greek, when ways were invented to represent the vowels that were essential in recovering the meaning of the words they wrote. Sometimes the existing elements were resignified to meet the needs of the reader. This was the case with the Romance reading of Latin. In every case, however, there is an interaction between the features of the notation and the representational needs of the user. This is not to claim that adaptation to a new language is the only reason communities change their writing systems. Some changes have strictly political reasons, totally unrelated to the links between language and script. Talking about cases in which a process of adaptation existed illustrates how this process affected both the system and the user.

The cases just analyzed highlight the fact that in the history of writing it is necessary to distinguish between the material evolution of the signs (paleography) and the creation of systems of writing, between the outward forms used for marking and the underlying principles. The same notational elements can be used, and were used, with different meanings in the context of different activities. This was the case with elements of writing that were read by people speaking different languages and that were used as logograms, syllabograms, or phonetic complements without a notable change in their outward form. This was also the case with writing systems used for the notation of number. But the opposite can also be true: Changes in the outward form of the elements do not imply changes in the underlying principles.

The purpose so far has been to support with historical evidence the role of writing and other means of external representation as sources for further development of the systems as such, and of the ways they are used. Systems for numerical notation and writing systems grew from other notational systems or from material intermediaries created to leave traces of human activities. Moreover, the need to adapt existing means to new functions or new languages was a historical constant. From the interpretation of the traces, from the reiterated use of the material intermediaries, from the adaptation of old means to new needs, notational systems improved or, to be more precise, users could find ways to improve their functioning.

The following are some key points in this chapter:

- The social history of writing and numbers highlights principles that have regulated these notational systems and that may differ from those that regulate current writing and number systems. Becoming acquainted with these principles is useful for interpreting children's production, whose organizing principles may also differ from the conventional systems they are learning.

- Taking a historical perspective helps to appreciate that many features of notational systems are not natural or obvious, but rather took centuries to be attained. This appreciation is useful for understanding some of the difficulties children may have in their learning process.
- The close relation in history between writing and numeration supports the decision to consider these two notational systems together.
- Crucial points in the history of writing and numbers reveal a constant interaction between the features of notational systems and the users' representational needs. From a dialectical interaction between users and notation both the system and the notational possibilities are modified to better fit the representational needs.

In the next chapter I will present another kind of history, the history of a child building knowledge about the writing system to which he is exposed. As pointed out at the beginning of this chapter, this is not to say that personal history replicates or recapitulates social history. Nevertheless, just as interaction between users and notational systems led to an improvement of the system and its representational possibilities as human beings created their own notational tools, children's interest and initial interactions with writing are the basis of their learning process.

3

What Children Know About Writing Before Being Formally Taught to Write

In the mid-1970s a number of psychologists from North and South America, working quite independently of one another, began to conduct a series of experiments that were unlike anything being undertaken in the field of psychology at that time. These psychologists asked very young children, ages 3 and 4, to read and write as the children believed this should be done. More than 40 years before, American and Russian psychologists had done something similar (Hildreth, 1936; Luria, 1929/1978), although they described what they were doing differently. Luria, who worked with Vygotsky in the 1920s, was looking for "the pre-history of written language," whereas Emilia Ferreiro (1985) studied the "psychogenesis of writing," and William Teale and Elizabeth Sulzby (1986) were investigating "emergent literacy." Put simply, however, all of these psychologists were exploring the way in which young children write *before* they start school and are taught to spell conventionally. What they did marked a turning point in the field of developmental psychology; these psychologists opened up a new domain of development. As a result of their work, psychologists started looking at reading and writing not only as abilities that should be formally instructed, but also as a kind of knowledge that undergoes reorganizational processes with age and experience, similar to what happens in other domains of development such as physical, linguistic, or mathematical knowledge.

   Although these scholars studied children of similar ages and sometimes asked the children similar questions, there was an important difference between these lines of work—the extent to which they were concerned with writing as a communicative tool and/or as a domain of knowledge. As mentioned in the introduction, writing is an efficient means for transmitting messages, but it is also a domain of inquiry. As an example of these two facets, consider chapter 1, which reviews the reflections of many semioticians studying the features of writing in comparison to other notational systems. These semioticians were using writing both ways: When reflecting about the features of writing, they related to it as a domain of inquiry, as an object of knowledge. But when transmitting their thoughts about writing, they used it as a communicative tool. Except for those in the psychogenetic line of work (e.g., Ferreiro), the scholars studying very young children's writing were mainly concerned with children's developing ability to fulfill communicative purposes, and they tended to neglect other aspects of children's knowledge of writing.

   In this chapter, I shall focus on the spontaneous development of writing both as a communicative tool and as a domain of knowledge. I use 'spontaneous' in the sense given to this word by Piaget when describing, for instance, the physical knowledge that children construct outside formal instruction through their interaction with objects and people. This interaction with the environment is only one of many possible sources of learning. Another major source of learning is the work we do internally with our thoughts and ideas; that is, with our own internal representations (Karmiloff-Smith, 1986, 1992). This kind of work may precede, be concurrent with, or succeed a person's interaction with the environment, yet regardless of when it occurs it constitutes a source of learning. Therefore, the term 'spontaneous' is used to embrace not only the sort of developmental processes that emerge as a result of children interacting with their environment and their own internal representations, but also the biological basis that permits these processes to occur. The three processes— interaction with the environment, interaction with one's own internal representations, and innate propensities—are all sources that will facilitate or impair learning.

   Piaget (1951) argued that symbolic expressions are dependent on general cognitive development. They are dependent in both senses of the word, in that they are determined by the development of operational knowledge and they occupy a lower rank than operational knowledge. This idea could have called for empirical verification in the domain of writing as happened with many Piagetian ideas. In the domain of language, for example, numerous studies have been carried out to explore the relation between language development and cognition (for a review, see Cromer, 1988). But this was not the case with writing. The conception of reading and writing as subjects to be studied in school, rather than as domains of development, was so strong that psychologists did not even believe there was any 'spontaneous' development to be studied. Psychologists could have explored, for example, how nonconservers read or write. But instead of doing this, they understood success in conservation tasks as a cognitive prerequisite for "entering the world of print." It was argued that if, according to Piaget, symbolic development is dependent on cognitive development then it is useless, "even deleterious" (Auzias, Casati, Cellier, Delaye, & Verleure, 1977, p. 40), to teach children to write until they are mature enough to start.

Such a position is based on a misunderstanding of the main Piagetian message, that is, that subjects are active learners and undergo constant cognitive growth. As such, learners have the ability to select and to focus on relevant features of their environment. Because writing is indeed part of their environment, children do not remain indifferent to its presence while waiting for formal instruction to begin. Therefore, questioning neither the influence of general cognitive development on writing nor the tremendous influence of schooling, it is indeed worthwhile to analyze the development of writing as something that is separable, although not separate, from both cognitive development and from schooling. Moreover, writing should be treated as a source of knowledge with its own course of development and not simply as an aggregate that amplifies knowledge of speech.

THE CHILD'S PATH TO ALPHABETIC WRITING

"The history of writing in the child begins long before a teacher first puts a pencil in the child's hand and shows him how to form letters," wrote Luria in 1929 (p. 145). He and Vygotsky were among the first psychologists to consider writing as an object of psychological interest. They argued that the aim of scientific psychology is to study "higher order psychological functions," "uniquely human functions," and because writing is uniquely human, it should be a concern of scientific psychology. Moreover, as with any other psychological function, they claimed, the child's acquisition of writing needs to be studied from its very beginning because the genetic method is the one recommended for scientific psychology. To Vygotsky's mind, reading and writing are not mere instruments or motor skills (Vygotsky, 1978, p. 55), they are tools that produce deep changes in the mind. Vygotsky was thinking about attitudinal and ideological changes far beyond changes in people's level of intelligence. He can be described as a "realistic optimist" with an almost unlimited faith in the power of instruction and language to change people from within (Zebroski, 1982). Reading and writing, for him, constituted sign systems that could change people "internally," as opposed to tools that change people and objects "externally."

Writing to Write

Luria and Vygotsky's study was carried out with Russian-speaking children just 10 years after the Soviet revolution. The time was ripe to demonstrate that the acquisition of cultural tools might lead cognitive revolutions. They performed a surprisingly simple test, although greatly daring: They had 3-, 4-, and 5-year-olds listen to sentences and, when they thought the children had heard too many words to be able to recall them word for word, they instructed them to write the sentences down *so that they could remember them better.* The request was strictly instrumental, because children had to write *in order to remember.* Luria reported that in most cases children were bewildered by the request, as they clearly believed that they were not supposed to know how to write. As found on numerous occasions since then, a child's refusal to write may indicate an awareness of conventionality; it reflects a child's conviction that writing, as opposed to drawing, requires special marks that must be known (Brenneman, Massey, Machado, & Gelman, 1996). Thus, the first task of the researchers was, and continues to be whenever similar experimental situations are used, to convince children that they should try. Of course, this approach has cultural limitations. For many Chinese communities, exploring writing, attempting to write, or inviting children to attempt to write without prior teaching would be quite inappropriate, because in these communities writing is strongly believed to be something individuals can do only if they know how to write (Chan, 1990).

At any rate, Luria and Vygotsky convinced the children to try. They found that regardless of the sentence, the youngest children produced similar "scrawls" for every word, whereas the older children did something very different (discussed in the next section). Figure 3.1 shows some of the examples discussed in Luria's paper.

Obviously, the children could not make use of their notes in recalling the sentences; their notes did not serve any mnemonic function. For this reason, Luria described this written output as *undifferentiated-noninstrumental.* Luria was so concerned with the instrumental aspect of writing as an auxiliary technique used for recording that he failed to acknowledge the extent to which children were beginning to grasp other aspects of writing. He could not see what children already knew despite their instrumental ignorance.

Just what is writing exactly in the eyes of very young children? Simply a discontinuous, linear pattern of wavy lines, a general visual pattern similar to many writing patterns that children have seen around them. Writing these lines brought to mind Lévi-Strauss, the French anthropologist, and his experience

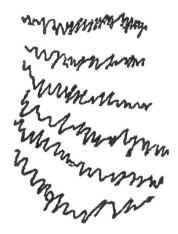

FIG. 3.1.   Undifferentiated writing by a Russian 4-year-old. From A. R. Luria, "The Development of Writing in the Child," *Soviet Psychology*, vol. 16, no. 2 (Winter 1977–78). English-lan-
guage translation © 1978 by M. E. Sharpe, Inc. Originally published in *Voprosy Marksistkoi
Pedagogikii* [Problems of Marxist education], Vol. 1 (Moscow: Academy of Communist Education, 1929). Used by permission of M. E. Sharpe, Inc.

with the Nambikwara in Brazil. As he did his field work, he usually took notes.
One day he decided to hand out sheets of paper and pencils to the Nambikwara.
At first they did nothing with them, but then, one day, Lévi-Strauss (1973) observed that "they were all busy drawing wavy, horizontal lines. It suddenly
dawned upon me that [they] were trying to use their pencils in the same way as I
did mine" (p. 296).

Sixty years after Luria's pioneering experiments, a group of Argentinian psychologists made very similar findings, although guided by Piagetian rather than
Vygotskian thinking (Ferreiro & Teberosky, 1979). Specifically, they worked
with the belief that even when children have to incorporate knowledge of a
conventional kind derived from their membership in a social community (e.g.,
through language), they must make that knowledge their own and reconstruct
it in their own terms. They believed that no knowledge begins from zero and all
knowledge has a developmental story. Accordingly, it is necessary to distinguish
between the child's acquisition of writing and the teaching of writing, and to
study the former process from the earliest possible moment.

As a student, I was part of this research group. From 1974 until 1976, the group
examined the way in which 4- to 7-year-olds went about reading and writing as
they think it should be done. I must confess that I was not very much aware of exactly what we were looking for. I was shocked, however, by the tremendous dispar-
ity between what children were supposed to know, according to the teaching
method used at school, and the knowledge they demonstrated in their individual

sessions. At that time, in Argentina, the most popular method for teaching reading was one called "mixed" or "word-type." Basically, it consisted in giving words (e.g., ALA 'wind' or OSO 'bear') that were considered easy because they have few and repeated letters and direct syllables (syllables formed with a consonant and a vowel). The words were then decomposed (A-LA) (O-SO) and recomposed (ALA) (OSO) and the children were required to read in a low voice the segments of the words and to complete the "missing segment." After teaching a few words, the words were integrated into short sentences. Imagine our surprise when we found that many children think that words containing few and repeated letters *cannot be read*. How could they manage with the words that they were taught? The previous case is just an example of the kind of dissonance found between what was taught at school and children's own developing ideas.

We used many different tasks, and they all unveiled the many things children were supposed to know and did not know. But, more illuminating, they also showed the many things that children were not supposed to know and did know. Some of the writing tasks had certain features in common with those employed by Luria. Children were asked to write words and sentences in the context of clinical interviews. But, in contrast with Luria, there was no instrumental aim to our request; children were not required to write for mnemonic or communicative purposes. Nevertheless, it turned out that many of the young Argentinian native Spanish speakers made similar "scrawls," regardless of the word or sentence they were asked to write. Ferreiro (Ferreiro & Teberosky, 1979) also termed this type of production "undifferentiated writing," because neither the child nor the adult could distinguish what had been written, be it a short word or a four-word sentence.

In the mid-1980s, I replicated many of these tasks with Israeli children who were native Hebrew speakers. They also produced "undifferentiated writing," as shown in Fig. 3.2, which provides an example of an Israeli 4-year-old's attempt to write a single word and a four-word sentence.

Looking at what the child did, it is impossible to recognize which "scrawl" represents the word and which the sentence. As usual, it is possible to describe what children do by examining what is missing from their products: There are no letters, no correspondence to the acoustic length of words, and no marks to distinguish between the sentences. But, more positively, it is clear that children's writing displays the "superordinate features" of writing (Gibson & Levin, 1975), that is, features of form common to writing in almost any language: linearity, presence of distinguishable units, regularity of blanks, and directionality. The marks appear organized around a horizontal axis, sometimes on a continuous line, sometimes relatively separated from each other with more or less regular blanks between them. Usually the marks are written toward the same direction, be it from right to left or from left to right.

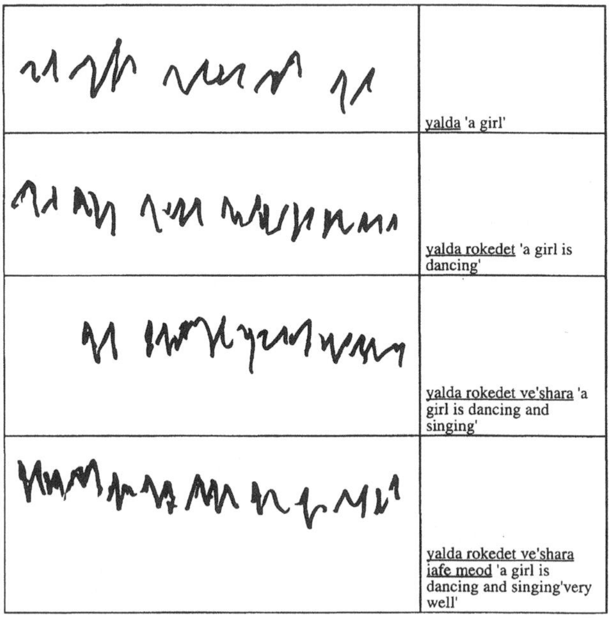

FIG. 3.2. Undifferentiated writing by an Israeli 4-year-old.

Superordinate features can be distinguished from "ordinate features," which are those features that distinguish different scripts: the specific direction in which they are written and the specific shape of their elements. The participants in the studies used the superordinate features of writing before the ordinate features of Hebrew script. By age 4, children's writing already appeared as a linearly arranged string of distinctive marks separated by regular spacing. These findings were further supported by numerous studies carried out in a variety of languages, including English, and seem to hold true independently of socioeconomic status, or microcultural milieu (Bissex, 1980; Clay, 1982; Gibson & Levin, 1975; Y. Goodman, 1982; Harste, Woodward, & Burke, 1984). These studies demonstrate that the graphic pattern of writing forms part of a child's mental space very early on. At 4 years, writing has been internally grasped by the child as a particular activity that produces a specific formal output distinct from drawing in that it is linear and discrete.

When comparing the writing and drawing of children between ages 3 and 5, they look different—the presence of superordinate and ordinate features clearly distinguishes one from the other. As for directionality in writing, the superordinate feature of unidirectionality was frequent after age 4, but the ordinate feature of writing conventional Hebrew from right to left only became dominant after age 5.

A recent study carried out in Hong Kong with Chinese-speaking children (Chan, 1990; Chan & Nunes, 1998) reported that even at age 3, the children used different representations to distinguish between drawing and writing. When drawing, their figures were large and usually had round edges; in contrast, the Chinese characters were usually smaller. Circles and whirls disappeared when writing, and instead strokes and dots were used to compose the word. Indeed, in all studies, very few children (and those only in the youngest age group) have been found to produce writing and drawing that cannot be distinguished. Just as their writing lacks the superordinate features of writing, so their drawing lacks the figurative features of a "realistic" representation. However, even when their products are indistinguishable, 3- to 4-year-olds' motor plans can be clearly identified either for drawing or for writing (Breneman et al., 1996; Karmiloff-Smith, 1992); each involves the performance of different actions. When drawing, children make wide continuous circular movements, whereas when writing, they lift their pencils off the page and interrupt their movements much more frequently. That is, although the graphic product does not look like writing to an external observer, children act differently when writing or drawing. The problem is that once finished, when separated from the "writer" and the writing task, the traces "do not mean."

When the characteristics of external representations were analyzed in chapter 1, one crucial characteristic they shared is that they can be interpreted outside the context of production—even when separated from the person who has produced them. In the first stages of writing development, this characteristic has not been attained yet; the product has not yet been detached from the process of production and from the producer.

A similar process was observed in the domain of musical notation, when children in a kindergarten were asked to record a tune on a paper so as to be able to remember it later (Cohen, 1983, 1985). The youngest children tried to "draw" the tune. They drew marks in a higher or lower position or changed colors as the sounds went from higher to lower pitches. The drawing procedure was determined by the tune, but the outcome did not reflect this systematically. While trying to draw the tune, it was a sort of action-in-the-graphic-space, but when finished, neither the same child nor another person in the same or a subsequent session were able to recover any of the features of the tune. As in the case of writing, the outcome had not yet become detached from the producer to become a potential source of information for an external interpreter.

How do children interpret their own written outputs during the stage of *undifferentiated writing*? They behave as though the place where writing stands or the writer himself, rather than any particular feature of the written display, will determine the interpretation.

Three- to 4-year-olds were shown pictures with a caption (e.g., a picture of a boat with a caption BOAT). Either as a result of their own guesswork or following a suggestion from an adult, they agreed that BOAT was written under the drawing of a boat. However, when the written word was "accidentally" moved to another picture, the reading of the word also changed (Bialystok, 1992; Ferreiro, 1984, 1988). So the same written word could come to mean "pipe," under the drawing of a pipe. Apparently, they did not see the written word BOAT as being a representation of 'boat,' independently of the changes in contexts, referents, or conditions of productions.

Another typical behavior that appears during the period of undifferentiated writing serves to illustrate this point further. In one study (Tolchinsky, Landsmann, & Levin, 1985), children were asked to write a list of various items: "a house," "a child playing with a ball," and so on. Their written products look very similar (see Fig. 3.2). And yet, when they were asked to read back to us what they had written, pointing in turn to the corresponding item, the children usually repeated the different words they had been asked to write. For the first writing pattern, they said /yalda/ 'a girl,' as a whole. For the second, they said /yalda rokedet ve'shara/ 'a girl is dancing and singing,' again as a whole, and so on. Note that they were saying very different things while referring to very similar written outputs. It is also important to remark that they usually did not pause between words or between parts of words; they did it in one breath. We shall discuss this apparently trivial reading behavior later in this chapter, but here it is just another example to illustrate that at this stage the meaning of writing is still circumstantial; it depends on the child's intention, and it changes with the adult instructions, or with the context in which the writing is presented.

Two things must happen to bring about changes in the representational status of writing: Children must realize that (a) the particular features of a text are what matter (not just the context, his intentions, etc.) and only certain forms carry potential meaning, and (b) the interpretable features are created when writing, not when reading. They must realize that the key for decoding is created during encoding. Certain processes have been observed during development that seem to indicate how these two realizations begin to take shape: Children gradually become more selective as to what forms or combinations of forms are accepted as "writable" or "readable." As a consequence, their own written production becomes more constrained. At the same time, they start to introduce in their productions certain graphic hints to the meaning of the words they are attempting to represent; their writing starts to be communicative. Each process is considered in turn.

Writing Becomes Formally Constrained

The merit of the work conducted by Vygotsky and Luria is beyond question. They were the first to draw attention to the possibility of a spontaneous development of writing and to the need for bringing the study of writing into the field of psychological research. Nevertheless, they failed to appreciate any feature in children's writing behavior that did not serve an instrumental purpose. Recognition of the formal work involved in early writing was one of the main contributions made by Ferreiro (1984, 1985). She discovered that even children who do not know how to write conventionally hold certain criteria concerning the *distinctive features* graphic displays must fulfil in order to be readable.

Developmental psychologists have learned the importance of discovering such *distinctive features* in other domains of knowledge. For example, the work of Susan Carey (1985) shows that giving birth is understood by children to be a distinctive feature of biological objects. In the child's mind, if an object gives birth, then it is a living object; if it does not, then it is a thing. Recall that the introduction referred to the usefulness of distinguishing what can be done with what; for example, what can be done with rubber bands is not the same as what can be done with worms. Distinctive features guide the kind of operations and the kind of questions people are prone to formulate. If an object is defined as living, they might wonder whether it feels warm or cold, whereas such thoughts would be nonsense for an inanimate object. By the same token, by recognizing certain *distinctive features* children distinguish between what is readable and nonreadable; if a text is readable, then it makes sense to wonder what it means. But, if it is not, then it would be nonsense to ponder its meaning.

Constraints on Legibility

Two criteria guide a child's decision as to whether or not something is readable: a minimal number of letters and a sufficient variety of them. The mere presence of letters is not enough for something to be readable; if there are very few letters, then it is "unreadable"; and, similarly, if the same letter is repeated many times, then it is also "unreadable." These criteria are manifest especially in sorting and writing tasks. The results of a sorting task conducted with Spanish-speaking children between ages 4 and 7, inspired by Ferreiro and Teberosky (1979), illustrate this point. Children were shown a number of cards containing between one and nine letters. Some formed words (PAPA), others did not (PE). Some were cursive, others were printed. Some contained a variety of letters (MANTECA), others contained a repetition of the same letter (MMMMMM, AAAAAA). Children were asked to separate the cards according to those that were 'good for reading' and those that were not (*fíjate si te parece que todas sirven para leer o si hay algunas que sirven para leer, y otras que no sirven para leer* 'look carefully and tell me if you think they are all good for reading or if some of them are good and others aren't').

Some children showed no criteria for discriminating among the cards and were unable to do the task. However, very few fell into this category and all were from the youngest age group. The first criterion that the other children applied was the *number of letters*. Letters that stand alone (T) *"are not good"* for reading, but too many letters (PERIMETRO) also led to doubt. The ideal number of letters for something to be readable was three or four. Cards containing strings of three to four letters were chosen without any hesitation as being suitable for reading. It was not enough, however, to have the correct number of letters, there was also a concomitant need for a limited variety. When they compared (MMMMMM), (AAAAAA), and (MANTECA), children had little doubt that only the last sequence was good for reading.

In many respects, this task resembles one used in English by Lavine (1977), who, working with a group of children between ages 3 and 7, asked the following question: "Does the card have writing on it?" Lavine was looking for the criteria that define writing from the perspective of the child and included among the cards pictures of familiar and unfamiliar objects, semipictorial elements and geometric shapes with either a linear or nonlinear orientation, and varied versus repetitive strings of elements. She also varied the type of elements in terms of their degree of similarity to Roman letters. Of the 3-year-olds, only 13% accepted the pictorial and only 27% the semipictorial graphic elements as writing, whereas the level of acceptance for the samples of conventional writing was greater than 80% for all age groups. The acceptance of linearity was more significant than that of nonlinearity, although not for individual age groups, whereas variety was significant at all ages. Sheer number of letters was a significant factor only among the youngest age group. For the older group, it was no longer the number of letters, but rather the quality of the elements that was important for deciding what was readable. As to degree of similarity to Roman letters, among the youngest group, radically different graphic designs such as a Mayan motif or a Chinese character were rejected, whereas Hebrew letters, signatures, printed and cursive words, and individual letters and numbers were accepted. At age 5, however, the acceptance of printed and cursive words differed significantly. The response to single unit displays also differed significantly with age. Five-year-olds clearly preferred conventional letters. Looking at the absolute results, there was a surprisingly high percentage of acceptance of repetitive strings.

Why was repetition generally accepted in the context of Lavine's study when it was rejected in ours? This would seem to be because variety is a criterion for judging whether something is *legible* although not whether it can be *written.* Although a great deal can be written, only some of it is readable. The constraints of quantity and variety are task sensitive but follow a clear rationale: They are stronger when children are asked to judge for readability rather than for "writability." Additional support for these findings comes from another study carried out in Spanish. Nemirovsky (1995) also devised a sorting task with cards containing single letters or long strings of repeated letters in cursive writing and in print. However, slightly different instructions were given. Instead of asking children to separate out those that were "good for reading," as Ferreiro did, she asked them to select those that were "good for writing." When using this instruction, the rejection of letters that stand alone and strings containing repeated letters did not occur. Reading is conceived of as a more specific activity with more specific requirements, whereas writing is conceived of as a more general activity that is synonymous to leaving traces on paper. A similar approach to reading and writing is encountered when looking at sorting numerals and considering illiterate adults.

Sensitivity to formal constraints was found not only for the number of letters and their internal variety, but also for the combination of letters. Camean Gorrias (1990) explored whether preschoolers, who are not yet looking for letter-sound correspondences, were able to distinguish between sequences of letters that are and are not possible combinations in their language. She was also interested in knowing whether acceptance or rejection of a certain sequence would take into account the graphic characteristics of a letter or its position in the sequence. Must every letter in the sequence be considered correct, or can some letters be rejected as being incorrect without rejecting the sequence?

Spanish-speaking Mexican children were asked to sort through a series of cards looking for those that were written correctly. Because the purpose was to explore "qualitative" differences, all the cards contained the same number (four) and style of letters (PRINT). Some, however, contained combinations that were possible, whereas others contained combinations that were impossible, including, for example, only consonants or consonants that could never appear at the end of Spanish words (in Spanish all the vowels but only nine consonants can appear at the end of words). With one exception, the word WEST, all the combinations were possible in Spanish.

The most readily accepted combinations were those that occur with greatest frequency in Spanish—those that do not contain letters that are rare in Spanish (k, w, x, y) and those without duplications. The most frequently rejected card was that containing the combination WEST, an English word that cannot occur in Spanish. In order to decide which combinations were "well written," children focused both on the letters within the string and on the general configuration of the string. These results are in line with those reported by Pick, Unze, Brownell, Drodzal, and Hopman (1978), who found that 5-year-old children rejected strings containing repeated vowels or repeated consonants, demonstrating their understanding that a word must contain both types of letter. The two studies coincide in demonstrating that before children map letters onto sounds they are sensitive to possible and impossible combinations and, in order to decide which combinations are "well written," children looked both at the letters within the string and at the general configuration of the string.

These results contradict suggestions made by Uta Frith (1980, 1989). Frith argued that the development of writing proceeds in three phases: logographic, alphabetic, and orthographic. During the first phase, she claimed, children relate to the written word as a whole because they are still unable to map graphic elements onto sounds. Only once children begin to identify correspondences between letters and sounds can they become sensitive to order and configuration (p. 24). However, Camean Gorrias (1990) and Pick et al. (1978) reported that even before the discovery of the alphabetic principle, children do in fact pay attention to the word components.

Constraints on "Writability"

During the initial stages in the development of writing, when writing is defined by children as a kind of action, almost every spoken utterance is written as an indistinct, linear, and discontinuous graphic pattern that imitates the general aspect of print in the environment. The fact that children imitate the overall appearance of writing indicates that they have noticed its existence, that writing is part of their mental space. When they produce those graphic patterns they are not reproducing something that stands in front of them at that very moment; rather, they imitate from an internalized pattern. The imitated traces may even provide "a partial, and perhaps implicit understanding of their significance" (Zelazo, 2000, p. 149).[14] On the other hand, imitation is never passive copy, but rather an active

---

[14]The quotation is from a chapter written by Philip Zelazo in which he described a theory of representational understanding and use, paying particular attention to the role of imitation in representation and development. As he explained, the theory draws on the philosopher Paul Ricoeur and the genetic psychologist James Mark Baldwin. Imitation is central to representational processes. It is always interpretative, never a mere copy; by a dialectical recursive process it scaffolds both the representational process and what is being represented. The quoted phrase is used by Zelazo when referring to Ricoeur's view of literary representation focusing on the creation of a story as a "narrative imitation of action." For Ricoeur, this narrative imitation depends on the existence of actions to be represented. Once the actions are available, even the most basic imitation of these actions is already interpretative, never a mere replica of the actions, and "the first moment of *mimesis* (*mimesis* ₁) prefigures these actions providing a partial, and perhaps implicit understanding of their significance." Although Zelazo used this reflection to underscore the interpretative, subjective nature of mimetic processes even when anchored to external events (the actions represented), it is used here to highlight the kind of understanding provided by imitation.

process of selection and interpretation. What children imitate from their environment functions as a sort of raw material with which they work out the constraints on interpretability: In order for a string of letterlike forms to be readable, it must be of a limited number and have sufficient variety. These two constraints also regulate children's writing, and they seem to hold true across languages and scripts. A number of examples drawn from a study examining the development of word writing in Hebrew and Spanish (languages that use different scripts) serve to illustrate this claim. Participants were Spanish-speaking and Hebrew-speaking children of preschool age through second grade, living in Barcelona and Tel Aviv (Tolchinsky & Teberosky, 1997, 1998).

The aim in this study was to determine the extent to which the characteristics of writing development can be considered general, whether similar constraints are operating in different scripts, or whether each script follows a different developmental route. This was not, however, the sole purpose. We were also looking for similarities and differences in the way children segment spoken words in different languages in order to determine whether the ability to analyze words into sounds is a prerequisite for identifying letter-to-sound correspondences. The differences between Spanish and Hebrew make the comparison of these two languages particularly appropriate for exploring the relation between oral segmentation and writing performance.[15]

Despite the differences between the two languages with respect to scripts and structure, they display similarities in the frequency of vowel and consonant distribution (an overall distribution of consonants and vowels close to 50% each), in the syllabic structure of words, in the typical number of syllables in words, and in the types of possible syllables.

We found that the written products of preschoolers, both in Spanish and Hebrew, were constrained by the same formal features of number and variety. These initial similarities were followed by an increasing divergence, as the dis-

---

[15]The Spanish alphabet includes consonants and vowels, whereas Hebrew includes only consonants. However, some of the letters, the *matres lectionis*, or "mothers of reading" (e.g., the letters *Yodh, Waw*), can serve as vowels, and quite often appear in modern Hebrew writing. Vowel denotation is achieved mainly through diacritical marks. Diacritics are used in holy texts, in poetry, in writing foreign names and, especially, in children's books and texts for the teaching of reading. There are also important differences in the structural features of the two languages. Spanish is far from being an isolating language—very few words consist of just one morpheme. Rather, morphosyntactic markers are usually affixed to the lexical root for derivation and/or inflection, and stem changes are uncommon (Green, 1990). In Hebrew, however, as in most Semitic languages, morphology works on roots having three, four, or occasionally two consonants that cluster around a semantic field, and the morphosyntactic system operates on these roots to derive words by a variety of alternations that are internal to the stem. Examples include the germination of the middle radical and the change in the way a stem is vocalized for active causative (*katav* 'wrote') and passive agentive (*nyktav* 'was written') forms. The vowel patterns are fixed, as are the systems of infixes, suffixes, and prefixes (Aronoff, 1985; Berman, 1978; Fevrier, 1971).

tinctive features of the respective languages began to exert their influence. Figure 3.3 illustrates two series of written productions highlighting these initial similarities.

Those on the left were produced by an Israeli girl named Maya, and those on the right were produced by a Spanish-speaking boy named Christopher; both were the same age. The letters used by each child are the conventional letters of each script. In general, children do not invent forms for letters, but instead use those provided by the environment. Yet, despite the different letters, the written outputs reflect the two formal constraints: (a) Every string should contain a similar number of letters, and (b) adjacent letters should not be the same. The most striking observation was that children used the letters in their own name as a sort of repository of conventional letter shapes. Both the Israeli girl and the Spanish boy used the letters in their respective names when writing each word. It was rather shocking to find such an original solution appearing in two different scripts.

Allow me to digress, momentarily, and make a few comments about the role of proper names in the development of writing. As discussed in chapter 2, personal names constituted the "locus" of qualitative shifts in the social history of writing. It appears that they also play a crucial role in the individual develop-

Maya's name   Christofer name

Coca Cola   Coca Cola

pizza   pizza

menta   menta

FIG. 3.3. Formally constrained writing in two different scripts.

ment of writing. In all studies, in all of the different languages that have been explored, whenever children are required to write their own name along with other words or sentences, the child's name always shows a higher level of development in any of the features that are being considered. This is true, for example, for superordinate features and conventional letters (Chan, 1990; Ferreiro & Teberosky, 1979; Tolchinsky-Landsmann & Levin, 1987).

Certainly, the aforementioned might be related to the strong affective meaning attached to our own name. But, personal names also constitute the first clearly meaningful text, resistant to being forgotten and unchanging in pronunciation. If 3- or 4-year-olds are told, even circumstantially, that a set of letters is their name, then they will likely remember it when presented with the written name at a later date, whereas for any other word this is not usually the case (Tolchinsky-Landsmann, 1993). This does not mean they will recognize the written pattern the next time; the claim being made is that the children recognize not the written pattern but the "text" that the pattern represents.

Undoubtedly, children may at times acquire the shapes of letters from other words they have learned, but most frequently the child's own name is the source and point of identification for the letters. This behavior, which has been reported time and again in many different languages, may also indicate that children come to identify one or more written words as prototypical exemplars of written texts, that is, texts that are meaningful and well written. The letters included in these words acquire a special status. In the words of a Spanish child: "*sirven para escribir,*" which is literally "they serve for (to) write." The child's underlying reasoning seems to be that they form part of meaningful texts that can be trusted to produce other texts.

The rules that children impose on number and variety are not mere inventions, they reflect the actual distribution of word length and intra-word variation found in real texts. English orthography also contains examples of this constraint. The only reason for repeating letters in 'egg' is to fulfill the constraint that nouns, verbs, and adjectives must have at least three letters. In Spanish no written word contains the same letter repeated more than twice in consecutive position, whereas in Hebrew very few words contain the same letter repeated three times in consecutive position. But this use of formal constraints is not a direct application of social learning. It reflects an active selection because, although it is true that there are very few single-letter words, single-letter words are the most frequently used in any text.

What is the origin of these constraints? They are neither a direct application of social learning, nor do they emerge from the functional use of writing. Children apply these constraints before they know how to, or indeed are willing to, produce a written message. Because the above is one of my central claims in relation to the development of writing, I would like to elaborate on it in more detail. If literate adults were asked why they thought there are so few one-letter words, then they would probably respond that it is because there are very few spoken words of one sound. Many of the formal constraints (although by no means all) result from the use of the system. But, for children in the process of becoming literate, it is actually the formal features that they initially see. The first things they observe in writing are the differing lengths of strings, the spaces between words, and the graphic variations in size and shape. These features are informative sources that guide children in their sorting of written materials. Children explore the features of writing, and the discovery that some of them are distinctive helps them to organize their written materials. Under these self-imposed limitations on number and variety, children start using, time and again, the same forms in different combinations rather than creating new forms. This is one of the necessary conditions of a notation, but, more important, it facilitates the attribution of meaning to individual letters. Before the application of the two constraints, writing was simply a discontinuous, linear pattern. After their application, however, it is made up of a small number of distinguishable and, therefore, manageable elements. It is not a concern for communication that leads children to inspect more closely the formal features of writing but a concern for these features in and of themselves. Thus, if writing is formally constrained it becomes manageable: first in order to create graphic differences and then to work out the value of the elements.

Writing Becomes Communicative

In Luria's pioneering study, a crucial observation was made. At a given point, children began to introduce graphic differences into their writing as some "scrawls" took on a longer or more rounded appearance. This occurred when the sentences referred to objects that differed in size and shape. For example, when writing that "The monkey has a long tail," children were found to use longer lines than when writing "It's cold in winter." Luria named this the "pictographic" use of marks. Instead of attempting to represent the sounds of the sentence, it seems that children try to represent their content. Instead of using the arbitrary conventional resources of writing, it seems that children are using direct, figurative means.

Ferreiro (1985) reported similar findings. Children suggested, for example, that "bear" should be written with more letters than "duck," because a bear is bigger than a duck. Ferreiro noted, however, that children's writing did not reflect differences in shape or color but *only* differences in number and size. That is, children are not producing an iconic representation, but looking for correspondences between one of the graphic resources of writing—number of marks—and a quantifiable feature of the referent. Similarly, in a study with Chinese-speaking children, Chan (1990) found that, when producing accurate Chinese symbols, even 5-year-olds would retain a figurative correspondence between what they wrote and the object to which they were referring. For example, in writing the word 'elephant,' they would overemphasize a long stroke to represent its trunk.

Levin and Tolchinsky-Landsmann (1990) and Levin and Korat (1993) further explored children's use of figurative elements. They wanted to find out whether children would use figurative elements only for certain features of the referent (e.g., size) or for every feature. For that purpose, 4- to 6-year-olds were asked to write pairs of words that had contrasting referents, for example, 'elephant' (in Hebrew *pil*) and 'ant' (in Hebrew *nemala*), which differ in contrasting size, or 'ball' (in Hebrew *kadur*) and 'rope' (in Hebrew *hevel*), which differ in shape. Note that in the pairs of words selected to represent size, the longer sounding word always stood for the smaller referent; this enabled researchers to distinguish between children's attempts at writing more marks for longer words and their attempts at increasing the number of letters for referential reasons.

At every age, children included referential elements in their writing, but the kind of referential elements varied with age. The use of color was very popular in all age groups. The use of shape was very rare and tended to decrease with age, and the use of more letters to write bigger or longer objects actually tended to increase with age. Children tended to translate both differences in size and length into number of letters; that is, they did not draw bigger letters for bigger objects but rather "translated" size into number of letters.

There are at least two conclusions to be drawn from the results of this study. First, they show that at a certain point in the development of writing, children attempt to represent differences in the *content* of words rather than differences in the *sound* of words. Second, they show that children are selective both in the features they attempt to reflect in their writing and in the resources they use to represent them. Whereas representation of shape is viewed as foreign to writing, representation of color is possible across the age range studied, and representation of size and length is the favorite. It seems that the preference for a particular graphic change is related to the extent that this feature is regarded by children as being *legitimate* in writing. Children discover at an early age that written strings contain different numbers of letters (and Chinese characters different numbers of strokes!), and they see that changes in number are frequent. Number of letters is for them a salient cue for distinguishing words, which they take advantage of when they attempt to reflect the differences. Moreover, there is congruity between the device they are using (i.e., more or fewer letters) and the feature of the referent they seek to reflect (i.e., size or length). In this view, this explains why children increase the number of marks when writing a word that refers to a bigger object and reduce the number when writing a word that refers to a smaller object.

In contrast, children realize very early on that direct replica is foreign to writing, and that is why the referential use of shape decreases with age. Similarity of shape is typical of drawing in a child's view (Brennemann et al., 1996) and not of writing, so they tend to disregard its use for writing. But, why then was color equally used in every group? Children continue to use color because they also see it as a permissible resource of writing, although fulfilling a different function from number of letters: Change in the number of letters produces another word, but a change in color merely has a decorative function. This might explain why the number of marks increased with age and eventually became the main representational device, whereas color, as a decorative resource, remained stable in the two age groups.

Luria and Vygotsky both argued that from the moment children resort to referential devices, the natural development of writing has become one of cultural development because children grasp the fundamental relation that something *stands for something else* (Luria, 1929/1978; Scinto, 1986, p. 73). That is, a symbolic relation has been established, although not in connection with the sound patterns of words. This is the point at which children start to look at writing as a communicative tool, and for that reason start to look for ways of introducing elements into their writing to show (to themselves or to others) what they have heard, that is, they make attempts to represent these words. They look for ways of correlating variation in spoken utterances, albeit in the content of these utterances, with variations in written displays because the features of the written output have now acquired an additional importance in communicating particular meanings. In other words, children begin to understand that in order to mean, they must put some cue in the writing—that the meaning does not just depend on the reader's intention or the context. Writing is beginning to become a potential source of information in itself; by looking at it, it is possible to discover what was said. This happens because children have started to link two activities, reading and writing, which up to that moment had been unrelated in their eyes.

Links Between Reading and Writing

From the perspective of a literate adult, it is understood that anything someone writes is readable (both at the time of writing and in the future), yet for children in the process of becoming literate, reading and writing start out as two unrelated activities. To illustrate, look at the following excerpt transcribed from an interview with a 4-year-old:

Experimenter: Write "a red ball." [Child writes something.]
                What does it say?
Child: You didn't tell me that I would have to read.

Children are able to recognize reading activities from a surprisingly early age. Indeed, research shows that even infants are intelligent participants in book-reading activities. Although young infants use books for sucking, eating, or squeezing (as they do with all other objects), this way of "understanding" books is relatively short lived. From 8 to 18 months of age, "children had progressed from an attempt to eat the page to being able to participate fully in verbal dialogue" while looking at the books (Snow & Ninio, 1986, p. 119). That is, children grasp the physical acts involved in reading—gazing, pointing, monitoring—and become familiar with the typical language associated with books (Bus, van Ijzendorm, & Pellegrini, 1995; Bus & van Ijzendorm, 1988; Heath, 1983; Ninio & Bruner, 1978; Sulzby, 1994; Teale & Sulzby, 1986). Initially, this verbal dialogue is produced in association with the pictures rather than with the text, and by age 2, most children have already discovered that they must look at the pictures in order to discover the story. Then, within a few months, children start to make distinctions between text and pictures (Ferreiro, 1986); they give each a different name. They state that it is the text and not the pictures that is read, "because there are letters."

    The kind of situations in which an adult functions as interpreter, putting words to texts and pictures, may have a strong impact in the development of literacy. They have a determinant role in transmitting to the child what reading means. To be clear, this does not mean that *only* bedtime stories or storybook reading have such impact. Rather, any situation in which someone who knows how to read pronounces words associated with certain text helps children to grasp how meaning is transmitted through texts and how this is related to writing.

    Ferreiro performed a series of longitudinal studies on the development of literacy in two groups of children from age 3 to 5 who differed in their exposure to literacy and notational artifacts. She observed that 3-year-olds raised in an isolated community had an internal representation of writing (i.e., to write meant the production of marks on paper), but for them reading had no definite meaning and was confused with writing. For example, a child who had just jotted down some marks on a sheet of paper was asked to read them back. He responded that he had already done so. Other children claimed that pencils were needed for reading. Although such manifestations might be interpreted as being a strictly terminological problem, Ferreiro's interpretation goes deeper. She suggested that the nature of writing is understood at an earlier age because it leaves visible traces. Writing changes the object visibly, whereas reading does not do so. To grasp the nature of reading, children must comprehend that marks *mean*, that is, they stand for something beyond themselves. It is in relation to this point, in particular, where someone who knows how to read and puts words to the text (by reading aloud for the child) may have a crucial impact on the child's understanding of reading. Reading aloud produces a trace that, even though short lived, can be repeated. When children establish links between written texts and reading behavior, they change their view about writing: They change from relating to writing as a special kind of object distinct from drawing (but which still "does not say anything") to understanding that writing "says something." This change is sometimes reflected in children's use of referential elements, but more generally it is reflected in their attempts to produce some visible difference in their writing.

During the period in which children produce undifferentiated writing, even when they produce similar "scrawls" for different utterances, there is no doubt that they perceive the differences between the utterances they are asked to write; it is not a perceptual problem. The point is that those young children do not find (or do not search for) any way of *recording* the perceived differences. The search for a graphic method to record the differences (albeit differences in the content of words) implies that children realize that what they do when making their marks (during the encoding process) will help them afterward when decoding the marks. Only when children attempt somehow to demonstrate via the graphic medium the differences they perceive, is there a manifestation of children linking writing and reading. Before this point, when they write, they merely write. And when they read (or participate in reading activities), they do no more than read. The two activities are juxtaposed but unintegrated. It is probable that the request to remember later, suggested by Luria, placed the children in a position where they sought a means of telling themselves (at another time) what they already knew.

A word of caution is perhaps in order at this point. It is necessary to take into account that the use of referential elements emerged mostly when children were presented with pairs of words or series of sentences that contrasted in selected features. Therefore, be wary of interpreting the developmental meaning of this resource. The production of differences using referentialization might not be a necessary step in development. What does seem necessary, however, is the introduction of certain graphic changes in the written output that covary with differences in the words the child is attempting to write. At a certain point in development, after a period of undifferentiated writing, the child starts to make modifications in the number of marks, shapes, and combinations of marks in order to differentiate one production from another. These modifications may or may not be referential.

Writing Becomes Regulated by Letter-to-Sound Correspondences

The process whereby writing becomes a system in which written marks represent the sound of words rather than their content or meaning is called *phonetization*. Chapter 2 discussed some historical factors that triggered the phonetization of writing systems. The following lines attempt to show how the process of interpretation triggers the process of phonetization in an individual's writing development.

Children's behavior when presented with writing that they have produced, or that has been produced by another person, is a source of information both for the researcher and for the child. For the researcher, it is a window on a child's understanding of the meaning of written texts. For the children, it is a motor for development because their own interpretative behavior will bring about a shift in their understanding of written texts.

Many children approach the task convinced that they know nothing about writing. But, after convincing them that they should nonetheless try to write, they are the first to feel surprised. Some may even exclaim: "I didn't know I could write!" The task, which exceeds their recognized level of expertise, enables them to change their attitude to their own knowledge. Once this happens, a new range of problems appears, among them the interpretation problem; and with the new problems, new possibilities are opened up.

How should children interpret what they write? A common strategy is by using the words the investigator asked them to write. In decontextualized situations, the words of the investigator are often the only cue available for interpretation. In contrast, in contextualized tasks or in real-life situations, children may resort to other sources of information to guide their interpretation. For example, if a text appears under a picture, they may use what they see in the picture to interpret the text. So no matter which source of information children use for interpreting what is written, the fact that they produce a verbal utterance for that purpose pushes the emergence of the next stage in the development of writing, that of phonetization.

During the period in which children are engaged in exploring the formal features of writing, their behavior shows they are aware that writing is *somehow* related to language. It has been shown that 3- to 4-year-olds, when required to read what they have written, will repeat verbatim the words they were asked to write. This behavior was discussed earlier to illustrate children's belief that the intention of the reader determines what is written; it may also be argued that a verbatim repetition indicates no more than the child's agreement to participate in a game of pretense—as if children were reasoning more or less in the following way: *You tell me to write something, so I make some scribbles that you accept and then, when you ask me to read what I have written, I repeat what you told me initially.* This indeed may be true. It may be that reading back what has been dictated to them constitutes little more than playing a game for the children. However, whatever the case, irrespective of the child's motives, this behavior of saying something for a written display scaffolds the development of writing.

When children repeat verbatim what they were asked to write for what they have just written, the occasion is created for a mapping of a verbal utterance onto a written display. Something said (a word, a sentence) is put into correspondence with a graphic pattern. At this point, it is important to take into account the characteristics of the graphic pattern to which children attempt to match the verbal utterance. It is very different to say a word while looking at a long discontinuous, linear pattern of wavy lines, the typical look of *undifferentiated writing*, and to do so in the face of a reduced number of written marks, the typical look of formally constrained writing.

Recall that children are at an age in which expectations about the number and variety of letters comprising words has already been established. These features of the written string pave the way to the possibility of providing a pronunciation for each of the graphic elements they are attempting to interpret. Parts of the utterance can be mapped onto parts of the written display and, vice versa, parts of the written display can be mapped onto parts of the utterance.

The phonetization of writing marks a turning point not only because it is the principle on which our writing system is based, but also because it constitutes the discovery of a stable frame of reference. Previously, children added figurative referential elements to their writing to hint at the meaning of the words they were representing. But the idea that writing reflects referential differences directly can only be applied in certain circumstances, when there is some kind of contrast between the referents of the words children are attempting to write. Note that children were found to use this strategy mainly when they had to write words that contrasted in size (e.g., ant vs. elephant) or in color (tomato vs. cucumber) or in any other feature. It is in this sense that the idea of referential correspondence functions as an ad hoc model suitable for solving particular situations. The emergence of this model shows a child's capacity to accommodate particular situations and to take advantage of the features of writing, but it is limited and it is not based on a working principle of the writing system children are acquiring. When children turn instead to the letter-to-sound correspondences to guide their writing, they turn to a general model suitable for every writing task, because every word and sentence has a phonic aspect (for a discussion of the differences between ad hoc and general models, see Inhelder & Celerrier, 1996, p. 55). The phonetization of writing implies a shift from covariation of graphic changes with some spoken words to the discovery of the actual general principle on which our writing system is based. Children have discovered that the number and variety of graphic elements (letters) is related to the phonological aspect of words.

But how do children segment words so as to make these segments correspond to the graphic elements in the written string? On which "units" is the mapping based?

The Syllabic Hypothesis

According to Ferreiro, once children have grasped the idea that writing is a representation of sound, they initially believe that each written mark roughly corresponds to a spoken syllable.[16] Evidence for the syllabic hypothesis is provided by case studies and in-depth longitudinal investigations of Argentine and Mexican children carried out by Ferreiro and her collaborators, by studies with Israeli children, and by further studies comparing Spanish-speaking and Hebrew-speaking children. However, the syllabic hypothesis has not gone unchallenged and it has been called into question by many studies, mainly those carried out in English (Kamii, Long, G. Manning, & M. Manning, 1993; Treiman, Tincoff, & Daylene Richmond-Welty, 1996). These studies suggest that children use alternative methods to understand the relation between written and spoken words. Before analyzing these alternative proposals, however, I would like to elaborate a little on the development of the syllabic hypothesis and provide some examples to show how this hypothesis functions in two different languages and scripts.

A child's first attempt at mapping letters onto parts-of-utterance appears when he reads back what he has just finished writing. Initially such attempts are nonsystematic. The child follows the written marks while segmenting the words into parts (e.g., saying *choco#late*), into syllables, or into a mixture of both. The need to accommodate the reading to the written form leads to different ways of breaking up the word. Sometimes children elongate the sound of a part, sometimes they cut it short. In developmental time (and probably with more experience with print or writing activities), segmentation systematically becomes syllabic and children look for a term-to-term correspondence between number of syllables and written marks.

---

[16]Spoken syllables are deliberately used because the definition of syllables is not clearly given in any of the studies quoted. Often they correspond to CV sequences (core syllables) and not to strictly defined syllables.

It is not surprising that the syllable has been hypothesized to be the initial unit of correspondence. Indeed, it has been established since the earliest studies by Bruce (1964) that when children are asked to break spoken words down into smaller parts, they tend to segment words into syllables before they segment into phonemes. This means *intentional* segmentation. Infants are capable of categorical perception of sounds almost from birth (DeCasper & Fifer, 1980; Eimas, Siqueland, Jusczyk, & Vigorito, 1971), but the intentional breaking down of a word into parts "smaller" than syllables rarely occurs before age 5. Researchers have created a whole range of tasks to verify this development (Adams, 1991; Stanovich, 1986; Treiman, 1985), but regardless of the changes they introduce, the results are invariably the same. At the age of 4, virtually no child is able to perform segmentation tasks successfully. At age 5, most children segment into syllables and only a few (usually less than 20%) can identify phonemic segmentation, even when tests are preceded by training and modeling. Finally, at age 6, most children perform the segmentation tasks successfully. This is the usual rate of development even in English, which is not a syllable-timed language. Syllables are natural units of segmentation because they have a phonetic substrate, whereas phonemes are linguistic constructs (Mehler, Dommergues, Frauenfelder, & Segui, 1984). Therefore, it is understandable that when children start segmenting words to map on to letters, they do so in terms of syllables.

Figure 3.4 contains a number of examples of the "syllabic period" in two languages, with different scripts to illustrate this period in the development of writing. The children were asked to write common nouns that form part of their typical out-of-school vocabulary and are similar in meaning and sound in the two languages. Two series of written productions can be seen for the same words. Those on the left were produced by a 5-year-old Hebrew-speaking girl, whereas those on the right were produced by a Spanish-speaking boy of the same age. The girl uses Hebrew letters and the boy Roman letters. Nevertheless, the two sets of products are regulated by syllabic correspondence. This can be proven by repeating the word the children were asked to write and by breaking it down into syllables (e.g., *sa#la#mi*). The number of letters maps onto the number of syllables. Initially, the main preoccupation within this age group is the correspondence between the *number* of syllables and the *number* of letters.[17] When children are concerned mainly with quantitative correspondence, any

---

[17]The two children used letters that were quite unrelated to the words. In the Hebrew example, the middle letter (L) might be thought to bear some relation to the same letter in the word (SALAMI); however, as the same letter reappears in every word, this possibility can be ruled out. In the Spanish example, the use of the letter (A) can be similarly ruled out. Obviously, it is impossible to determine whether children are applying syllabic correspondences by looking at just one written production. What is needed is a comparison between productions.

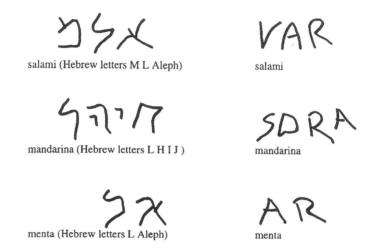

FIG. 3.4.   Syllabic writing in two different scripts.

letter will apparently do. At this point, a child's specific knowledge about letter-names and their respective sound values plays an important role.

Two processes are active in this undertaking. On the one hand, there is the
analysis of the word, and on the other, a child's knowledge of the conventional
sound-value of the letters. It may be the case that some syllables, usually the initial
one, are written with the corresponding conventional letters, whereas others are
written with any letter. It may also occur that some children can identify one or
more letters by their sound-value and use them, in a nonsystematic way, when
they recognize the presence of that sound in a word. For example, the Spanish boy
whose writings appear in Fig. 3.4 seems to have identified the letter A. He uses it
in every word, but only one time instead of two in the first and second words (*salami* and *mandarina*), and he uses it in the wrong place in the third word (*menta*).
Therefore, there may be some words that have not yet been analyzed and are written with any letters, some words that have been partially analyzed and are written
with some letters the child knew, and other words in which, by chance, the child
knew all the letters and used them. These various possibilities are typical of any
process of transitional knowledge. Eventually the two processes of writing and analyzing the sound-values of letters concur. Then, the written product will include
a letter with its conventional sound-value for each syllable.

Writing Becomes Language Specific

The study comparing Hebrew- and Spanish-speaking children demonstrated
that it was at this juncture that the developmental paths in these two languages,

which up to this point had been very similar, became differentiated. This splitting of roads is illustrated in Fig. 3.5, which shows two series of production for the same word.

The productions on the left were written by an Israeli boy, and those on the right were produced by a Spanish girl. As in the previous example, the two sets of written products are regulated by syllabic correspondence. The two children analyzed the word into syllables, but the letters used are no longer just any letter; they are chosen based on with their phonic value. However, for each syllable, the Hebrew-speaking boy used consonants and the Spanish-speaking girl used vowels. They did so even for *Coca-Cola* or *Pizza*, words that are written alphabetically, that is, one letter for each sound. Both words appear with great frequency in both Tel Aviv and Barcelona, the two cities where the children who participated in the study live. This point stresses that visual information is particularly relevant for understanding writing at some stages. For example, it is relevant during the stage of undifferentiated writing when children imitate graphic patterns or during the period of formally constrained writing when children are defining the formal constraints of writing. But, at this stage, the interaction between graphics and phonics acquires greater importance.

It may come as little surprise that Hebrew children mainly use consonants; this is, after all, what the system is based on. However, it should be noted that the boy could have used any of the *matres lectionis* (see footnote 15) as vowels. In any case, the argument that "this is what the system is based on" cannot explain why the Spanish girl mainly used vowels, because the Spanish alphabet

mandarina (Hebrew letters N R D M)   mandarina

Coca Cola (Hebrew letters L K K K)   Coca Cola

pizza (Hebrew letters S P)   pizza

FIG. 3.5.   Syllabic writing using mainly consonants or mainly vowels.

includes both consonants and vowels. It is necessary to look elsewhere in seeking an explanation.

In Spanish, at least four reasons might contribute to the preferential use of vowels. The first two are related to the phonological structure of Spanish. Unlike English, Spanish vowels are highly stable and not subject to contextual variations. There are only five vowels to remember (in English there are 14 at least!),[18] and they are obligatory constituents of syllables. Unlike English, syllabic consonants (as in the word *bottle*) are not possible. These two reasons, however, are not sufficient to explain the different use of vowels and consonants because both arguments are equally valid in Hebrew.

The two additional and differential reasons are related to Spanish orthography. Spanish spelling is completely transparent as far as vowels are concerned; there is a one-to-one mapping between vowels and letters. Also, the names of vowels coincide with their sounds. It would seem indisputable that it is the combined effect of both factors that determines the massive presence of vowels in Spanish during the syllabic period.

Perhaps for similar reasons, English-speaking children rarely use only vowels. Vowel instability, as well as their context dependency and the lack of term-to-term correspondence in orthography, may explain this difference. There is no mention of a "syllabic period" in Glenda Bissex's (1980) case study of the literacy development of her English-speaking son, Paul, although some of the examples she provided might be interpreted in terms of syllabic mapping. Although several authors, as well as many parents and teachers, have noted that preschoolers and first graders "miss" letters (writing VKT for vacation; Kamii et al., 1993), this is not interpreted as syllabic mapping. The usual interpretation given is simply that children omit letters (Shimron, 1993). Kamii et al. (1993) suggested that in English there must be a sort of consonantal stage rather than a syllabic one.

The strongest attack against the "syllabic hypothesis" has come from Rebecca Treiman and her associates (1996). As an alternative process, they suggested, in line with Linnea Ehri (1993), that "children begin to create links between printed words and spoken words from a very early age by finding links between letters in printed words and the names of the letters in the spoken words" (Treiman et al., 1996, p. 512). North American children learn this very early in the context of preschool or family activities. In order to provide further evidence to support these claims, Treiman and her associates designed two

---

[18]The 14 vowels in English that are commonly identified are: "/ai/ as in pie, /au/ as in out, /æ/ as in at, /A/ as in odd, /e/ as in aid, /E/ as in etch, /«/ as in up, sofa, /i/ as in eel, /I/ as in it, /o/ as in oat, /oi/ as in oil, / / as in audit, /u/ as in ooze, and /U/ as in put." (Treiman, 1993).

studies: the first to demonstrate children's familiarity with, and use of, letter-names, and the second to demonstrate that children do not link print to speech at the level of syllables, but rather by using their knowledge of letter-names. The first study showed that 5-year-olds found it easier to say the initial letter of a word if it was the name of an English letter rather than its corresponding sound. For example, they found it easier to say the initial letter in *beach* than in *bone* because the spoken form of *beach* starts with /bi/, the name of the letter *b*; whereas the spoken form *bone* starts with /bo/, which is not the name of a letter in English. Similar findings were reported for final letters, although letters at the end of words were more difficult to identify. Treiman concluded that knowledge of letter-names helps children to understand that print represents spoken language. This knowledge is a condition for learning the specific mappings between spelling and phonemes and seems to constitute a stronger link than syllabic mapping, as was shown in their second study.

In the second study, Treiman used monosyllabic and bisyllabic words. In the monosyllabic words, the name of the letter coincided with part of the syllable, whereas in the bisyllabic words, it coincided with the whole initial syllable. For example, in the monosyllabic word *bead*, the name of the letter /bi/ coincides with the initial consonant and a vowel segment (a CV segment), whereas in the bisyllabic word *beaver*, the letter-name coincides with the first syllable. The results revealed no differences in the ease with which the initial letter of the bisyllabic words versus the monosyllabic word were identified. This suggests that children are not mapping at a syllable level but rather using their knowledge of letter-names.

The results of these studies are particularly significant because they highlight the influence of the structure of words on children's behavior, both in segmentation and in spelling. In addition to the other factors that create crosslinguistic differences, it is the structure of the word that children are attempting to analyze and write that is determinant. Children's success at spelling will vary according to the position of the letters in the word they have been asked to identify (initial or final) and according to whether the letter-name fits the segment of the word they are asked to spell.

But, do these studies challenge the place of the syllabic hypothesis in the development of writing? In Treiman's studies, children were not asked to write but rather *to spell orally*, and from this Treiman deduced that they would apply this knowledge when writing words. As already seen, what children *know* about a notation is one thing, and how they *use* the notation is another. These two aspects of knowledge will eventually overlap. But they do not overlap all early in development. Close observation of children's behavior in different tasks suggests that children may recognize the name and the shape of the letters, both when isolated and in the contexts of words, and yet not use them for writing (chap. 5). In order to appreciate how children use their knowledge of oral spelling and letter names, children should be asked to write words displaying relations similar to those studied orally.

There is no doubt that children's knowledge of letter-names plays an important role in the acquisition of writing. This same theory has been used to explain the preference of Spanish-speaking children for vowels during their syllabic period. Knowledge about letter-names is one of the factors that influences writing development but it does not operate identically in every language and script.

An exact correspondence between letter-name and sound is not a crosslinguistic phenomenon. In Hebrew, the name of the letters differs greatly from their sound, and studies such as that performed by Treiman would be difficult to carry out in Hebrew because there is no possibility of parts of words coinciding with letter-names (the name of certain letters does, however, coincide with some words like *yod* and *zayn*).

Besides, oral spelling is a social practice that, as with most such practices, is far from being universal. In English-speaking countries, it is used particularly for proper names, but it is also used for any word considered difficult or unknown. In languages with shallow orthographies—that is, orthographies in which there is a closer correspondence between letters and sounds—oral spelling is far less common and is used almost exclusively for foreign names. If Spanish first graders were asked to spell orally, they would not understand what was required of them, even though they offered the name of the letters spontaneously when asked to segment the words (Tolchinsky & Teberosky, 1998). In Hebrew, asking a child to spell a word would be interpreted as "how do you write it." These differences point to the need to evaluate the role of letter-names in the development of writing, taking into account the uses and practices of different linguistic communities and scripts. It is possible that in certain languages and communities the name of a letter is just one of many factors contributing to the development of writing, whereas in others it is the main factor that leads children to make the link between print and spoken language.

Similarly, one possibility is that the syllabic hypothesis holds true for syllable-timed languages such as Spanish, Italian, and Chinese, but not English. This possibility is quite reasonable because segmentation strategies are influenced by the phonological structure of the language.[19] However, many more crosslinguistic studies are needed before a definitive answer can be reached.

---

[19]In Italian as well as in English, children find it much easier to segment into syllables than into phonemes or morphemes (Devescovi, Orsolini, & Pace, 1990). But, preschool Italian children have segmentation skills that are far superior to those of appropriately matched American children (Cossu, Shankweiler, Liberman, Katz, & Tola, 1988). This seems to be because Italian has a relatively shallow phonology with little morphophonological alternation and a basically open syllable structure. The influence of the phonological structure of a language on segmentation strategies is also found among adults (e.g., Cutler, Mehler, & Segui, 1986).

An alternative possibility is that the units on which children initially base their letter-to-sound correspondences are neither absolute nor stable. Rather, they may depend on the structure of the words that children are trying to write and on the level of the utterance they are being asked to write. If syllables are absolute units of mapping, then any word or sentence should be written on the basis of its syllables, regardless of their length and structure. If, on the other hand, they constitute relative units, then some words might be analyzed and written syllabically whereas others are not; or, words might be written syllabically whereas sentences are not. This framework is useful for interpreting Treiman's findings. Thus, Treiman found that when words are bisyllabic and the name of the letter coincides with the syllable, children will use this information to isolate the first letter. But when the words are monosyllabic and the name of the letter coincides with the initial sequence of consonant and vowel (CV), they will use this cue to identify the letter. Bear in mind that the CV sequence is the smallest *pronounceable* segment and it corresponds to core syllables*. In other words, when the identification of letters requires an analysis at the level of phonemes, which are not pronounceable, children find it more difficult to use their knowledge of letter-names. This explains why children found it more difficult to identify the letter /bi/ in *bone* than the same letter in *beach*. In the case of *bone*, in order to identify the letter /bi/, they must analyze the word into phonemes, which are unpronounceable. But, to find the same letter in beach it is enough to identify the initial CV sequence. Once one pronounces this first sequence, one "discovers" the letter /bi/. The hypothesis that children use "relative units" in their segmentation and letter-sound correspondences is compatible with Treiman's findings. Moreover, it is supported by various studies conducted on spoken and written development.

Research into adult perception of speech has provided evidence of the relativity of the use of linguistic units (McNeill & Lindig, 1973). For example, even adults find it easier to detect a particular phoneme when asked to look for that particular phoneme in the context of a syllable rather than in the context of a word. In the case of children, Fox and Routh (1975) demonstrated that when 5-year-olds have to say words "in little bits," they usually tend to say the syllables, but when asked to say short phrases "in little bits," they break the phrases down into words, or part of words.

To determine the effect of different linguistic units (syllables vs. words) on children's writing, Hebrew-speaking children, from ages 4 to 6, were asked to write pairs of words and series of sentences (Tolchinsky-Landsmann, 1991; Tolchinsky-Landsmann & Levin, 1987). Words were monosyllabic and bisyllabic, and sentences ranged from one to five words, with the syntactic category of the words being different in each case. In one of the series, most words were nouns (*Tami ve'Eran bonim migdal* 'Tami and Eran are building a tower'). In the other series most of the words were verbs (*yalda rokedet ve'shara* 'a girl is dancing and singing'). The analysis of children's written products showed that correspondence in terms of syllables appears more frequently in single words than in multiple word sentences. In multiple word sentences, children could resort to words as a unit of correspondence. Moreover, word category also had an effect on the unit of correspondence. Words were more frequently used as units of correspondence in sentences containing a predominance of nouns than in sentences containing a predominance of verbs.

In sum, children's discovery of links between letters and sound is a turning point in the conceptualization of writing. It means discovering a stable principle useful for representing any word. The first unit of letter–sound correspondence, at least in certain languages, is the syllable because it is a pronounceable natural unit of segmentation, in contrast to the phonemes that are unpronounceable abstract units. It might be the case, however, that during this period of writing development, children do not have a fixed, stable unit of correspondence. So, depending on the structure of words or on whether they are trying to represent a word or a sentence, they may vary the unit of correspondence between letters and sounds.

The Alphabetic Principle

Most studies conducted on early literacy identify the child's main task as being the discovery of the alphabetic principle. According to Byrne and Fielding-Barnsley (1989), the alphabetic principle is the "usable knowledge of the fact that phonemes can be represented by letters, such that whenever a particular phoneme occurs in a word, and in whatever position, it can be represented by the same letter" (p. 314). The "syllabic period" is, therefore, nonalphabetic because children use letters to represent syllables rather than phonemes. More precisely, they use letters to represent one component of a syllable—Spanish-speaking children use vowels, and Hebrew-speaking children use consonants. Spanish-speaking children, however, need to go one step further in the exhaustiveness of their representation. In order to write conventionally, they need to use a letter for each component of a syllable. In simple terms, writing conventional Spanish means the representation of each of the consonants and vowels in a word.

Reconsider the case of Hebrew-speaking children. Hebrew script works successfully without the representation of vowels at the level of letters. Therefore, children who only represent part of the syllable in their writing, in this case the consonant, are much closer to writing Hebrew conventionally. Indeed, many children were found to be doing this already, although probably without any great awareness.

Many children, even before being formally taught, discover the alphabetic principle. That is, they produce a letter for each vowel and consonant in the word. How do children discover the alphabetic principle? As with most of the acquisitions so far described, the transition to alphabetic writing is gradual, demonstrates a sensitivity to word structure, and is related to children's previous knowledge. There is not a sudden shift from one stage in which words are regulated by syllabic correspondences to a different stage in which words are regulated by alphabetic correspondences. Instead, intermediate phases can be identified in which children produce syllabic-alphabetic mapping. That is, some syllables are fully represented, whereas others are not. For example, the word *gato* 'cat,' might be written GAO, where the first syllable is completely represented (#*ga*# written GA), but the second #*to*# is not. Situations also arise in which information stemming from different sources creates conflict and children regress to more primitive ways of writing. There are also privileged situations in which children arrive at more advanced solutions that cannot yet be generalized to other situations.

The transition to the alphabetic principle is also word sensitive; certain words are regulated by alphabetic correspondences before others, depending on several factors. These factors include the structure of the word, the extent to which word components present any pronunciation difficulty, the way word components are represented orthographically, the child's previous knowledge of the word (i.e., whether this word forms part of a child's inventory of well-written meaningful texts), and the child's previous knowledge of the letters used to represent the word.

It is in this transition to the alphabetic principle that these specific characteristics of the phonological and morphological structures of a language, and the way in which these characteristics are reflected in the script, play a crucial and distinctive role. But, as in the emergence of syllabic correspondences, the search for a more exhaustive means of representation involves an interaction between spoken segmentation for writing, the features of the written product, and the child's interpretation of the written output. A child's knowledge of the names of the letters and the conventional sound of each letter intervenes, but this knowledge does not seem to be a necessary precondition for the child's acquiring alphabetic mapping. Some examples drawn from the Hebrew/Spanish study described earlier in this chapter may help to clarify these processes.

Recall that children from preschool up to second grade were asked to write a number of words that are pronounced similarly in both languages. One of the analyses examined the percentage of children who produced alphabetic mappings for each word. The percentage of children using alphabetic writing increased from preschool to first grade, and by second grade all the Spanish-speaking children were writing alphabetically. This general tendency aside, however, the differences in the number of children who wrote each word alphabetically were marked in both languages. The first word to be written by alphabetic mapping in Spanish was *te* 'tea,' which in Spanish is monosyllabic and coincides with the name of the letter T. Three preschoolers "discovered" the possibility of alphabetic mapping in the process of writing this word, although each arrived at different products.

Miriam, a Spanish-speaking preschooler, wrote every word by syllabic mapping and by using the letters of her name (see Fig. 3.6). The exception to this was *mandarina* 'mandarin,' where she used two other marks that can be interpreted as being either numerals (5 and 0) or letters. For the remaining words, she only used letters from her name. The monosyllabic *te* 'tea' was the only word in which she used two letters. A closer observation of the production process should shed

IAM

salami

5OMA

mandarina

IRRM

Coca Cola

RRAMI

pizza

AM

menta

MI

te

FIG. 3.6. Transition to alphabetic correspondences.

some light on her decision. Miriam wrote silently but slowly, and the pace of her writing seemed to indicate that she was anticipating the number of letters, performing a syllabic analysis of the word. When she was asked to read back what she had written, she repeated the word pausing between syllables, where each syllable was a letter. This procedure worked well for four words. When it came to *te*, however, Miriam started to do exactly the same—she drew an M and then stopped, but then, after a short while, she added another letter (I) so that the word *te* was written MI. When reading back her own writing, she ran her finger over the two letters pronouncing *te* in one breath. Implicit in her reading back, but explicit in her written product, was an alphabetic mapping.

Was it Miriam's understanding of an isolated letter, which acted as a constraint on legibility, that led her to add another letter? This is the interpretation provided by Ferreiro (1985). This interpretation explains why, for children who are already working under syllabic constraints, monosyllabic words might constitute the privileged locus for the discovery of the alphabetic principle. In Miriam's case, the conflict between a segmentation hypothesis and a self-imposed constraint on the written output apparently led to the emergence of alphabetic mapping. Note that only quantitative correspondences were involved both in the process of encoding and in the process of decoding. It is this search for a balance between both processes, while at the same time considering the constraints on legibility, that leads to a more complete representation.

In the other cases of preschoolers acquiring alphabetic mapping, a similar search for balance between encoding, decoding, and constraints on legibility would also seem to be involved. Two of the Spanish-speaking preschoolers (Raquel and Marcel) already recognized some letters by their conventional sound-value, yet each of them used this knowledge differently. Marcel used syllabic mapping. Thus, for *salami* he wrote SLNA, for *mandarina*, MAAIA, and when it came to writing *te*, he did not hesitate, and wrote a single T and read back *te*. His knowledge of the conventional sound of the letter facilitated his selection of the initial letter. However, immediately after reading back the word, he added another (unrelated) letter, yielding TL. Perhaps he acted for the same motives as Miriam, described earlier, in deciding to add another letter. In any case, he then tried another reading, this time pausing shortly between the pronunciation of the first and the second letter. The syllable was decomposed in the act of interpreting his own writing.

Raquel also wrote by syllabic correspondences. Thus for *salami*, she wrote AIOA, for *mandarina*, AIIA, and for *Coca-Cola*, AOAO. When it came to the word *te* she repeated it to herself *te*, again and again, and then wrote TE. Unlike Marcel, however, she did not pause between the first and the second letter, and it is was impossible to determine whether she was using the name of the letter as an unanalyzable whole to solve this situation or whether she was using it as an alphabetic representation of the word *te*.

Table 3.1 presents in a very synthetic way the main features of the three periods in the development of spontaneous writing (focusing on the writing of words).

It should be noted, however, that it is difficult to grasp the many dimensions that intervene when children attempt to write words after the period of undifferentiated writing, At times it is a painstaking process during which they seek to coordinate online information from different sources previously stored representations. In an effort to make at least part of this process understandable, this discussion has focused on the transition to alphabetic writing and on just part of the very many "preoccupations" that are at play. Children are not concerned only with letter-to-sound mapping, which sometimes leads to unwanted products. They may also be worried about the outward shape of the letters, which do

TABLE 3.1

Development Sequence in Spontaneous Writing

Developmental Phase	Features
Undifferentiated writing	• similar "scrawls" for every word • displays the superordinate features of writing • cannot be interpreted outside the context of production • the words children have been asked to write and/or other contextual sources (e.g., pictures) guide the interpretation of their own writing

Formally constrained writing	• emergence of the *distinctive features* that graphic displays must fulfill in order to be readable and writeable: minimal number and sufficient variety of letters
	• displays the ordinate features of writing
	  – use of own name letters in different combinations to form other words
	  – modifications in the number of marks, shapes, and combinations of marks to differentiate on production from another
	• when interpreting their own writing, children attempt to match the verbal utterance to the graphic pattern

Phonetization of writing • Syllabic mappings • Syllabic-alphabetic mappings • Alphabetic mappings	• writing becomes language specific: The phonological and morphological structures of a language, and the way in which these characteristics are reflected in the script, determine further development. • letter–sound correspondences, increasing exhaustiveness in the representation of a word's sounds • increasing use of letters with conventional sound values

not always come out as planned, and about what they have already written on the piece of paper, which sometimes acts as an aid but at other times gives rise to conflicts that are not easy to overcome. Eventually, however, these different sources of information become integrated and children learn to write conventionally.

THE DEVELOPMENT OF EARLY WRITING
AND INVENTED SPELLING

Why, you might well be asking, do I insist on speaking throughout this book about writing development and not about spelling, or invented spelling? The reasons have to do with the different denotations of the words "writing" and "spelling" and the particular focus that research on "invented spelling" has had, mainly in the United States.

In general, "spelling" refers to naming, or printing, the correct letters of a word. If someone asks you "how do you spell it?," then you are supposed to answer with the correct letters. The term "writing" instead embraces not only the choice of the right letters but can also refer to the process of tracing letters or other signs on a surface. The term includes not only a concern for the letters, but also for the configuration and organization of the signs in the graphic space. And it also covers the general process of producing texts, any text, from single words to novels, poetry, or scientific articles. Therefore, the reason for using "writing" throughout is to embrace the developmental period during which, as discussed in this chapter, children are not producing the right letters for writing words or sentences but are still writing.

During the late 1960s and early 1970s, a number of researchers observed that very young children who were not formally taught to read showed a creative ability to spell. Dolores Durking (1966) suggested that the ability to spell precedes formal teaching of reading. More than that, "the ability to read seemed almost like a by-product of [the] ability to print and spell" (Durking, 1966, p. 137). A few years later, Carol Chomsky and Charles Read published some highly influential papers on the development of spelling. It was a time in which psychologists and psycholinguistics were very much involved in demonstrating the creative nature of learning. Many mistakes that young children produced when acquiring spoken language—like saying *goed* instead of *went*—were taken as clear evidence that children were able to deduce the rules of their language even without formal instruction. In this spirit, evidence that children might also be creative in discovering the rules of spelling, and even go through a process in which they "invent" their own spelling but otherwise attend to the rules of the domain, was most welcomed.

When working on his doctoral dissertation in linguistics and education at Harvard University, Read observed many children who began to write, when they were between about age 2½ and 4, before they were able to read. He noted that these children produce "spellings" that are often incorrect by conventional standards but still represent the sound structure of each word. In their spelling, these children are not trying to remember strings of letters, or to put on paper words that they have seen written. On the contrary, they are attempting to represent the sound structure of the words they are trying to write. Indeed, an analysis of their spellings shows that these children have a deep appreciation of the phonemic structure of their language. Read was among the first to discover the important role of letter-names in identifying phonemes and also the importance of a child's own name in this discovery. Very often, children learn the names of the letters of the alphabet, and then realize that their own name includes the phoneme for which a particular letter stands, for example, when a boy called Tommy discovers that the first letter *t* stands for /t/. These children then reply on their knowledge of the sound of such letter names to spell each word as it sounds to them. For example, they may write *Thank you* as THAQ. Children thus exploit the names of the *letters* rather than the sounds that these letters represent (C. Chomsky, 1979), as when they write *nature* as NHR.

The most interesting situations occur, however, when children attempt to write phonemes that do not occur in the name of any letter. For example, no English letter contains the vowel /E/ (as in the word bed) in its name. In such cases, children may resort to an adult for help or invent their own spellings. For example, children may use the *a* whose name sounds similar to /E/. In so doing, children demonstrate that they implicitly recognize the similarity between /E/ and /e/ (Read, 1971, 1973, 1986).

Inspired by Read's work, Treiman (1993) conducted an in-depth study of a group of American first graders who were learning to read and write in English. In common with an increasing number of children in the United States today, these children were encouraged to write in their own way, and Treiman analyzed their spelling. As in Read's study, Treiman's study involved detailed linguistic analyses of large collections of beginning spellings produced in natural situations. Unlike Read, however, Treiman did not study children who were beginning to read and write on their own but rather first graders who were already involved in formal teaching. Another important difference is that Treiman considered both misspellings and correctly spelled words so that she was able to answer not only what are the difficulties that children are facing and how they solve them creatively, but also which words are easier for the children to spell. Finally, in her analysis of children's spelling she considered how children's experience with printed words, that is, their visual knowledge of orthographic patterns, might have an influence on their spelling decisions. She showed that some spelling decisions are affected not only by the kind of letter-to-sound correspondence that children are looking at, but also by what they have seen in writing. Treiman (1993) explained that "even first graders are beginning to learn about which letter sequences may occur in English and which may not" (p. 167). This kind of knowledge may sometimes help and at other times interfere with children's phonological analyses. For example, the first graders made a number of errors like FASS for *face*, using a double consonant to end a word because this is a rather common orthographic pattern in English. But they made fewer mistakes, including double consonants at the beginning of a word, such as spelling MMNE for *money*.

By emphasizing the creative character of spelling, the work of these researchers brought about a paradigmatic change in the way the process of learning spelling is viewed. This work was revolutionary in viewing spelling as a linguistic process in which children attempt to map the sound structure of words onto letters. Moreover, it demonstrated the role of orthographic knowledge in developing spelling. Many reasons that led to the study of invented spelling are similar to those that motivated researchers working from a constructivist stance to look at early writing. Both lines of research attempt to provide evidence for creative learning in a particular domain of knowledge, and they proceed with a conviction that children's mistakes might be necessary steps in the learning process and a useful window for researchers to access their implicit knowledge.

There is, however, a crucial difference between research on the development of writing and that on invented spelling, and this difference relates to the main focus of the research. Research on invented spelling focuses strictly on how children use letters for representing words—attempts at writing in which letters are not involved, or in which the use of letters might be completely unrelated to the sound structure of words, is not their concern. In a sense, research on spelling is a part of the more inclusive research on the development of writing. Thus, a developmental perspective on writing might start with a full exploration of the initial phases of acquisition during which children explore the formal and referential communicative features of writing system, as this chapter has attempted to do, and then turn to the development of spelling, including a full consideration of the different knowledge dimensions that must be mastered by children to become literate (Ravid & Tolchinsky, 2002). Thus, children certainly need to learn the way in which phonological segments are represented in the writing system, that is, the *phonological dimension*. But, in our writing system, learning the link between letters and sounds is not enough for 'correct' spelling. The reasons why we should write KNOW for /nou/ or for the use of double consonants like in EGG are historical, not phonological. So, children must also figure out this *graphic-orthographic dimension*. And this is not all about spelling; as we shall see in chapter 6, many spelling decisions are related to the morphological features of the word, rather than to its phonological features. The grammatical inflections that mark number or tense are spelled always in the same way, independently of whether and how they sound. For example, English *passed* and *past* share a final *t*, however in *passed* this *t* represents past tense, which is associated with the consistent spelling *<ed>*. Learning to identify and spell *<-ed>* *correctly typically takes several years and lasts into the middle of grade school* (Nunes, Bryant, & Bidman, 1997).

The study of children's struggle with the different dimensions of knowledge involved in spelling is still only part of what a comprehensive view of developmental writing should cover. Beside being a notational system, writing is a means for producing different types of texts; knowing how to write means learning how to use the different genres of written language, and the study of this learning process is an essential part of a developmental study of writing. Indeed, the developmental sequence outlined in this chapter is only a tiny part of the many facets that must be explored in trying to understand the child's path to writing and literacy.

THE DEVELOPMENT OF EARLY WRITING
AND SOCIOCULTURAL APPROACHES TO LITERACY

Throughout this chapter I have tried to provide evidence of principles that operate to organize children's interpretation and production of written materials. These were evident in children's categorization of written displays into legible/not legible, in their decisions regarding the number and the kind of letters they have to use for writing words, and in their mapping of letters to sounds. Notational information is such a vast and diverse domain that, as in other domains of knowledge, some channeling of attention to relevant environmental inputs is necessary (Karmiloff-Smith, 1992). The organizing principles serve to channel relevant information, to separate writing from drawing, to single out variation in number of letters as a licit representational resource of writing, to link spoken utterances to written strings and then parts of the spoken utterance to parts of the written string. Where do these principles come from and why do they change with age? Certainly, children come into the world equipped with a propensity to extend knowledge by systematically monitoring variations both in their environment and in their own active exploration of the environment. Thus, successive interactions with the environment bring about changes both in the way the environment is perceived and in the way it is explored. Because interaction with writing is almost unavoidable, it is reasonable to find children's ideas changing with age and to progress by transformations and correspondences, as in other domains of knowledge (H. Sinclair, 1988). Children's ideas are not idiosyncratic inventions—although they may often appear as such—but rather reflect the selection and elaboration of the information provided by the environment. Such elaboration can bring about certain transformation in the rules of the respective writing systems, for example, when children establish the minimum quantity principle, but they are constantly confronted with the features of the writing system, with the social uses of writing, and with the knowledge significant others have about writing.

Sometimes, however, studies on emergent literacy within a sociocultural context focus on the information provided by the environment and neglect children's transformation of this information. In an effort to stress that children's interest in the written word does not emerge "naturally," many attempts have been made to describe the circumstances that might trigger, propitiate, enhance, or provoke reading and writing activities at home, or in school settings. The benefits of sociocultural approaches to emergent literacy are beyond doubt. Rather than conceiving of literacy as an individual process of acquisition, they see it as a process of situated learning in which children and adults interact to facilitate or hinder a child's integration into the literate practice of the community. These studies have clearly demonstrated the extent to which family literacy practices can be of fundamental importance when it comes to succeeding at school (e.g., Heath, 1983; R. Scollon & S. B. K. Scollon, 1981). The focus in this chapter, however, has been on the individual, on the child's personal work imposing certain principles on the information provided by the environment. This is an aspect that is sometimes neglected in sociocultural approaches. Maybe an example will help to clarify exactly what is meant by neglecting the child's work on writing. In a very vivid manner, McLane and McNamee (1990) described the writing activities of a 4-year-old at home. In one observation, the boy asked his mother for "the letters that spell 'danger'" because "he wanted to make a danger sign." His mother interpreted the request and suggested he start writing the letters one by one (some were very difficult, according to the mother—the D, N, G, R—while the other two—A and E—were much simpler). From this situation, a rich explanation is obtained about the child's understanding of the function of writing in relation to his fantasy and to the importance of a supportive environment in developing literacy. Unfortunately, no comment is provided by McLane and McNamee about the specific knowledge the child displays by relating a set of letters to a spoken word or by accepting that isolated letters can be written to form a word. Not a single word is dedicated to an analysis of why certain letters are more or less complicated than others.

Another example from the same authors demonstrates very much the same point. A boy is reported to have written with his parents' typewriter "what looked like a random assortment of letters" for a list of titles of stories. Again there is an interesting description of a game of pretense and of a supportive father willing to treat pretend writing as real writing, but there is no attempt to analyze whether the arrangement of letters was indeed random. It is a cute analysis of a cute situation, but alas, it sheds no light on the kind of cognitive work a child is performing when trying to make sense of a notational system.

WRITING AS A SOURCE OF KNOWLEDGE

The path children take to alphabetic writing has been examined through a discussion of several case studies and experimental tasks in which children were asked to write and read in their own way. These have served to identify the different aspects involved in children's construction of knowledge about writing. Obviously, these form just a minute part of the many other situations that could have been used, and the many that have indeed been used, to observe children's path to alphabetic writing. This discussion highlights not just the particular task, but the underlying hypothesis—the hypothesis that there is a construction process to which it is possible to gain access by having children interpret and produce writing. The basic rationale underlying this approach is that writing activities are both the source and the outcome of knowledge about writing.

Human beings have a specific propensity to leave intentional traces and a special sensitivity to features of writing such as linearity and periodicity. Writing appears to be an interesting object to explore even before formal instruction has begun. Therefore, if notational artifacts are part of a child's environment and writing activities form part of constant interactions, children will turn them into a problem space. Consequently, children observe regularities, they map talk onto the observed graphic shapes, and they make inferences about functions and functioning. Children are constantly using socially transmitted knowledge as raw material on which to build their strategies for representational purposes.

This is particularly evident in the emergence of the formal constraints of legibility, and also in children's search for syllabic correspondences and their gradual recognition of the rules of correspondence within the scripts to which they are exposed.

To what extent is this out-of-school knowledge then used and extended once children enter school? The answer to this question is far from being straightforward. A large number of schools in Argentina, Brazil, Spain, Israel, and other countries have already opted for what is sometimes termed the "constructivist" approach to literacy or other approaches to literacy that take children's out-of-school knowledge as the starting point for instructional processes. However, programs in other schools, throughout the world, pay less attention to the quality of preschoolers' ideas concerning writing. They still see reading and writing as two abilities that must be taught letter by letter (or sentence by sentence).

The approach suggested by the psychological research that I have reviewed would be just the reverse. At a very early age, children's knowledge about writing should be taken into account and expanded. As a referential communicative tool, the use of writing should form part of daily school activities, and multiple texts should be integrated into these activities—from writing their own name and the names of the rest of the children, to writing prescriptions when playing at being doctors, letters to the mayor, poetry, songs, or newspaper stories. The list is a very long one, but the principle is a very simple one. Whatever the project to be developed in kindergarten, preschool, or first grade, written representation should be included without any limit concerning the letters or the text to be used. The criterion is the interest of the theme or project and the need to write, not the particular difficulty of a sound combination. Note that this suggestion concerns the functional use of writing, but this is only one of the aspects that should be taken into account and extended. Besides the referential communicative aspect, there is also the need (and the interest) to use and expand a child's concern for writing *as a domain of knowledge.* Dictation, comparison of words, sentences, and texts, and rules of spelling *as such* are meaningful activities that help children to discover regularities and to look for an explanation for these regularities.

Therefore, producing texts in their own way must be accompanied by reading activities and by the specific intervention of many aspects of the writing process. The main conclusion is that the principal source of knowledge for understanding writing is writing itself. It is by being exposed to writing and by using writing that children will learn to master it.

The following are some key points in this chapter:

- Prior to formal instruction, there is a spontaneous development of children's understanding of writing both as a communicative tool and as a domain of knowledge.
- When acquiring knowledge of a conventional kind (e.g., language), children must make that knowledge their own and reconstruct it in their own terms.
- The first stage in the development of writing is called "undifferentiated writing," because children produce similar writing patterns re-

gardless of the word or sentence they were asked to write. At this stage, children's writing displays the general, "superordinate features" of writing (linearity, the presence of distinguishable units, the regularity of blanks, and directionality), and it is distinct from drawing in that it is linear and discrete and is interpreted in a global way.

- At a second stage, children construct the criteria by which to determine whether written strings are readable, and their writing becomes formally constrained in terms of number and variety of letters. Before children map letters onto sounds, they are sensitive to possible and impossible combinations of letters in their language. During this stage, children may introduce some graphic or figurative elements that hint at the meaning of the words they were asked to write. Once writing is formally constrained, it becomes manageable: first, in order to create graphic differences, and then, to work out the value of the elements.

- At a third stage, children work out the links between letters and sounds, and their writing undergoes a process of *phonetization*. Children find a stable frame of reference useful for representing any word. The first unit of letter-sound correspondence is the syllable, and a syllabic stage can be detected at least in certain languages.

- At a fourth stage, children discover the alphabetic principle—the fact that phonemes can be represented by letters such that whenever a particular phoneme occurs in a word, and in whatever position, it can be represented by the same letter.

- The basic rationale underlying the developmental approach reviewed in this chapter is that the principal source of knowledge for understanding writing is writing itself. This approach suggests that from a very early age children's knowledge about writing should be taken into account and expanded on both at home and in school contexts.

In the next chapter we turn to the other main notational system of our culture, the written system of numeration. To discern the various factors involved in children's construction of knowledge about the written numeric system I will discuss numeration in the context of experimental and school situations in which children are asked to identify and use notational artifacts to represent quantities and to compare numerals.

4

What Children Know About Numerals Before Being Formally Taught and Immediately Afterward

Infants are able to match the number of drumbeats to the number of objects in a visual display, rats can learn how many times they need to press a lever in order to receive a reward, and all known human cultures have developed words for counting. Yet, mathematics is generally considered one of the most difficult subjects at school, and mathematical illiteracy is a worldwide phenomenon (Paulos, 1995). What happens to our natural propensity for mathematics? Researchers speak of insufficient mathematical education, psychological blockage, and fallacious, romantic ideas about mathematics. Psychologists and many mathematics teachers believe there is a problem because there is a divorce between the mathematics involved in day-to-day life and the symbolic representations used when teaching at school. Classroom instruction in mathematics is likened

> to learning about an environment by studying guidebooks and maps without ever exploring the actual territory or by studying recipes without ever cooking anything. Although symbolic representations can be helpful—even essential in the activities of learning to inhabit environments and as important resources for use in reasoning and communication—they should not replace experience in conceptual environments as the main learning activity that we provide for students. (Greeno, 1991, p. 177)

According to Greeno, notations are viewed positively as a useful aid in a particular place or in a particular process, as when cooking; they are indeed considered helpful in communicating ideas. But, the advice is not to confound them with the real thing; notations are a tool, but "conceptual environments" are the "actual territory." Apparently, difficulties with mathematics stem from the ill-defined relation between these two entities: the notational and the conceptual. But to solve these difficulties, attention should be dedicated to the conceptual territory; learning stems from experiencing the conceptual territory. The idea is clear, if someone wants to learn about a particular place (i.e., its routes, its rules, and its available resources), then the best thing to do is to get direct experience rather than resorting to a map. This is the particular view about the relation between domains of knowledge and notation that was characterized in the introduction as the "derivative view." According to this view, knowledge of a domain, in this case knowledge of mathematical concepts, paves the way for understanding the notation of that particular domain.

Most developmental research in the domain of numbers has been devoted to children's understanding of the conceptual territory. That is, developmental studies have focused mainly on the development of mathematical concepts. In this chapter, in contrast, I will focus on the notational territory. I will concentrate mainly on the way children take to understanding the written system of numeration. As with alphabetic writing, children's understanding of the written system of numeration is separable, although not separate, from children's notional knowledge. Therefore, knowledge of numbers can be explored as a domain of development and not only as derivative from conceptual knowledge.

Children are exposed to numerals from very early on and they participate in many activities in which numerals are used. Taking elevators, blowing out birthday candles, buying an ice cream, or taking a bus are among the many diverse occasions in which numerals are used, named, and compared. In this chapter, I will try to show that looking at numbers, attending to their names, perceiving the ways in which they are commented are, for the developing child, experiences as real as the sensorimotor experiences with balls, cars, sand, or people. Numbers, as well as writing and other notational artifacts, are territories for exploration as real as conceptual environments. Moreover, the written system of numeration is a source, and not only an outcome, of numerical knowledge. So information that children gather from notations, as well as the information they are able to produce, is not simply a supplement to previously acquired notions that serves to amplify these notions. Instead, it is a permanent ingredient of developmental processes.

NOTIONAL COGNITION
AND NOTATIONAL COGNITION

Piaget was among the first scholars of cognitive development to propose an explanation of how children construct the notion of number. He explained that children understand what numbers are when they succeed in synthesizing in their mind two logical relations: the relation of order (or seriation) and the relation of classification. To establish a relation of order means focusing on the differences between elements, or groups of elements, whereas classification means focusing on their similarities. Consider the following example. If, in front of me, I have a pile of oranges and just a few apples, and I say that I have more oranges than apples, then I am focusing on a difference between the two groups. If, on the other hand, I say that I have two groups of round objects, then I am looking at what the two groups have in common. If I arrange the fruit by size, from the biggest to the smallest, I am focusing on the differences between elements. If, on the other hand, I put the dark oranges and apples in one group and the light oranges and apples in another group, then I am looking for a common feature among different pieces of fruits, regardless of type of fruit.

Note that each case suggested possible differences and similarities between apples and oranges. Indeed, objects of any kind have a variety of features (e.g., size, shape, color, etc.), but similarities and differences are *discovered* or *created* by the observer. The similarity or difference relation is not inherent in the objects themselves, but imposed by the observing subject, the one who creates the relation. Notice the work of the subject in the different criteria that can be taken into account to order or to classify the same group of objects. I have just done it in the example with oranges and apples. First, I used the criterion of quantity to order the two groups (I wrote that there are *more* apples than oranges), then I moved to size as another criterion of order (I wrote that I can arrange the fruit *from biggest to smallest*). Similarly, first I used a criterion of shape for classification (I decided to group them together because they were all round). Then I moved to a criterion of tone and compared dark to light pieces of fruit. There is a diversity of distinctions that can be made between apples and oranges. Each time a criterion is fixed, some features are highlighted and others are neglected. To decide that oranges and apples all belong to a class of round objects is to disregard the differences between them and concentrate solely on their roundness. It means *abstracting* this relation instead of many other possible relations. Similarly, when I decided that the group of oranges was larger than the group of apples, I *abstracted* just one of the possible relations between the two groups.

Imagine that the oranges and apples were arranged in pairs—groups of two. In order to appreciate this, a child would have to abstract this property from the oranges and apples. It does not matter whether there are big or small apples in each group, or whether in one group there is a light apple and a dark orange, or any other possible combination. The child must focus on the particular property that is common to all the groups: their *twoness*. Number is a property of sets (groups), as opposed to tone, color, or size, which are qualities of objects. (Notice that we cannot say *a two apple* but we can say *a red apple*.)

That is why Piaget suggested that children could not abstract the property of number by observing the features of the objects. He believed that only by reflecting on their own actions with the objects (putting them together, separating them, comparing them, etc.), are children able to abstract the relations of order and class inclusion and the numerical property of groups. He called this mechanism of abstracting properties from actions with objects "reflective abstraction." A point of clarification is important here. When Piaget referred to actions he did not mean only manipulation. Sometimes actions are manipulative (e.g., moving blocks, putting something on top of something else), but many other times actions are mental (i.e., they involve working with internal representations). Children, or adults for that matter, can be completely still but very active mentally (comparing, adjusting, or transforming mental objects).

However, and this is perhaps the most difficult part of the construction process, to construct the notion of number, it is not enough to understand the *twoness* of a group or a group of groups. The child must grasp that being two is more than being one and less than being three. Understanding number means understanding that each number represents all the possible groups having as a property that particular number, and *at the same time,* that that particular number is more than the preceding ones and less than the following ones.

Imagine that it is possible to construct all the possible groups of objects, different or similar, that have in common the property of being two—whatever the objects are, whatever their pattern, what they have in common is being two. Each number represents a class of all the possible sets having this number as a property. Yet, at the same time, each number is larger than the preceding one and smaller than the subsequent one in the series. It cannot be said that children have understood what numbers are if they merely understand that (x x) (! #) (Ç •) (+ !), are all "two," but they do not understand that "two" is more than "one" and less than "three." In the notion of number, the two relations of order and class inclusion are synthesized, or as Piaget put it, they are reciprocally assimilated.

The quality and property of being "two" is called the *cardinality* of a set, whereas the property of being "more or less than" is called the *ordinality* of sets. In Piaget's view, the process of understanding cardinality cannot be separated from the process of understanding ordinality. However, this process of constant interaction between cardinality and ordinality proceeds in gradual steps via a slow "arithmetization," starting from an intuitive perception of 1, 2, 3, then from 8 to 14 or 15, then from 15 to 30 or 40 and then above 30 or 40 (Bergeron, Herscovics, & H. Sinclair, 1992).

Piaget viewed the process of understanding number as part of the general development of logical thought. Within this process, activities such as counting or reciting numerals are not considered very important. In general, the information children can obtain from looking at spatial configurations (e.g., those used in domino pieces), from listening to the number series, or from drawing numerals are not seen as essential contributors to the constructing process. Indeed, according to Piaget, children need to construct this understanding by going beyond perceptual cues, by "acting" internally and coordinating actions on objects. That is why educational proposals based on these ideas organize classroom activities around daily living situations and group games in which children need to form groups according to different criteria, look for different orders, find alternative ways to get to a particular point in space, or compare alternatives to reach a solution. The basic idea is to have children "try to think of other possibilities" (Kamii & De Clark, 1985, p. 35) and compare their own point of view with other points of view, rather than working on fixed symbolic representations or verbal explanations. Only in this way will they be able to abstract relations of order and class. Verbal and notational information serve simply to reflect notions acquired by reflecting on actions performed on objects and with other people—they do not in themselves lead to the construction of a notion. It is possible to represent it externally, only after the notion has been acquired, and then it is possible to represent this notion by any means.

Among Piaget's most creative contributions were the tasks that he designed to tap children's notion of number as opposed to counting, spatial, verbal, and notational knowledge. A paradigmatic example is the conservation task commented on in the introduction. In this task, Piaget demonstrated that even children who "know how to count" the number of marbles laid out in each row failed to recognize that the number of marbles remains the same when the marbles in one row are spaced out in such a way that the row becomes longer than the other one. Conservation of numerical equivalence—recognizing that the two rows have the same number of marbles despite perceptual and spatial changes—was considered essential to the notion of number. And, he insisted, "it is no exaggeration to say that the verbal factor does not play any role in the progress of correspondences or equivalence" (Piaget & Szmeniska, 1941/1967, p. 82, my translation).

For Piaget, until children can perform the mental operations necessary to compensate for spatial movement, they cannot have the concept of number. In order to get this knowledge, they must reason as follows. "The longer the array, the lower the density, and because the arrays were the same in number and nothing was added or subtracted, they still be the same." Once they are able to perform these mental actions, then they are able to "quantify" reality. But again, according to Piaget, "spoken numeration does not have any role in transforming the mechanism of thought that constructs the numeration system" (Piaget & Szmeniska, 1941/1967, p. 82, my translation).

Piaget was also very careful to distinguish between recognition of canonical configurations (e.g., arrays on a domino), and building the notion of number. He stated clearly that he was concerned not with "the perception of number" but with the elementary operations that constitute the logic of number. The concept of number cannot be taught by social transmission; rather, it is "an idea in the child's head [that grows] out of the child's natural ability to think" (Kamii & De Clark, 1985, p. 19). This idea is supposed to be universal and independent of the notational system that embodies it. That is, the idea of number belongs to the universal realm of logic and mathematics, which is independent of the verbal names or graphic shapes that numbers may acquire in different cultures or languages. Notational activities, conceived of as the mere exercise of a skill, are considered unnecessary, undesirable, and possibly even harmful to mental action (Kamii & De Clark, 1985, pp. 78–79). If notational activities such as a substitute for direct experience with objects, then children may acquire ritualistic memorized verbal habits that may hinder the growth of logical understanding. The fundamental difference lies in whether children are asked to accept from outside an already organized discipline, which they may or may not understand, or whether they are invited to discover (or to invent, as Piaget would say) relations and ideas by themselves.[20]

After Piaget, many psychologists sought to challenge his idea that the concept of number is independent of counting and of the magnitude of sets, and that it does not rely on the perceptual cues provided by patterns of dots or other shapes arranged in a particular way. Researchers were keen to demonstrate that preschoolers could conserve "small" sets of objects. In their view, children may have the concept of two, then of three, and so on. It is only a matter of additive change to arrive at the conservation of large quantities (Siegler, 1981). Some claimed that the reasons for children's difficulty in conserving the equivalence between sets was due to the experimenter's wording of questions (Markman, Horton, & McLanahan, 1980). Others demonstrated that small changes in the experimental setting or in the layout of the objects led to success in conservation tasks at a younger age. If a careless teddy bear, instead of the experimenter, moved the marbles by accident (McGarrigle & Donaldson, 1975), or if one row was placed in front of the other, instead of side by side, and the child saw when marbles were

---

[20]Nevertheless, one of the leading Piagetian scholars in the domain of number, Pierre Greco (1963), was among the first to recognize the role played by counting in determining equivalence between sets and the use of verbal labeling. Again, he was careful to distinguish between *denombrement*, or counting, and conservation of quantity, and between *quotité*, or saying the numeral of the set, and quantity. But, clearly, he appreciated the function of these two notions in the construction of number.

added or subtracted, then he could conclude whether the total amount had changed or remained the same (Gelman, 1982). Most of these studies sought to demonstrate that it was precisely those linguistic and perceptual factors that Piaget aimed to separate from the logical mathematical understanding of number that were in fact crucial determinants of children's performance.

As it happened, however, these studies proved insufficient to challenge the main thrust of the Piagetian argument. On the contrary, they provided further support to Piaget's central claim: Whereas children's answers on conservation problems clearly depend on linguistic and perceptual factors, the concept of number is just as clearly still in the process of construction. Only when children's judgment becomes independent of such factors, and generalizes to any unspecified quantity, can this concept be considered consolidated. From a Piagetian view, conservation is imposed by logical necessity, and thus should not vary with changes in verbal or perceptual cues.

Nevertheless, if the notion of number is a unique concept in the child's mind, independent of such factors as magnitude, or verbal and notational symbolism, then several questions need to be answered: Why is it that the construction of the notion of number proceeds in gradual steps? Why is it that once children have discovered the logic underlying the conservation of small sets, it takes such a long time for them to generalize to any pair of sets? If the conviction of equivalence is one of logical necessity, independent of magnitude, then why is there an enduring effect of magnitude both in the construction of number and in arithmetical operations? Why is it that many concepts that children seem to have clear for small numbers (1 to 9), need to be reorganized for numbers from 10 to 99, and later for thousands, and so on? Finally, if spoken numeration does not have any role, then why is it that children have less trouble understanding the functioning of the written system in those languages where the names of the numerals provide clues about how they should be written.

Indeed, one of the main contributions of the post-Piagetian studies mentioned earlier was to show the range of details—wording, magnitude, purpose of the task—that influence a child's grasp of numerical situations. Moreover, these studies contributed greatly to highlighting the role that social knowledge in general, and symbolic systems in particular, have on the development of the notion of number. They also identified processes, occurring with small quantities and at young ages, that cannot be explored in the framework of conservation tasks.

NUMERICAL NOTIONS BEFORE NOTATIONS

As mentioned in the introduction, psychologists have revealed newborn babies' ability to distinguish between their mother tongue and other languages, and between faces and other patterns. But this is not the whole story about infants' re-

FIG. 4.1.   Quantitative similarities.

markable 'capabilities'; babies are also sensitive to quantitative or quantifiable features of patterns. What exactly is meant by quantitative or quantifiable differences? Examine the pictures in Fig. 4.1. Despite the fact that the two sets are made up of different objects, and all the objects in one set are different and all the objects in the other are identical, each set comprises the same number of objects. Now, examine the pictures in Fig. 4.2, where the objects are the same in each set, but the number of objects differs. Having the same number and having a different number are quantitative or quantifiable features of the sets.

In a number of highly ingenious experiments, psychologists discovered that infants apparently discriminate between arrays of objects on the basis of the number of items presented. For example, a few weeks after birth children can perceive the difference between an array of three dots and an array of four dots.

FIG. 4.2.   Quantitative differences.

Although it is true that they can make such discriminations only with small sets, they are able to do it with any shape of item (i.e., dots, rectangles, triangle) and even when the items are in motion (Antell & Keating, 1983; Starkey & R. G. Cooper, 1980; Strauss & Curtiss, 1981; van Loosbroek & Smitsman, 1990). More surprisingly, between 6 and 8 months of age, they are able to coordinate information presented visually with auditory information. In one study, 7-month-old infants were shown photographs of two and three dots and simultaneously heard either two or three drumbeats. It turns out that they looked longer at the photograph that matched the number of drumbeats (Starkey, Spelke, & Gelman, 1983, although Moore, Benenson, Reznick, Peterson, & Kagan, 1987, failed to replicate this finding).

Not only that, another study showed that infants as young as age 5 months appear to add and subtract small quantities (Wynn, 1992a). The infants were shown one Mickey Mouse doll in a display area. A screen was then raised to block the infant's view of the doll. The infant then saw the experimenter place a second Mickey Mouse doll behind the screen. The screen was then lowered to reveal either one or two dolls. Infants looked longer at the one-doll display, presumably because they expected to see a two-doll display.

In contrast to these demonstrations of early competence, however, recognizing that an array of three dots has fewer dots than an array of four appears to develop only after 15 months of life (R. G. Cooper, 1984). Strauss and Curtiss (1984) managed to teach infants to touch the side of a panel that contained an array with the smaller (or larger) number of dots. When the researchers wanted to see if the infant was able to recognize the smaller array, they put three dots in the smaller array and four in the larger, but when they wanted to test for recognition of the larger array, they used two dots in the smaller condition and three in the larger. In this way, the researchers were sure that infants were not reacting to absolute numerosity but to the order relation between arrays (larger or smaller). Only 16-month-old infants demonstrated sensitivity to the ordinal relation. (And this is considered a late development!)

Certainly everything infants appear to do with number—differentiate numerosities, match across modalities (sound and vision), add and subtract, and later on, appreciate order—is restricted to sets with *less* than four items. Looking at this capability from the point of view of the Piagetian notion of number, it cannot be said that it is a manifestation of the concept of number. Nevertheless, should this capability to recognize and operate with numerosities below four be dismissed as peripheral to the number concept (von Glaserfeld, 1982)? And, if it is peripheral to the number concept, then what is the nature of this capability and its role in further development? Psychologists do not agree on the nature of this capability, but at least they have a name for it (Dehaene, 1997):

They call it *subitizing* or *subitization*. Remember that *subitizing* was discussed in chapter 2 in relation to the historical development of notations. That discussion suggested that the evolution of numerical notation owes very much to the limits of *subitization*. Indeed, most written systems, in different times and places, developed some special sign or some way of grouping marks beyond four because the human eye found it difficult to deal simultaneously with more than three or four items.

Moreover, *subitization* is also used to characterize nonhuman numerical capabilities—that is, the ability that pigeons, rats, dolphins, and nonhuman primates have demonstrated to recognize and operate on small sets of items. Indeed, one main question concerns which nonhuman species, if any, are capable of perceiving number beyond *subitizing;* but there is no doubt that they are able to subitize (Gallistel & Gelman, 1991). In other words, this is an ability that seems fairly universal. It has appeared in every time and place, and it is shared with numerous nonhuman species. So, what is the nature of this ability? There are two contrasting opinions, one advanced by Randy Gallistel and Rochel Gelman, two American psychologists, and the other offered by the French cognitive psychologist Stanislas Dehaene.

Gallistel and Gelman (1992) claimed that when we subitize, we always count all the objects one by one, but very quickly and without words. For babies this would be a preverbal counting procedure and for adults it would be a nonverbal counting procedure. We attend to each object in turn, and then we know how many there are. This would explain why it takes about half of a second to identify a set of three dots. *Subitizing* is very rapid but not instantaneous. And, more important for Gallistel and Gelman's claim, this duration is not constant; it slowly increases from sets with one to sets with three dots. Thus, the more there is to count, the longer it takes. Perhaps something else that supports their claim is that there is one situation in which *subitization* fails. When the objects are superimposed so that we cannot see them occupying distinct locations, then we have to count to determine how many there are, even if we perceive them simultaneously (Trick & Pylyshyn, 1993). It is precisely on this point that the two theories on *subitization* diverge. Dehaene (1997) posited that there is no fast serial counting of objects (one by one, in turn), but that "all the objects in the visual field are processed simultaneously and without requiring attention" (p. 69). Dehaene, together with Jean-Pierre Changeux, a leading French neurobiologist at the Pasteur Institute in Paris, developed a computer simulation to show how this computation is implemented by simple cerebral circuits. The simulation shows that the "number detectors" start to respond at about the same time whether one, two, or three objects are present and they do not require each object to be singled out in turn; rather, all were taken in at once in parallel.

Dehaene supported his view on subitization with neuropsychological evidence. For example, he told us about a woman referred to as Mrs. I, who suffered from a cerebral lesion due to high blood pressure during her pregnancy and consequently lost the ability to count numbers greater than three. When four, five, or six dots were flashed for her on a computer screen, she consistently failed to count some of them. But, Mrs. I had no difficulty in enumerating sets of one, two, or three dots.

Whether by a fast serial preverbal procedure or by a parallel simultaneous processing, healthy infants—like healthy adults and nonhuman animals—find their way quickly and easily in numerical worlds comprising up to three items. After many years of research on infancy, researchers are starting to take these abilities as natural facts, but it was a revolutionary finding in developmental psychology to discover not just *what* infants are able to do with numerical displays, but the fact that they see them as being quantifiable. How is it that they react at all in numerically relevant ways to sets of objects? Both Gallistell and Gelman, and Dehaene are correct that it is due to our genetic endowment. We are apparently provided with a "number sense" (Dehaene, 1997) just as we are provided with a "language instinct" (Pinker, 1995). These channel attention to what counts as relevant input in either domain.

Moreover, and this may be the most delicate point, according to these researchers, human beings are not endowed just with a sort of number-detecting mechanism that demarcates number-relevant territory; they also have an internal accumulator that provides a quantitative interpretation for this information. This internal accumulator is very precise for small quantities, up to three, and only approximate for larger ones. This accumulator turns discrete elements (elements that are countable, such as dots or bricks) into magnitudes (which are continuous, like current or temperature). Gallistel and Gelman (1992) suggested that the numerical preverbal processes in both infants and nonhuman animals are similar to "histogramic arithmetic." An examination of the process of building a histogram will explain how the purported accumulator functions.

When building a histogram, each time there is an increment in a certain variable it is shown in the height of the column. For example, if a histogram is built for the distribution of pupils according to the scores they get on a math exam whose possible scores range from 0 to 60 (see Fig. 4.3), the pupils cannot be counted directly in the histogram columns because they are continuous. However, it is clear that as there is an increase in the number of pupils who get a certain score, the column gets higher, and each time the number of pupils decreases, the column gets lower.

The number of pupils is not explicitly displayed in each column, but the differences in number have a direct effect on the height of the columns: Increments

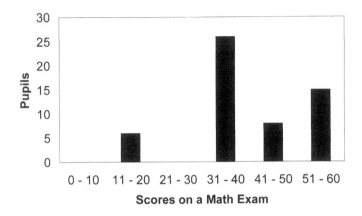

FIG. 4.3.   Example of a histogram.

and decrements are *analogically* represented. Because no pupil got a score lower that 10 or between 21 and 30, there are no columns for these scores. Representing the absence of something by nothing, as many children do when asked to represent zero, is an analogical representation. Except for no element, through analogical representation it is hard to know *exactly* how many elements are being represented, but it is possible to approximate and to evaluate differences.

If we count with an internal accumulator, then this means that after the precise perception of number provided by *subitization* we enter a numerical world of approximation. Were we to count only with our accumulator, this would have been the style and the limit of our numerical knowledge. The cultural artifacts that we have created—spoken and written numeration systems—are to provide a more precise representation for these approximations. In the same way that our number sense channels attention to number relevant input, the numeration systems guide children's attention to adult talk about amount, size, or quantity. From very early on, infants recognize what aspects of the world to which this talk applies. This sensitivity helps to single out spoken and written numerical messages from the mass of other verbal and visual input, and to relate these messages to quantifiable aspects of the world very precociously.

According to Dehaene (1997), however, "the availability of precise number notation does not obliterate the continuous and approximate representation of quantities with which we are endowed. Much to the contrary, experiments show that the adult brain, whenever it is presented with a numeral, rushes to convert it into an internal analogical magnitude that preserves the proximity relations between quantities" (p. 86). There is a simple but very ingenious study by Robert Moyer and Thomas Landauer (1967) that measured the precise time it takes for an adult to decide which of two numbers is larger. They flashed pairs of digits such as 5 and 7 and asked participants to indicate which was larger by pressing one of two response keys. Surprisingly, it sometimes took half a second to respond to such an apparently simple task, and people made mistakes. Even more important, the time people took to decide was directly related to the distance between the two digits; they were quicker to decide which was larger for a pair like 4 and 8 than for a pair like 5 and 6. But, when the distance between the two digits was the same for different pairs, the response time slowed down as a function of the quantity the numerals stood for; they were quicker to decide between 2 and 3 than between 8 and 9. The experiment has been replicated with many variations, for digits and multidigits, but the results remain similar. It is even possible to calculate in very precise terms the time it will take to decide among pairs as a function of distance between the numerals in the pair and the quantity they represent. How should these results be interpreted? It is clear that adults do not store an automatic set of responses to such comparisons, even though they look very common and easily automatizable. Apparently, what happens is that adults do not approach the numerical meaning of numerals directly. When they are required to compare, they translate the numerals into an analogical representation (like the columns in a histogram) and therefore, if the distance between numerals is a big one, no problem, but if the distance is very small, then it takes more time to decide.

The claim is that not even adults can understand the numerical meaning of numerals without translating it into an analogical representation that provides the "feeling" of quantity. This argument helps explain why different forms of analogical representation will reappear all along the path children take toward an understanding of the written numeration system. Despite the fact that they know the numerals, children will not use them directly for representing quantities; instead they look for alternative representational strategies. These strategies all have in common the fact that they show the quantitative meaning of numerals by more direct analogical means. Apparently, children need to see multiplicity and iteration before accepting that they are embodied in a numeral. Moreover, even though children recognize forms and functions of numerical symbols very early on, there is a long way to go until they use these forms communicatively.

Cognition of Environmental Notations

Children's environment is filled with artifacts displaying numerals—clocks, watches, calendars, telephones, scales, counters, elevator buttons, and so on; children are also immersed in adult talk about these artifacts. How do they interpret the different environmental uses of numerals? Numerals fulfill different functions; they are used for noting cardinality, order, and arithmetical opera-tions. But they also serve nonquantitative purposes. Phone numbers do not rep-resent quantities and Bus 39 is neither smaller nor bigger than Bus 43. In nonquantitative domains, the use of numerals would represent real social knowledge in the sense used by Kamii and De Clark (1985). The sources of so-cial knowledge are conventions worked out by people. There is no logical rea-son why Bus 39 is called Bus 39, and phone numbers are decided for geographic not mathematical reasons. Social knowledge is embodied in the many cultural artifacts used in daily life and transmitted through social uses. Are children able to make sense of these different uses?

When children between ages 3 and 6 were shown numerals on birthday cakes, bus stops, buses, lifts, speed limit signs, car license plates, and price tags, they were not only able to recognize them but also to interpret many of their regularities (A. Sinclair & H. Sinclair, 1984). As in the writing domain, when asked about numer-als, 3- and 4-year-olds were mainly concerned with the variety of shapes, but they also attributed to them a global function linked to the context (e.g., numbers on buses are "for the driver to look at"). At a later age, they said numerals provided information of a specific nature related mainly to quantity (tickets indicate "the price of the bus"), but also to labeling ("to tell which one it is").

According to Anne Sinclair's (1997) observations of her own child, children make sense of the different functions of numerals very early. At the age of 2 years, 8 months, her child turned to the telephone and said the names of the graphic shapes deployed on it; as Sinclair noted, "The number words zero-nine were in this context labels for certain printed shapes" (p. 2). However, they were also used in other contexts besides that of the phone, as when the child said he would be back "in three minutes." The same child could also write the numerals 1 and 0 as well as a few letters. At age 3, the child was using the number words one, two, and three correctly to describe quantities, saying for example "I want three cookies." As expressed by Sinclair, "the match between subitizing and the first three number words occurred invisibly as part of vocabulary acquisition, during the second year" (p. 1).

Children are certainly more familiar with some functions than they are with others (Ewers-Rogers & Cowan, 1996), but these observations show that there is no developmental progression from a period in which children are engaged merely in physical actions but remain indifferent to notations. On the contrary, at ages 2 and 3, number-words and number-shapes are objects as interesting to act on as any other kind of object. There is no notional construction to be ap-plied to a system of notation but rather different sources of information that must be coordinated. This process of coordination becomes evident when tod-dlers and preschoolers produce notations.

To discover more about children's use of numerals for different purposes, children from ages 4 to 5 from a low-income district in the outskirts of Barcelona were asked to complete a blank card with their name, their date of birth, age, address, phone number, number of brothers and sisters, and their ages, eye color, and hair color. This "identity card" task was originally designed by Eva Teubal and Julie Dockrell (1997) in order to explore how children used numerals in quantitative (age, number of brothers and sisters, and date of birth[21]), and nonquantitative domains (addresses and phone number), and whether they would use numerals to represent verbal messages (names and colors).

In Spain, talk about children's age, number of brothers and sisters, and their ages is part of regular talk at school. Every day the teacher writes the date on the board, and play phones displaying numerals are used in play activities. Besides, teaching numerals is part of nursery school and preschool curricula, and children learn to draw and identify the name of numerals very quickly. In general, children find it easy to learn the conventional shapes and names of digits: They have less graphic variation than letters, and their names coincide with their numerical meaning. Also, their numerical meaning is preserved in normal talk about prices, measurements, ages, locations, phone numbers, bus numbers, time, weight, and speed (see chap. 5 for a more detailed discussion). Moreover, in Spanish a very explicit verbal formula is used to ask one's age: ¿Cuántos años tienes?, literally, 'How many years do you have?' This request in Spanish clearly points at quantity, unlike in English where the request to state age, 'How old are you?', is relatively obscure concerning quantity. This means that the toddlers and preschoolers who participated in the study were familiar with the domain of reference and the graphic shapes, although for most of them it might have been the first time they had been asked to write the information down. The results were clear-cut. No child used numerals for representing verbal messages, but they did for quantitative (e.g., age) and nonquantitative (e.g., addresses) domains. However, numerals were not used with similar frequency for the different functions. Table 4.1 shows the distribution of children according to the forms used in quantitative and nonquantitative domains.

For representing their age, half of the children at age 4 years used numerals, whereas the rest used either letters or icons. At age 5, the vast majority used numerals and only a few used letters. No child mixed letters and numerals in the

---

[21]Date is a domain of measurement and quantification. Calendars are notational objects in which different systems of measurement are involved. In the experiment, children were not supposed to know the day and year of their birthday. They were told this and merely asked to write it down. Despite the fact that every morning the teacher wrote the date on the board, the request sounded very strange to the children.

TABLE 4.1

Distribution of Children According to the Forms Used in
Quantitative and Nonquantitative Domains (in Absolute Numbers)

			Graphic Elements				
Domain	Age	n	Numerals	Letters	Mixed	Icons	No Answer
Own Age	4	15	8	4	0	3	0
	5	16	14	2	0	0	0
Number of siblings	4	15	7	4	4	0	0
	5	16	6	6	4	0	0
Siblings' age	4	15	6	4	4	0	0
	5	16	10	3	3	0	0
Address	4	15	0	9	6	0	0
	5	16	3	9	4	0	0
Phone number	4	15	2	10	0	1	2
	5	16	7	4	0	0	5

same string. As for representing the number of brothers and sisters, half of the children at age 4 used numerals but the other half was equally distributed between those using letters and those using mixed notation. Unlike the representations for age, the number of children using numerals did not increase from age 4 to 5. More than half the children were equally distributed between those using letters and those using mixed notation. Thus, it seems that using numerals for representing number of siblings is more difficult than, or at least different from, using numerals to represent one's age.

To represent their brothers' and sisters' ages, there was a slightly different distribution. Almost half the 4-year-olds and more than half of the 5-year-olds used numerals, and the rest of the children at both ages were equally distributed between children who used letters or mixed notation. No child used icons for representing the siblings' age. Why should the use of numerals to represent one's own age differ from the use of numerals to represent number and of siblings and siblings' ages? Why do children resort to mixed notations for representing number of siblings and siblings' age(s) but not for their own age? Before attempting to answer these questions, consider what happened with the use of numerals in nonquantitative domains.

A different picture emerged for nonquantitative domains. When writing their addresses, no 4-year-olds used numerals. They clearly preferred letters or a mixture of numerals and letters. A similar pattern was found at age 5. For phone numbers, only 13% of the children at age 4 used numerals, whereas more than half used letters and the rest either did not answer or produced icons. At age 5, almost half the children used numerals but the other half was almost equally divided between those who used letters and those who did not answer. There are two main differences here compared with quantitative domains: First, fewer children used letters for phone numbers, and second, more children did not answer. Thus, taking together the results of quantitative and nonquantitative domains, despite knowing numerals, they do not use them equally for every purpose.

Why is it that children who are familiar with numerals do not use them across the board for every function? One possible explanation is sociocultural. Children might have more experience with numerals in one particular function than in another. It is difficult to believe, however, that children in an urban environment, albeit from a low-income environment, are not exposed to telephones and addresses. Another possible explanation is that differential use reflects a need to map different functions of numerals onto different forms. Thus, in domains where numerals fulfill a labeling function, children prefer to use letters to numerals. But still, why should 5-year-olds use a numeral for representing their age but not always for representing the number of siblings (or even more striking their siblings' ages)? I think that although children process numbers as a particular category of objects, different from pictures, letters, and icons, and despite the fact that they are familiar with the shape and the names of numerals, numerals have not yet been detached from what they represent. Despite children's sensitivity to and familiarity with numerals, there are certain cognitive obstacles they must overcome to treat them as notational elements fulfilling different functions. To use numerals as a notational system whose forms can convey different messages requires something more. It requires the child to overcome two related ideas. First, there is the idea that representation of quantity is *motivated* versus arbitrary (see chap. 1); that is, the idea that the formal features of the notational elements used for representing quantity reflect the content or the features of the quantified objects. And, second, there is the idea that multiplicity must be explicitly displayed. Any quantity beyond the unit is multiple; if multiplicity were to be explicitly represented, then people would be unable to use one single sign for representing quantities beyond one.

To overcome these ideas means to grasp two basic features of numerical notations: their arbitrary nature and the *compiled* way in which numerals represent quantity. As discussed at length in chapter 1, the shapes of notational elements have nothing to do with the content they represent; they are arbitrary. Thus, the same form can be used to represent a diversity of contents and to fulfil different functions. As seen in chapter 2, sets of multiple elements (e.g., # # # #) can be "compiled," and represented by only one sign (4), in contrast to token-iterative systems in which there is one mark for each element.

An example will help to illustrate how children's representations disregard these two features of numerical notations. After writing his name, Ruben, a

4-year-old boy, was asked to jot down how old he was. He then asked, *¿con la mano?* 'with the hand'?, and immediately proceeded to draw the outline of his hand. The physical gesture he usually used to show his age is now brought, directly, into the graphic space. This gesture is, for him, the one that best shows the meaning of his age. Ruben is producing a motivated representation instead of resorting to the arbitrary way in which a numeral represents age. He knows the form and the name of the numeral but he is not taking advantage of its representational capacity. (See Fig. 4.4.)

Next, the interviewer asked Ruben to write down how many brothers and/or sisters he had. Without hesitation he wrote two letters and the numeral 1. While writing, he said *tengo uno y se llama Raul* 'I have one and his name is Raul.' For Ruben, quantity of brothers could not be represented separately from his name, and so he wrote both. To be meaningful, the numeral 1 had to be attached to the brother's name. Ruben was not alone in this approach. Many other children represented the number of brothers and sisters in similar ways, accompanied by similar explanations.

In the next task, the interviewer asked Ruben to write down his brother's age. Very carefully, Ruben wrote six letters and exclaimed: *cierto que es muy grande, tiene seis* 'He is indeed very big, he has six.' Ruben seemed unable to rely on a single numeral to show how big his brother was, and thus he resorted to six letters. He was using writing with a different representational pur-

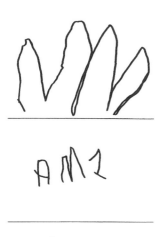

FIG. 4.4.   Representation of age, number of siblings, and siblings' age.

pose—not for representing a verbal utterance, but for conveying quantitative meaning.

The example illustrates the extent to which the representation is attached to the content of what is being represented. To preserve this attachment, children are reluctant to use the same numerals for different content (e.g., their own age and the age of a sibling).

If we examine in detail the process of production and an analysis of the notational strategies of children who did not use the same numerals for different functions, we see that children are attached to the specificity of the situation and they attempt to show as directly as possible the quantitative meanings they are representing. No matter what elements they use (i.e., numeral, icons, or letters), they use them iteratively and look for one-to-one correspondence with age or any amount they are attempting to represent. Eighty-five percent of the children who, at age 4, used letters or icons to represent age produced an explicit one-to-one correspondence, and 55% did so when representing their brothers' and sisters' ages. They are certainly resorting to means of representation specific to quantitative domains (iteration and one-to-one correspondence) but, in so doing, they demonstrate that they are not satisfied with the compiled form in which numerals represent multiplicity. Or, to put it another way, before accepting the compiled way in which numerals represent quantity, they need to go through a stage of explicit analogical representation in which quantity is shown figuratively. As is discussed later, the use of multiple and repeated shapes that explicitly display amount reappears in other notational situations and plays a crucial role in understanding the meaning of numerals.

Interpreting and Relating Digital and Analogical Representations

When young children are asked to represent quantitative information such as age, some use conventional numerals and others use letters or icons but in an iterative and one-to-one correspondence pattern. These are two different formats for representing quantitative information: a *digital format*, where only conventional numerals (digits) are used; and an *analogical format*, where elements (dots, letters, or even numerals) are used in an iterative, and one-to-one correspondence pattern. Earlier in the chapter, reference was made to another kind of analogical representation in which a continuum (e.g., a column of a histogram) is used to represent discrete elements (number of items in a collection). Now consider another variety of analogical representation: Discrete elements (dots) are used to represent other discrete elements. In *analogical* formats, the quantity is more explicitly displayed, whereas in *digital* formats, it is hidden behind a single digit. This compiled way of representation is not very well accepted by young subjects; they look for more explicit ways of representing quantity. In many cases, the same child may use both digital and analogical formats but for different functions. It was important to find out how children see the links between these two formats. Do they see them as interchangeable? Do they stick to the same format when asked to record the same content?

Teubal and Dockrell, who designed the "identity card" referred to in the previous section, were also responsible for designing a very clever way to check how children see the links between analogical and digital formats. They invited children between ages 4 and 5 to participate in a dice game. There were two kinds of dice: spot dice, where one face was unmarked and the others were marked with from one to five spots, and numeral dice, where the faces were marked with numerals (0–5) instead of spots.

Each child was given three throws with two spot dice and three throws with two numeral dice and they had to write down six notations. The interviewer tried to ensure that the child threw a certain variety of digits smaller and larger than 5, and that they got a zero. Each time the dice were thrown, the children were asked to look at the result, to read it, and to jot it down. The ostensible purpose for recording was to remember, providing a context in which recording made sense. Once they had finished writing down the results, the children were asked to read what they had written.

In contrast with tasks in which children generate a notation without any model, the dice game requires the production of one notation but the use of another notation as a source. The task, therefore, enables exploration of whether numerals are recognized, reproduced, or translated into another notational format. Teubal and Dockrell (1997) found that the number of times in which the notation corresponded to the display correlated with age, and that developmental progression was independent of the quantity displayed and the nature of the display. That is, young children were more likely to stick to one way of representation, regardless of whether they were playing with the spot dice or with the numeral dice, whereas older children tended to use spots when playing with the spot dice and numerals when playing with the numeral dice, regardless of the quantity they had to represent. An analysis of the types of notation produced by the children showed that the majority of responses were attempts to mark quantity in some way. Overall, iterative responses declined with age and there was a corresponding increase in digit notation, but young children provided as many iterative responses for spots as they did for digits. Teubal and Dockrell (1997) interpreted this to indicate that children are able to extract information from the two formats and they are governed by a "representational system" rather than by motor skills or direct mapping of the display.

I replicated "the dice game" with Spanish children of the same age range and found that, with the exception of two 4-year-olds, the children interpreted both the conventional numerals and the spot patterns without hesitation. The two 4-year-olds counted the spots before saying the corresponding number-word. As to whether toddlers and preschoolers consider analogical spot patterns and conventional numerals to be alternative formats, the results showed that more than half of the 4-year-olds and most of the 5-year-olds decided to write numerals independently of the nature of the dice they were playing with (see Table 4.2).

In other words, the children considered the two formats as two versions of the same content, but they preferred conventional numerals. This happened because the spot dice already displayed analogically the quantity that children were attempting to represent. Therefore, they could rely on the digital information. Otherwise, if there was no analogical representation to provide an explicit visualization of quantity, then they would create it in order to convey analogically the specific quantity they were attempting to represent. The following section indicates that this interpretation regarding the need "to see" the quantity on paper (i.e., explicitly) is supported by the developmental path observed in young children's representation of small numerosities.

Creating Graphic Representations of Quantity

Many studies have explored toddlers' and preschoolers' recognition, interpretation, and creation of graphic representation of small numerosities (Allardice, 1977; Hughes, 1986; Merlo de Rivas, Scheuer, & Criados, 1993; Scheuer, 1996; A. Sinclair, Melló, & Siegrist, 1988; A. Sinclair, Siegrist, & H. Sinclair, 1983; Terrigi, 1991). Few developmental processes are so revealing of children as active,

TABLE 4.2

Distribution of Children According to Notational Behavior for Digital and Analogical Patterns (in Percentages)

Age (years)	n	Use of Same Format		Translate Numerals to Dots	Translate Dots to Numerals	Other Group
				Notational Behavior		
4	15	digital	31	6	56	16
		analogical	25	25	25	25
5	16	digital	5	5	70	15
		analogical	88	88	58	64

constructive learners using their own previously acquired knowledge in constant interaction with the information provided by the environment. In few other cases is it so clearly shown that social knowledge is not directly absorbed but rather transformed through the children's own ideas and representational needs.

In most studies on the development of the representation of quantity, children between ages 3 and 6 are shown either cards depicting collections of objects, usually the same type of object one, or groups of real concrete objects—for example, toy bricks—and they are asked to represent how many objects there are. The situation is very simple, and it might be expected that the children's solutions will depend mainly on whether they know the digit corresponding to the quantity to be represented. That is, if a boy, for example, knows the digit 3, and there are three toy bricks depicted on the card, then he will use the numeral; but, if there are eight toy bricks, then he will probably resort to other means. As reasonable as this expectation may sound, it contradicts the diverse uses of numerals discussed in the "identity card" situation (earlier in this chapter). As pointed out earlier, children may know the shape and name of the numeral that would be appropriate for representing a certain collection but will not necessarily use it. There is a *décalage*, or dissociation, between children's knowledge of culturally transmitted shapes and the use they make of these shapes in conveying the numerosity of a collection. This delay in using the numerals they know has to do with the two obstacles concerning arbitrary and hermetic representation that children must overcome. Here, too, they must realize that notations function detached from the content they convey, in this case the enumerated objects, and multiplicity is embedded in the conventional digits.

The general developmental path observed in children's representation of small numerosities (Cowan, Rogers-Ewers, & Chiu, 1997; Pontecorvo, 1985; A. Sinclair, Melló, & Siegrist, 1988) proceeds in four steps, in which five notational strategies are deployed.

The earliest notational attempts by 3- to 4-year-olds, many of whom know the numerals, are in the form of a kind of *letterlike pattern* accompanied frequently by a drawinglike pattern. The quantity of the objects is not reflected at all in the *letterlike pattern*, although the kind of objects (whether they be bricks, or toy cars, or whatever) can sometimes be guessed from the drawing. If asked by the interviewer, they point at the pattern and say that it states 'the name.' This does not mean these children are confounding names with quantities; rather, children use the term 'names' as the most generic term for writing. They are saying that what they have done is something that is written (as distinct from something depicted or drawn).

The next step in this developmental process occurs when quantifiable features of the situation are reflected on paper in the form of iterative marks. Initially, children produce what is described as a "global notation of quantity;" they produce lines or dots, the number of which diminishes or increases with the reduction or increment of the objects in the collections the children are seeking to represent.

At a later age, children manage to deploy a one-to-one correspondence with the objects in the collection. However, this correspondence may be obtained by icons, tallies, dots, crosses, letters, or even numerals. The point is to obtain a controlled variation of graphic marks that covaries with the quantity of objects in the collection. So, if children are required to represent four toy bricks they use four tallies, and likewise if they need to represent six toy bricks they have to increase the tallies to six. Sometimes they might succeed in a perfect one-to-one correspondence and sometimes they might not, but the intention to covary is clear. This is by far the most popular means of notation, in which a mark is repeated for each object.

A notational strategy some children produce at this level of development is particularly illustrative of children's constructive assimilation of the conventional forms. This refers to those cases in which children attempt to obtain a one-to-one correspondence to represent quantity but using numerals. For example, when representing a collection of four buttons, a child might produce 1 2 3 4, whereas another child will repeat the same numeral as many times as the number of objects that have to be represented: 4 4 4 4. Children use conventional shapes, but they do so according to their own representational concern at that moment, which is to produce a visible term-to-term correspondence to represent quantity.

It is important to note the progress implied in this notational solution as compared with the previous one at this same level of development. Although children still need to produce explicit term-to-term correspondences, the same numerals are now used to represent different objects. In the notational strategies already described, when children produced iconic iterative marks, they needed to make explicit both the *quantity* of objects and the *quality* of objects: They had to show what objects were included in the collection and to individualize them as being distinct from one collection to another. In contrast, this new notational strategy focuses on making explicit only the quantity of objects included in the collection.

The fourth step in development corresponds to the production of unitary notations. Although the cardinality of the collection is sometimes conveyed by an incorrect numeral, the important point is that it is conveyed by a single numeral. Children no longer need to show explicitly either the numerosity or the quality of the objects included in the collection.

The previous description of the different steps taken by children in tasks in which they were asked to represent collections of objects shows that they begin with a conception that in representing quantity they are doing something different from drawing (the writing pattern at the very beginning), even though the meaning of what they are representing is conveyed by a drawing. They then move to an explicit representation of both the quality and the quantity of objects included in the collection through iterative, one-to-one correspondence, followed by a representation of just the quantity of objects. Finally, they progress to a conventional compiled representation of quantity. Although children learn the conventional shapes and names of numerals very early on, they do not apply them directly to convey numerosity. So when the purpose of the notation is to communicate a certain content, children between ages 4 and 5 prefer to reflect in a more direct and explicit way the quantity of elements included in a collection. This seems to be a necessary step before single digits—in which multiplicity and iteration are compiled—become useful for external representation of cardinality.

Numerals are part of children's repertoire of forms from a very early age, but the construction of the representational links between numerals and numbers advances through the explicit rendering on paper of the objects (through drawing) and the quantity (through direct graphic mark-to-object correspondence). Only after this explicit rendering has been performed are children able to rely on the use of single numerals to denote multiplicity. This use of single numerals is a fundamental step along the path toward understanding the meaning of the elements in our numeration system. Children come to realize that single forms represent sets of elements having this number as a property. Chapter 2 discussed how important it was for the historical development of notation systems that notational elements *for a group of marks* be created. By so doing, notations became much more economical and efficient; with fewer elements, larger quantities could be marked without the burden of mapping once and again. However, one drawback of this approach is that notation became more obscure and more ambiguous. The one-to-one correspondence that was explicit in ungrouped notations became embedded, and therefore implicit, in this new kind of notational element. It is interesting to see how, in the developmental path followed by children, as they appropriate the conventional system, they *undo* the historical development in order to clarify the meaning of notational elements and make explicit what is embedded in them. Only after taking this step can children start working on the relation between elements.

So far we have attempted to infer the nature of children's understanding of written numbers by looking at the way they represent quantities. Their notational productions have been used to catch their understanding of the notational elements. I will soon use the same approach to tap children's understanding of the principles that regulate the relation between elements in our written system of numeration. But first look at children's understanding of this written system through a different window: the invention of notations.

Inventing Numerical Notations

In general, psychologists qualify notations as "invented" whenever they ask children to make something that exceeds their supposed level of expertise. Thus, if they ask a toddler to jot down how many toy bricks there are in a tin and the child produces an iterative multiple pattern, they might call this "an invented notation." From the child's point of view, however, they are not inventing, they are simply trying to solve a task. The situation, however, is very different when children are asked directly to invent a notation.

Xesca Grau i Franch (1988) asked first graders to invent "a new way for doing numbers," that is, to create their own "numerical code" (p. 190). She conducted her study in the context of class activities with the purpose of improving children's understanding of written numeration. Many doubts have been raised, however, concerning whether invention tasks help children to discover the principles of the system. Educators who have used this type of task for teaching the *grouping principle*, for example (see chap. 2), found almost no transfer of the acquired skills to situations where children were required to use the conventional system. For example, Bednarz and Janvier (1988) asked children to create alternative groupings of a collection of objects to express how many objects there were in the collection. Take the case of a collection of 22 toy bricks. It is possible to group them in *two groups of tens* and *two units* following the grouping criterion of our system. In this case, using our written system we would write 22. The two on the left represents the two groups of tens, and the two on the right represents two units. The purpose of this task is precisely to teach children about the difference between face value (two) and positional value (tens and units) of the same numeral. Now, the authors thought that a good idea for helping children understand these notions might be to ask them to invent a notation for *two groups of tens* and for *two units*, instead of using conventional numerals. This was supposed to help them to generalize the idea of face value and positional value, independent of any particular numerical representation. However, what these authors found was that, despite the fact that the children could invent special signs for groups of units and for units, their understanding did not generalize to conventional numerals. They continued to produce all kinds of mistakes in relation to the positional meaning of numerals or in relation to the amount bi-digits represented.

In my opinion, an examination of what children invent is of greater use in discovering what they already know than what they still have to learn. Invention tasks are also particularly useful for gaining access to knowledge that people cannot express verbally, but that is somewhere in their mind. There are many levels at which people can say they know something. Thus, some knowledge is implicit—people are not aware that they know—and yet from the way they do things an external observer can deduce that they do indeed know. This is the case with many rules of grammar. People are seldom able to explain them but they certainly know them, judging from the way people talk. At another level of knowledge, individuals know of something in a very clear and explicit way; they are able to explain the main point and many details about this something without difficulty. When they write about a particular topic, they usually state verbally their explicit knowledge about the topic. There are, however, many levels of intermediate knowledge, which is a kind of knowledge that only emerges in certain circumstances. For example, as we shall see in chapter 6, children can be perfectly able to analyze a word into individual sounds for writing it, but may be completely unable to do so when asked to say that word "bit by bit." The different levels at which knowledge is represented in the mind is discussed in chapter 5. But, for the present purpose, it is sufficient to say that a certain level of knowledge about the written system will emerge when inventing a notation and it is worthwhile to tap this knowledge. To be clear, this is not recommending the task as a didactic strategy, but rather as a window on children's understanding of the written system.

Note that when Xesca requested children to create their "own code for numerals," she was asking them to engage in a notational activity for its own sake. They were not asked to represent content or to perform numerical operations, just to produce an alternative version of numerals. Once the children had invented their own codes, the teacher asked them to write the following six numerals, 68 - 39 - 17 - 52 - 88 - 40, using their own code. These examples illustrate what can be learned about a child's understanding of the principles underlying the written system from looking at their invented notations.

I must confess that I was shocked by the code invented by Joan, a Catalan 7-year-old in Xesca's class. It seemed he had read Gallistel and Gelman's article on "histogramic arithmetic" discussed at the beginning of the chapter! Joan created an analogical code in which the length of the invented sign generally increases with the size of the represented numeral (see Fig. 4.5). He knew that each successive numeral in the series was "bigger" than the preceding one, but he did not show any explicit understanding of the internal structure of numerals. For Joan, each numeral had a magnitude that increased with the numerals in a rather systematic way for the digits and in a much less systematic way for *larger* numerals. He performed an analogical representation of different magnitudes. This was indeed a very different way of representing quantitative infor-

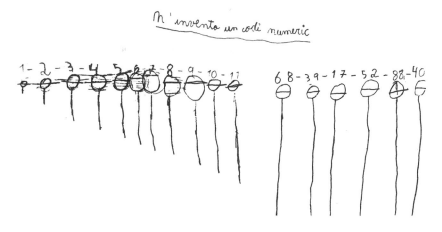

FIG. 4.5.   An analogic histogramic code.

mation, in a continuous approximate way without the precision of discrete or digital representations.

The code invented by Susana resorted to a different variety of analogical representations. It comprised just one notational primitive (a dot). For each digit, she created a multiple iterative analogical representation of its cardinality (see Fig. 4.6). The same principle was also applied when writing the numerals proposed by the teacher. Susana's system, therefore, was a purely token-iterative device. It consisted of the same marks with no differentiation being made for the objects to be counted, even when they were put into one-to-one correspon-

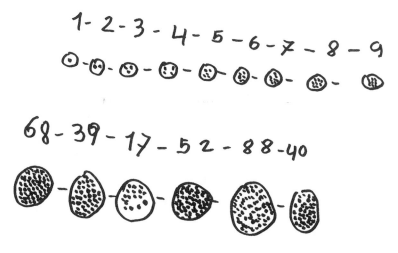

FIG. 4.6.   A multiple iterative analogical representation of digits.

dence with the enumerated set. In many senses, Susana's notational strategy resembles the earliest historical notation (chap. 2), based on term-to-term correspondence. There was no possible way to get at the cardinality of the set without counting all the items.

The children who based their codes on iteration or analogical representation managed to write the six numerals suggested by the teacher without any problem. Token-iterative devices are very easy to generalize for any quantity; their limitation lies in the burden they create for coding and decoding. With no elements that represent groups of marks, users must count each item anew every time they use their marks. However, these children did not seem bothered by the burden their system might create for decoding.

Another group of children demonstrated a different conception of the system by producing a limited set of notational primitives, that is, by inventing a range of graphic shapes. The shapes produced for the digits were then used in combination for multidigits. (See Fig. 4.7.) There was neither an indefinite iteration of a unit nor an indefinite creation of new shapes—the children were applying a recursivity principle. For example, they used the same shape they had invented for 1 and for 7 to write 17. Their systems, however, displayed neither a base 10 grouping principle nor a zero. The items invented ranged from 1 to 10, where 10 was presented as just another primitive not as a composite. Consequently, the children could not write 40, because they did not have a symbol for zero. When the invented primitives were applied to multidigits, this was achieved by juxtaposition of two notational primitives.

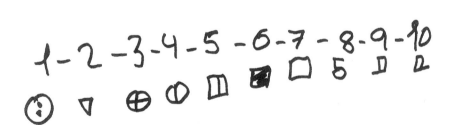

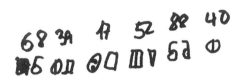

FIG. 4.7.   Use of invented notational primitives.

Two main conceptualizations of the written system emerge from these invented notations. According to the first, numerals are a sort of labeling of magnitudes (Joan's code) or sets of iterated objects (Susana's code). The children are focusing on the magnitudinal meaning of numerals. In this conceptualization, neither carving principles nor recursivity are considered. The second conceptualization is closer to the underlying principles of written numeration. There are primitives, each representing a set of elements, and the system is recursive; the same shapes are used to create composites, but combinations are created by juxtaposition of primitives. This system has neither a grouping principle on base 10 nor a "zero element." Clearly, understanding the written system requires the identification of the values of the elements, but also the relation between them, the meaning of position, and the usefulness of a zero element. Apparently, the defining features of our written system are not part of children's internal representation of the written system, at least judging from their invented notations.

Understanding Combinations of Numerals

Indeed, one of the defining features of our written numeration system is that it is positional. Children need to understand that the meaning of each digit depends not only on its face value, but also on the position it occupies in the string. Many researchers (Brun, Giossi, & Henriques, 1984; Kamii, 1986; Richards & Carter, 1982; A. Sinclair & Scheuer, 1993) have explored the development of first and second graders' understanding of place value. They usually confront the child with a particular numeral, say 18, and have him respond to questions such as: "How many does this number represent?" (pointing at the 8) and "How many does that number represent?" (pointing at the 1).

Children between ages 4 and 6 did not typically attribute to the whole numeral its conventional numerical meaning, and when they did, they did not attribute any meaning to the individual digits. Slightly older children (5-, 6-, and 7-year-olds) interpreted meaning conventionally and attributed meaning to individual digits, but the sum of the digits did not account for the whole. Thus, each digit was read as standing for its face value and the whole may have been read correctly but the two readings were juxtaposed. The children did not seem to be bothered by the "contradiction." For example, when confronted with 27, they read *twenty seven*, but when asked to read each digit separately they may say that the first means *two*, the second *seven* and all together *it makes nine*, without being bothered by the fact that they had just read *twenty seven*.

It is only after the ages of 6, 7, and 8 that children begin to understand the relation between the parts and the whole. But, as A. Sinclair, Tieche Christinat, and Garin (1992, p. 205) wrote, "The idea that the whole must equal to the sum of the parts is constructed quite early, … well before children have any intuition at all concerning groups of tens." In fact, some children managed to partition the collection and account for the whole in a nondecimal way. Different partitions were proposed, such as attributing face value to one digit and the remainder to the other. Finally, the precise meaning of tens and units are interpreted. It is important to note that here again there is a magnitude effect. Children's realization of the meaning of tens and units is only very slowly generalized to hundreds and thousands.

Another way of testing children's understanding of place value, which was discussed in relation to the invention task, is to ask them to construct an alternative representation of a given numeral using building blocks or pen and paper. Usually children are placed in situations in which different groupings are created for collections of objects (recall the previous example of toy bricks). Once children have experimented with different possible groupings, they are supposed to realize that it is not the same to talk about 'one' when referring to a single toy brick as when referring to one package of 10 grouped toy bricks. Children are encouraged to represent each level of grouping by using a different block; for example, they may be encouraged to use cubes to represent groups of tens and strips for units. After they have decided on a particular symbol for each level of grouping, children are asked to represent multidigit numbers using the symbols they have chosen. For example, if they are asked to represent 77, they are expected to use 7 cubes and 7 strips, which is a partition on base 10. They could also produce other partitions like 6 cubes and 17 strips or any other combination in order to represent the multidigit number. As a rule, this is a very difficult task until the age of 8; only then are children able to represent partitions on base 10 (7 cubes and 7 strips). They find it even more difficult to represent other partitions, such as understanding that 77 stands for 6 cubes and 17 strips (Bednarz & Janvier, 1984a, 1984b, 1988; Resnick, 1983; Ross, 1986).

Until almost age 9, children have difficulty understanding positional value. Karen Fuson (1990, p. 273) described the representation underlying children's responses very clearly—the same underlying conception identified from observing their invented notations: "Initially children's conceptual structures for number words are unitary conceptual structures in which the meaning or the referents are single objects (as in counting objects) or a collection of single objects (as in the cardinal reference to a collection of objects)." Nevertheless, to understand multidigits and, in particular, to operate with numbers greater than 20, "children need to construct multi-unit conceptual structures" (Fuson, 1990, p. 273). This is an essential condition for understanding the meaning of multidigits and for performing basic arithmetical operations. It is extremely difficult to understand what we are doing when we "carry one" when adding, for example, 38 + 3, if the additive composition of the system is not understood.

Why does it take such a long time to build up this multi-unit structure? According to some, the difficulty lies in the need to deal with numerals whose value changes with their placement in a string (8, 80, 8000), which requires an operational understanding of part–whole relations. It is also claimed that at school, instead of developing the logical operation underlying the system, the focus is placed mainly on cardinal values. Arguably, explicit teaching of positional value should be postponed and more time should be dedicated to comprehending grouping and seriation (Kamii & De Clark, 1985; Kamii, 1986). Others have suggested that the comprehension of positional value is an outcome of a child's understanding of addition. Thus, neither counting nor learning the written system will help; only a change in children's addition procedures will act as the spur for understanding the base 10 system (Nunes & Bryant, 1996).[22] Finally, there are those who claim that mathematics curricula actually prevent children from understanding the positional nature of the written system by overlooking children's ideas and ignoring the sources of their mistakes (Bednarz & Janvier, 1986). According to these authors, different activities should be designed to make the hierarchical grouping of our system more ex-

---

[22]Nunes, Schlieman, and Carraher (1983) carried out a number of studies in Brazil to test the relation between the understanding of additive composition and success in writing multidigit numerals. Children were asked to participate in a shopping game (i.e., "the shop task") using coins and bills of different values. The currency system consisted of units of different orders (100 cents was equivalent to $1, a $5 bill was equivalent to five $1 bills, etc.). Let's say that a child has one $10 bill, two $5 bills, and four $1 bills, and he must pay $7 in the shop task. If he chooses to pay with one $5 bill and two $1 bills, or he asks for change from his $10 bill, he displays an understanding of this feature (additive composition). If, on the other hand, he counts out seven bills without paying attention to their different values, he displays no such understanding. Nunes and Schlieman found that children who solved the shop task had no problem with a "compact" representation of place value. Nunes replicated the findings of this study by asking children between ages 5 and 6 to write single digits (8), two-digit numbers (14, 25, 47), three-digit numbers (108, 129), one four-digit number, and "round numbers" (10, 60, 100, 200). They were also asked to read numbers. Almost all the children were able to write single-digit numbers and the round number, 10. The four-digit number was the one most children failed to write, followed by 129. (The children were not always successful with the rest, but they were easier to write.) Some children (4%) appeared to use a type of one-to-one correspondence between a number word and a digit (25 was written with two digits, 60 with one digit, and both 100 and 1,000 with two digits). Many children wrote the two-digit numbers (e.g., 25, 47) and the round numbers correctly, but when writing the three-digit numbers they made mistakes of concatenation—they changed the order of numbers or added zeros where they were not needed. A relatively small percentage of the productions (21%) presented either wrong digits or an inversion of digits (e.g., writing 74 for 47). Nunes included inversion of digits with lexical mistakes. The number of syntactic mistakes was consistent with those reported by Power and Del Martello´s study (1990) with French and Italian children. Here, children were placed in two groups: those who had been successful in the shop task and those who had not. The percentage of correct productions for the critical number differed greatly. The authors concluded that learning to write the conventional numeration system does not lead to an understanding of additive composition but rather the process operates the other way round: Understanding the additive composition of the system facilitates learning the conventional system of numeration.

plicit, as well as to challenge children to invent nonconventional notations for different groupings.

These suggestions seek to circumvent the written system, with the reasoning being that if the difficulty lies in the written system of numeration, then alternative, more accessible routes should be sought that will eventually enable children to understand the written system.

There are others, however, who believe that what is happening in schools is that children are prevented from interacting fully with the whole system (Fuson, 1990). Instead of allowing the child to explore the way in which the written system functions, school curricula progress in a piecemeal fashion. Thus, children are first introduced to small numbers, following the notion of increasing arithmetization of number and neglecting the role that children's experience in the notational environment may have on their understanding of place value (Lerner & Sadovsky, 1994). This way of approaching the teaching of the numeration system fails to recognize that place value, as an underlying principle, is not something that needs to be explained or precisely formulated by a competent user of our numeration system, "it is inherent to the system itself and in some sense implicit" (Scheuer, 1996, pp. 193–194). The discovery of this implicit principle can be facilitated simply by allowing the child to experiment with the system. The following section tackles how much children can learn about the written system simply by using it in meaningful situations.

CHILDREN'S PATH TO THE WRITTEN SYSTEM OF NUMERATION

Many suggestions that have been made to help children with their difficulties in understanding positional value take into account what toddlers and preschoolers know about the written system of numeration but fail to acknowledge how much children can gain from their interaction with this notational system. In contrast, a number of psychologists and teachers of mathematics (Gil & Tolchinsky, 1997; Lerner & Sadovsky, 1994, Scheuer, 1996; Tolchinsky, 1995) have promoted a different approach. They assumed that children might learn to understand the system only by using it. Thus, rather than bypassing the use of written numeration, they suggested exploiting its use in the context of meaningful tasks so that children will come to understand its intrinsic features. The basic idea underlying this approach is that only by looking at the criteria children use to guide themselves in the written environment is it possible to design situations in the classroom that will help them understand it better. Some studies have examined these criteria in the context of regular classroom activities in preschool (5-year-olds) and first grade (6-year-olds), whereas others have operated in the context of controlled or clinical interviews. For example, children were asked to play card games in which the winner was the one who obtained the highest number. They had to decide which card had won and justify their decision; they were asked, for example, to justify why they thought 28 beat 19. This task requires interpretation of notations and reveals the criteria children use in determining the winner. Similarly, in more controlled situations and using a full range of comparison strategies (Scheuer, 1996; A. Sinclair & Scheuer, 1993), children had to choose between pairs of numbers that varied in magnitude, number of digits, the repetition of digits, the position of the same digit, and the presence or absence of zeros. In other tasks, children were required to produce a "big number." Working in pairs, the children had to compare the notation they had each produced and decide which numeral was "bigger" and why. This task also requires the production of notations, revealing the criteria that children use when writing a big numeral and explaining their decision.

A close observation of the verbal explanations given by the children, the questions they formulated, their reactions, and their notational behavior in the contexts of these tasks, led Lerner and Sadovsky (1994) to conclude that, initially, three criteria guide children in deciding which numerals are bigger and why: (a) the number of numerals included in a string, (b) the position of numerals in a string, and (c) the early recognition of the "round" numbers (e.g., 1,000). These three criteria coexist rather peacefully between age 5 and 6 until children start grappling with certain cases of conflict between magnitude and number of numerals. Solving this conflict brings about a qualitative change in children's understanding of written numeration.

Criterion 1: The Number of Numerals Is a Good Indicator of Magnitude

In deciding which of two cards displays the higher numeral, one criterion was particularly apparent before age 6: The greater the number of numerals, the higher the number. This criterion was, in most cases, strictly based on the features of the notation, given that children were unable to say the numerals. However, when they also knew the spoken version they were able to complete the explanation—"this one is bigger because it comes after this one." As a rule, choices were correct in cards containing pairs of numerals smaller than 10. Five-year-olds usually had no problem in distinguishing bigger numerals from smaller ones in the domain of single digits. When it came to a comparison of numerals with a different number of digits, the number of numerals was the feature they used in determining the highest numeral. For example, if asked to decide between 34 and 254, they would point to 254 as the biggest one.

The criterion that the number of numerals makes one numeral larger than another was not immediately generalized to each pair of numerals or to multidigits in general. The children remained doubtful when asked to compare pairs of numerals in which there was an extreme difference in the absolute value of the individual components of the multidigit numerals, for example, when they had to decide between 112 and 89. Because 1 and 2 are so much smaller than 8 and 9, they doubted despite their conviction that what counted was number of numerals. The children were attempting to coordinate two kinds of information: one provided by the absolute value of the numerals, which they already knew, and the other provided by the number of numerals in the string.

There might have been, however, another source of conflicting semantic and syntactic information. The children may have been of two minds as to the purported value of the numeral as a whole and the number of numerals in the string. As one of the children clarified, "Two numbers form one number" (Lerner et al., 1994, p. 16). They were aware that the string had a value as a whole, yet they did not have a clear idea about how the whole value was obtained. Some children tried to add the values of the numerals and decided that 112 must be less than 89, "because the first is just four and the second is seventeen" (Lerner et al., 1994, p. 116).

The number of numerals was a very useful criterion to apply when the number of numerals differed. However, when the children had to choose between pairs of numerals containing the same number of numerals, it was apparent that this was not the only criterion they used in reaching a decision.

Criterion 2: The Position of Numerals Is Also Important: The One Coming First Wins

This criterion appeared, in particular, when the number of numerals in each pair was the same. The children explained that "the first number—starting from the left—wins." Their explanation reflected that, in the context of this task, they had discovered the role of position in determining the value of a numeral. They were aware that the value of a numeral is determined by its position with respect to other numerals in the string. Therefore, if two numerals have the same number of digits, the face value of the digit furthest to the left will determine which is the highest. Thus, for 35 versus 43, 43 was considered higher. Children would even go a step further and argue that when the first digit is the same in both numerals, they need to look at the following digit. So, presented with 73 and 79, they considered 79 to be higher.

In general, independent of the magnitude of the numerals, pairs of numerals that contained the highest digit in the position furthest to the right caused greater problems than numerals in which it was only necessary to look at the face value of the digit furthest to the left. Thus, for example, the children found it more difficult to compare 19 and 21 or 88 and 79 than 50 and 40 or 301 and 501. In the case of 19 and 21, the difference between 9 and 1 is so great that it gave rise to doubts, despite the fact that the digits furthest to the left differed. In the second case, 88 and 79, the conception of 9 as "a big number" was so strong that it also sowed the seeds of doubt. Once again, this shows the major effect of the absolute value of digits and is a further example of the kind of conflicting information children have to coordinate in determining order relations between numerals.

Clearly, children between ages 5 and 6 are not aware of the reasons underlying the criterion: "The one coming first wins." They are unaware that because the system is positional and ruled by recursive grouping in base 10, in bi-digits, the digit furthest to the left represents groups of 10; whereas the digit furthest to the right represents an amount smaller than 10. However, children do elaborate on the notational consequences of positionality and recursivity in base 10. This is a case of practical knowledge without awareness of the underlying principles. Why is 19 smaller than 21? Because the first digit represents one ten in 19, and two tens in 21.

Their interaction with numerals in different situations enables children to perceive the regularities. Indeed, they may begin to wonder about the meaning of the number of numerals when they become aware that numerals sometimes appear in isolation, whereas on other occasions they appear in long strings. If only single digits appear in a child's environment, they will never realize that this is a relevant criterion for differentiation. Thus, they set out on their search to justify the observed regularities, a search that seems to be enhanced by the need to explain verbally the reasons why one number wins and the other loses.

But if this is the case, does a clear understanding of positional value and the additive composition of the system help children understand the functioning of written numbers or is it rather the use of numerical writing that facilitates their understanding of positional value? Or, to put it in more general terms, is an understanding of the underlying principles of the system a condition for understanding how to use numerical writing or does the use of written numeration lead to an understanding of its underlying principles and, via a bootstrapping process, to improvement in its use? We should consider another characteristic of children's path to written numeration before turning back to this question.

Criterion 3: Round Numbers Receive a Privileged Treatment

In the Lerner et al. (1995) study, children between ages 5 and 6 were asked to write "big numerals." If the belief is that notational knowledge derives from conceptual knowledge, then this request does not make much sense. This may be one of the reasons why so little developmental research has been conducted into this issue.[23] If the numerical series is acquired little by little, starting from small numbers and proceeding sequentially, it does not make much sense to ask children questions that extend beyond their sequential understanding. However, in those circumstances in which the sequential constraint was overcome (by the researcher or by the teacher), it was clear that the children's construction of conventional numerical notations does not follow the sequential order of the numerical series. Numerals such as 100 or 1,000,000 are learned, for example, before 16. This was also found to be the case among the participants in the Lerner et al. study.

Most 5-year-olds' attempts to write "big numbers" start with round numbers comprising tens or hundreds, for example 10, 100, 500, or 1,000,000, which seem to function as prototypes of "big numbers." Exact units of tens, hundreds, or thousands have a clear notational pattern: a numeral and a set of zeros; they have an exact correspondence with spoken words (in Spanish as well as in English). They are used in currency, and in daily talk we tend to use "round numbers" rather than exact numerals. We are much more likely to say, for example, 'he earns more than a hundred dollars' than 'he earns more than one hundred and thirty two dollars.' All these are perhaps factors in explaining the ease with which they are learned.

When children are requested to write big numerals, the round numbers are always first to emerge. Regardless of their magnitude, they identify these before the numbers that lie between them in the number series. In their attempt to produce big numbers, they juxtapose two round numbers that sound to them like big numbers for getting an even bigger number. For example, children write 60020 for six hundred twenty—they know that six hundred is written 600 and that twenty has to be written 20, so they copy the verbal utterance and place one after the other. These kind of notations have become known as "oral-based notations" because they are based on children's knowledge of round numbers and the idea that the order of written numerals follows that of utterances. When children are producing oral-based notations they are putting into operation linguistic and functional knowledge, what they know about number words and their use in different contexts. But, are children aware that 100209 represents a much bigger magnitude than 129? Is there a semantic interpretation or just a mapping of a linguistic expression to graphic shapes? When children between ages 5 and 6 are explicitly asked to compare numerals, they usually comment on how long they look instead

---

[23]Bergeron et al. (1987a, 1987b, 1990, 1992), however, carried out a series of studies aimed at discovering the roots of multidigit notations—in particular, children's understanding of positional notations. They asked preschoolers "to write down all the numbers they knew." They stopped, however, at 30, and they only considered the sequence of numerals up to the point at which the sequence was complete. So if the child wrote 1 2 3 4 5 6 8 9, then the child was considered to know 6 numerals.

of how much they amount to (the quantity to be represented). Moreover, certain round numbers are always considered "bigger." A thousand is always considered bigger than transparent notations comprising five or six digits (e.g., 200304). What seems to happen is that, at age 5, children "dissociate the transcoding activity—the translation from spoken expressions to written notations—from their knowledge about the numerical magnitude represented by the spoken numeral" (Power & Del Martello, 1990, p. 100). However, in these two kinds of knowledge, the quantitative (i.e., evaluation of magnitude) and the notational (i.e., the information provided by the number of numerals), lies the source of the conflict that will eventually ensure that the written notation is grasped. The process of understanding numerical writing undergoes a qualitative change when these two kinds of knowledge, quantitative and notational, which initially are in juxtaposition, first come into conflict and later become successfully coordinated.

Criterion 4: Conflict Between Magnitude and Number of Numerals

In the development of numerical notation, different notational strategies coexist. Five-year-olds may use conventional numbers for bi-digits, but a strictly oral-based notation for multidigits. Initially children are untroubled by these inconsistencies within their own knowledge. They are convinced that a *thousand* is bigger than *three hundred twenty nine* and that if a numeral contains more digits it is larger. But, when they write 1000 for a *thousand* and 300209 for *three hundred twenty nine,* they do not seem to realize the contradiction between these two pieces of knowledge. As interaction with written notation is promoted, children's sense of a conflict begins to emerge. Some Spanish-speaking children when producing an oral-based notation for *ciento cuarenta,* 10040, will comment that it has too many zeros. This may be the first indicator that children are aware of a conflicting situation, when they express a certain uneasiness concerning their own production. Other children will start to compare their own oral-based notations and the notations they produce for round numbers. Below is a short extract from an interview with a 6-year-old child during her first months of her first year in elementary school. The investigator is slowly dictating numbers to her, but giving her time to look at her production.

Investigator dictates:	Child writes:
five hundred	500
four hundred fifty three	400503
	Says: *five hundred is more, but this one has more*
	(and starts erasing digits)

SPOKEN AND WRITTEN NUMERATION

Spoken language is an important source of information for writing numerals. However, reliance on the spoken names of numerals (at least in some languages, e.g., English) may lead children to produce unconventional notations, because the two systems differ in a number of fundamental ways that derive from the fact that spoken numeration is not positional (Hass, 1990).

If spoken numeration were positional, then the numeral 732 would be uttered as seven-three-two and the temporal order of pronunciation would indicate the different values of each numeral. But speech is ephemeral and maybe for that reason the system of spoken numerals marks the value of the different levels of the units (tens, hundreds, thousands) not by temporal order of utterance, but by certain marks internal to the word (morphemes) or by special words. In spoken numeration, units of different sizes are given a different expression, not only a different location. In *twenty,* the morpheme "ty" indicates tens; in *three hundred and two* it is the word "hundred" that indicates the different level of the unit. Moreover, in spoken numeration, the juxtaposition of words always implies an arithmetic operation—this might be addition, as in *a hundred and two;* or multiplication, as in *three hundred;* or sometimes both, as in *three hundred and two.* Any change in the order of words implies a change in the operation: compare *two hundred* and *a hundred and two*—there is multiplication in the first case and addition in the second.

Written numeration is more regular: Numerals are always multiplied by the power of the corresponding base and then the results are added. For example, $(4 \times 10^2) + (5 \times 10^{1)} + (3 \times 10^0)$. However, written numeration is more hermetic (less explicit) because the only graphic cue for the different value of each numeral is the position it occupies in the string, and not any particular marking in the numerals, as in spoken numeration. Another major difference is that in speech the zero is not pronounced, whereas it is always present in writing. If the explicit pronunciation of zero were required, then the numeral 7032 would have to be uttered seven-zero-three-two. The following table summarizes the differences between written and spoken systems of numeration.

(continued)

Differences Between Spoken and Written Numeration

Spoken	Written
The value of the unit at each level is expressed by internal marking of words or by special words.	The value of the unit at each level is expressed by position in the string of numerals.
examples: Twenty Two hundred	examples: In 20, the 2 means two In 200, the 2 means two hundreds In 932, the 2 means two units
Production is open to different arrangements.	Writing is not open to different arrangements; each has a different meaning.
example: 1920 may be spoken as: *one, nine, two, zero* *nineteen, twenty* *nineteen, two, zero*	
Zeros are not always pronounced Juxtaposition of number words implies an arithmetic operation.	Zeros are always written down Numerals are always multiplied by the power of the corresponding base and the results are added.
examples: Addition: *a hundred and two* Multiplication: *three hundred.* Addition/Multiplication: *three hundred and two.*	example: $453 = (4 \times 10^2) + (5 \times 10^1) + (3 \times 10^0)$

The extent to which written and spoken numeration reflect each other is known as *transparency*. In Asian languages (e.g., Chinese, Japanese, and Korean), by listening to the number words individuals know exactly how to write them. Children speaking these languages have to learn the word names from 1 to 10, but then numbers between 11 and 20 are formed by compounding the decade with the unit. So, for example, *eleven*, *twelve*, and *thirteen* are spoken as *ten-one*, *ten-two* and *ten-three*; *twenty* is spoken as *two-ten(s)*, and so on. Thus, the spoken numerals in these Asian languages correspond exactly to their written form. So in more transparent languages, children find it easier to write numerals.

Transparency also helps to understand the additional structure of the system. In languages where there are more spoken cues about the additive structure, children understand place value at an earlier age and more efficiently (Miller & Stigler, 1987; Miura, Okamoto, Kim, Steere, & Fayol,

(continued)

1994). When Chinese, Japanese, or Korean children were asked to represent a multidigit number using building blocks, some of which represented tens and others represented units (as in the tasks used to test children's conception of positional value discussed earlier in this chapter), they were able to combine them to build the required number better than their English-speaking counterparts. For example, for the number 43, they used four blocks representing tens and three representing units. The English-speaking children, in contrast, tended to build the number using the blocks that represented the units, that is, they used forty-three blocks. Here again, as indicated earlier, English-speaking children see numbers as the grouping of counted objects. Transparent counting systems facilitate learning in a more global fashion, enabling children to understand the additive structure of the system.

English-, Spanish-, and French-speaking children would probably love to have a transparent language. This is clear in the oral-based notations they produce. Indeed, when they write, for example, 800308 for 838, they are writing as the number is said, as though the language were transparent. During a period of time in children's development toward conventional written numeration, notation based on spoken numeration may coexist with notation based on written numeration. Thus, children may write 29 conventionally, but then write 100209 when they attempt to write *one hundred twenty nine*.

When children realize the conflict between what they know about magnitude and what they know about the role of number of digits in determining magnitude, they try different solutions. They may either change their interpretation or, as in the excerpts, their written production. When they decide to change their written production, they start to delete numerals in a clear attempt to be consistent with the number of digits that best fits their idea of magnitude and approaches conventional writing.

Coming back to the question formulated earlier: Is an understanding of the underlying principles of the system a condition for understanding how to use numerical writing, or does the use of written numeration lead to an understanding of its underlying principles and, via a bootstrapping process, to improvement in its use? The previous description clearly illustrates how children find their way in the system by using written numeration in different situations. They do not construct notions about its underlying function from outside the system and only then apply them; rather, they discover the underlying functioning of the system by interacting with the system itself. A similar process is to be found with regard to another principle of our numeration system, the zero element.

The Representation of Absence and the Use of Zero

Various sources suggest that children have difficulty with zeros. Errors involving zeros are the most common in the four operations (addition, multiplication, subtraction, and division) and in writing numerals. Perhaps this is not unrelated to some of its properties. Zero is neither positive nor negative. The use of zero in arithmetic gives rise to many contradictions (how much is zero divided by zero?) and mathematicians have long argued about the characteristics of zero as a number. There is no doubt, however, that historically the zero emerged to solve a computation problem in writing. The representation of no quantity (absence of quantity) in accounting, for example, was never a difficult problem; even the most primitive systems were capable of solving it leaving empty spaces. But it took thousands of years to invent a specific symbol for zero and to use it for computation.

For young children today, however, zero has a strong environmental presence, similar to that of any other numeral. It appears in many notational artifacts—phones, calendars, clock faces, temperature scales—and, at least in Spain, it appears in almost every list of prices. Ewers-Rogers and Cowan (1996) compared the way in which 3- and 4-year-olds represented small numbers with their representation of zero using the tin game (Hughes, 1986). The purpose of the game is to identify the number of toy bricks in each of several tins. Children are invited to produce labels to indicate which tin contains which quantity. In this task children are required to use notations as a communicative-referential tool.

Here, once again, is a very familiar situation: "While most children managed the task, few used numerals to represent quantity and even fewer used the numeral zero to represent no bricks" (Cowan et al., 1997, p. 3). Most of the notations the children used were of a written form; others chose an analogical solution: They simply did not write anything at all. I have made similar findings when using the dice game previously discussed.

Recall that there were two kinds of die, a spot die, one face of which was unmarked and the others of which were marked with from one to five spots, and another a numeral die, the faces of which were marked with numerals (0–5) instead of spots. In the dice game study, 4- and 5-year-olds had to note down the blank side of the die when they were playing with the spot, or the zero when they were playing with the numeral. When comparing the kind of graphic shapes children used for zero with those used for any other number, numerals were used much less frequently to represent both no spots and zero than for any other quantity of spots or any numeral. Table 4.3 displays the distribution of children according to

TABLE 4.3

Distribution of Children According to the Forms Used for Notation of Zero
(in Absolute Numbers)

| Age | n | Spot-dice | | | | Numbers-dice | | | |
| | | 1–6 | | 0 | | 1–6 | | 0 | |
(years)		Numeral	Other	Numeral	Other	Numeral	Other	Numeral	Other
4	16	9	7	2	14	13	3	2	14
5	17	15	2	15	2	15	2	14	3

whether they used numerals, another form of notation such as letters, or if they left a blank space (note that some children used more than one form).

Some children did use zero, others resorted to analogical representation by leaving an empty space, but for no other number was the use of a writing pattern so frequent. They interpreted this pattern as saying *nothing*. They stated something like *it says that there is nothing*. In other words, they preferred to note absence through a written description of the situation. This means there was no problem with the referential use of zero—if all these different ways of notation are accepted; from age 4, children clearly understand that zero means *nothing* and *nothing* can be represented by zero, but they prefer to write about it rather than produce an analogical representation.

The problem lies with the syntactic function of zero in the written system of numeration. Besides its referential function, zero performs a syntactic function in the written system and is used as a placeholder in multidigit numbers. Zeros are used in writing multidigit numerals to indicate the lack of units of a certain order. So if the numeral is written 203, then it means there are no units of ten, whereas the '2' clearly refers to hundreds. The use of zero is one of the main points of mismatch between spoken and written systems (see Aside: Spoken and Written Numeration), especially in European languages. The intermediate zero is not always pronounced in the spoken version. It is in this sense that placeholders are said to be "silent," and it is this aspect of spoken numeration that likely gives rise to so much trouble when young children are asked to write down dictated multidigit numbers.

Research involving the reading and writing of multidigits by British and Taiwanese children suggest a substantial effect of language. In one study by Cowan et al. (1997), Taiwanese children typically said the zero when reading multidigits that contained them, and they were more successful in reading three- and four-digit numbers than British children. In general, they also made fewer mistakes when writing. However, the extent to which *transparency* helps beyond correct translation from speech to writing is still a matter of controversy. The children who succeeded in writing the number were unable to say what the digits stood for. In contrast, no child understood place value but failed to write numbers correctly.

To conclude, at age 4, children seem to have a clear idea of the referential meaning of zero—it means "nothing." However, they are reluctant to use the numeral zero for notation of absence, preferring to write (or attempting to write) that *there is nothing*. The psychological basis of this notational strategy is likely similar to the one involved in analogical strategies used for representing other numerosities. In the case of other numerosities, children must show (and see) the cardinal composition. Therefore, for a long time they use iterative marks or even conventional numerals iteratively. Similarly, in the case of zero, children need to make *emptiness* explicit or to express it in writing. The graphic shape zero is not explicit enough; they need to show it analogically. At this age, the syntactic use of zero is not yet understood, although some 4-year-olds may already recognize that zero is used in making big numbers.

Finally, at age 5, zero is more systematically used as a distinctive feature for big numbers (adding zeros makes a number bigger) and to form oral-based notation (e.g., when *three hundred twenty nine* is written 300209 and the zeros serve to match the *hundred* and the *tee* morpheme). At the same time, children use it more readily for the notation of null sets. That is, they abandon analogical representations and use zero to represent no element. But, it will still take a long time for children to generalize the use of zero for representing lack of units at any level.

NUMERALS AS A SOURCE OF KNOWLEDGE

The child's path to written numeration was tapped in the context of different experimental and school situations: identification of the different functions of numerals in "cultural artifacts" such as buses, birthday cakes, or identification cards; recognition, interpretation, and production of graphic representation of small numerosities; number comparison and production of *big numerals*. These contexts served to detect the various aspects of child's construction of knowledge about the written system. Obviously, these contexts constitute just a small selection of the many other situations that could have been used and that have been used to observe a child's path to written numeration. What needs to be highlighted here is not just the particular task, but the underlying hypothesis that there is a construction process to which it is possible to gain access by having children interpret notational artifacts, compare numerals, produce notations, and use notations as representational communicative tools. The rationale underlying this approach is that written numerals are both a source and an outcome of knowledge and not just a means for representing knowledge acquired independent of written numerals.

Human beings appear numerically inclined from birth, with the potential to discriminate numerically relevant input from other graphic and spoken environmental features, with a specific sensitivity to those features that are numerically relevant such as iteration, multiplicity, and discretionality (presence of disunited elements as opposed to a continuum). As development proceeds, numerals appear to be interesting objects to explore even prior to, or in the absence of, formal instruction about their shape and function. If notational artifacts are part of a child's environment and written numerals form part of their constant interactions, then children turn them into a problem space. Consequently, they observe regularities, they map talk onto the observed graphic shapes, and they make inferences about functions and functioning.

This was particularly evident in the ideas children displayed when asked to compare multidigits and to note *big numerals*. When asked to note bi-digits, many used conventional numerals in the conventional order and used zeros as distinctive marks. Spoken sequences and the names of numerals were used as a guide to constructing multidigit notations, whereas rules of generation of numerals were used for comparison and for generation of novel numerals. In general, conventional, socially transmitted knowledge was used as raw material on which children built their representations.

Representation of content posited different constraints on children's use of notations. When children were placed in a situation in which they had to represent the meaning of a numerical message, when they wanted to convey a certain content, they tended to reflect in a more direct and explicit way on the quantity of elements they wished to convey. But, they always resorted to representational strategies using features that are relevant in the domain of number, mostly iteration and multiplicity but sometimes size.

All the studies show, however, that children go through a period of time in their notational development in which they need to represent these features (iteration and multiplicity) explicitly before accepting that they are embedded in conventional notation. This is why it takes time for children to resort to compact notations for every numeral. This is also why the process proceeds by increasing arithmetization, each step embracing larger parts of the number series, but also by an increasing "place-valuation" of the system. When issues of place value appeared to be solved for the tens, they reappeared for the hundreds and then for the thousands. The reasons for this might be the difficulty of grasping increasing magnitudes and the difficulty of grasping a recurrent system of counting. However, other reasons, more related to symbolization processes of the kind discussed here (e.g., the need for explicitness in the notation of multiplicity and grouping, and the influence of spoken language) may also be adduced to explain these difficulties.

To what extent is this out-of-school knowledge used and extended once children enter school? School mathematics is built in a piecemeal fashion and works mainly on the meaning of the numerals and the lexical primitives of our written system (Lerner & Sadosky, 1994; Walkerdine, 1988). What does this mean? In crude terms, the prevailing idea is that children need to understand the meaning of 2 before they understand 3, and so on. Once the meaning of single digits has been mastered, children can proceed to the meaning of bi-digits and then to multidigits. Moreover, in order to acquire the meaning of digits, children must have a clear notion of the represented magnitude. Therefore, the quantity represented by digits has to be materialized in as many ways as possible so that children will have a clear sense of what a particular digit represents (e.g., pictures displaying different kinds of repeated objects, concrete collections of toys, wooden blocks of different kinds). The use of multidigits is mostly excluded from preschool programs.

Based on the psychological and pedagogical research reviewed here, I would like to make a few suggestions. From the very beginning, a child's notational knowledge should be taken into account and expanded—as a referential communicative tool, allowing and enhancing uses of numerals in a diversity of contexts and functions, be they numerals in phone books, diaries, lists, dates, birthdays, number of children present or absent from class, counting children in a group but also groups in a class, and classes in a school, counting glasses on a table and calculating the remaining number of glasses to be bought, prices to be compared, currency to be used, measures to be measured compared and ordered, and so forth. The list is a very long one, but the principle is a very simple one. Whatever the project to be developed in preschool or first grade, written representations should be included without any limit concerning magnitudes. Magnitude should not be a limiting factor. The selection criteria are the interest of the learner, the subject matter dealt with at a particular point, and the real need for notation, not the magnitude of the numeral. Let children find a way to compare the ages of parents, for example, and not only their number of brothers and sisters. Let them calculate budgets for school trips and not just the glasses on a table. This concerns functional uses of numerals and quantitative and nonquantitative contexts. But this is only one of the aspects that should be both taken into account and extended. Besides the referential communicative aspect, there is also the need (and the interest) to use and expand children's concern for numerals and relations among numerals as domains of knowledge. Dictation, comparison, ordering, and observation of similarities and differences between series are meaningful activities that serve to help children to discover regularities and to seek an explanation for the regularities.

Therefore, producing an external representation of numerals with different materials, or showing the composition or recomposition of construction as proposed by Bednarz and Janvier (1986), needs to be accompanied by an intense exploration of conventional written numeration and its use in multiple contexts. The knowledge children obtain from their contact with the conventional system is not acquired by mechanical, rote learning. Reconstruction processes will occur in many situations (e.g., when children are trying to put prices to different objects to show differences in magnitudes, or when children discuss which is the winning card in a card game) because in these cases they are required to talk about the system at the same time as they are using it.

This is the main conclusion I would like to draw from the preceding discussion. The main source of knowledge for understanding the written system of numeration is in the interaction with the written system of numeration. It is not only by being exposed to the written system that children will master numerical writing, they must explore the confines of this territory in a variety of tasks and for different purposes. Even before using numerals as communicative tools, before grasping the magnitudes numerals represent, children are sensitive to the elements and the combinatorial regularities of numerals. The precocious consideration of numerical notation facilitates the handling of conceptual and procedural components of number. Some conceptual requisites necessary for grasping the functioning of our written system, such as understanding its operating principles, can be obtained through the use of numerical writing in solving numerical problems. The knowledge that children demonstrate of round numbers, their early realization that number of numerals in a string is a good indicator of magnitude, and that the position of numerals is also a relevant cue, show clearly that they work on the regularities of the system, and they use both notational and verbal information. In trying to solve notational and arithmetic tasks, they come to grips with the additive structure of written numeration. But, if children's interaction with written numeration is controlled, if their access is regulated piece by piece under the assumption that an understanding of the additive structure, or of positional value, must be acquired outside the system and only later applied to conventional numeration, then these effectively become pre-conditions for using written numeration. If, on the other hand, significant interactions with notational artifacts are not only allowed but also encouraged, then conceptual understanding and notational knowledge become reciprocally enhanced.

The following are some key points in this chapter:

- Piaget's unified model of numerical cognition is challenged by the fact that the construction of number proceeds in gradual steps, by the enduring effect of magnitude, and by the effect of different symbolic systems on children's understanding of numbers.

- There is a numerical capacity we share with babies and some nonhuman species: the ability to identify and operate with a small set of numbers, up to four items. Beyond that, quantitative meaning is provided by approximation, whereas notational systems provide precision and means of calculation.

- Children include numerals in their repertoire of notational forms very early. However, there is a delay in their use of numerals for representing quantities and for using the same numerals for various functions, apparently because this requires them to detach quantity from the quantified objects.

- Two obstacles must be overcome before the generalized use of conventional numerals: Children must accept the arbitrary nature of notational elements and their compiled way of representing multiplicity.

- The use of numerals to convey the numerosity of a collection is not a direct application of social learning. Although children learn the conventional shapes and names of numerals very early on, they do not apply them directly to convey numerosity. When the purpose of the notation is to communicate a certain content, children between ages 4 and 5 prefer to reflect the quantity of elements included in a collection in a more direct and explicit way. This seems to be a necessary step before individual digits—in which multiplicity and iteration are compiled—become useful for external representation of cardinality.

- Two main conceptualizations of the written system emerge from the invented notations of first graders: First, numerals label magnitudes or collection, but neither grouping principles nor recursivity is considered. Second, numerals are integrated into compounds by recursivity, but no grouping principles or zero elements are considered.

- Place value is inherent in the system itself and in some sense implicit. The discovery of this implicit principle can be facilitated only by allowing the child to experiment with the system.

- A child's route to our written system of numeration is guided by the number of numerals in a string, their position in the string, and the recognition of round numbers. The three criteria coexist between approximately ages 5 and 6 until children start to perceive certain cases of conflict between magnitude and number of numerals. The children's attempts to solve this conflict bring about crucial changes in their understanding of written notations.

- Spoken language is an important source of information for writing numerals, but it may lead children to produce nonconventional notations because spoken numeration is not positional and zeros are not always pronounced.
- From age 4, children have a clear idea of the referential meaning of zero but are reluctant to use it for notation of absence, preferring to convey the idea using words or to resort to analogical strategies. Later, zero is more systematically used as a distinctive feature for big numbers and to form oral-based notations. But, it will still take a long time for children to use zero to represent lack of units at any level.
- The information children gather from notations, as well as the information they are able to produce, is not an aggregate on top of previously acquired notions that serves to amplify these notions, but is a permanent ingredient of developmental processes.
- The precocious consideration of numerical notation facilitates handling some conceptual bases of the functioning of our written system. That children work on the regularities of the system and use both notational and verbal information is clearly shown by their early realization that the number of numerals in a string is a good indicator of magnitude, and that the position of numerals is also a relevant cue, and by the knowledge they demonstrate of round numbers.

So far we have followed the developmental path taken by children in each notational territory separately. Chapter 3 traced the developmental route to writing and this chapter has focused on the notational principles that regulate our written system of numeration. In the following chapter we will look at how children view the relation between writing and numerals, the main notational systems in our culture.

5

What Children Know About the Relations Between Writing and Number Notation

A child's environment is rich with displays of letters and numerals. These letters and numerals have multiple functions. Letters are usually used to form words in written messages, but they also may indicate order (e.g., in outlines) or location (e.g., on a compass). Numerals may serve an ordinal function, as in elevator buttons, or they may provide geographical information, as in zip codes. Their more obvious use is to indicate quantity. Do very young children perceive the differences between letters and numbers? Do they attribute letters and numbers similar or different functions?

In the process of the acquisition of writing, as discussed in chapter 3, children impose constraints on the *distinctive features* that graphic displays must fulfill in order to be readable even before they have learned to read in adult ways. They believe, for instance, that strings of letters must be made up of three or four different letters. These self-imposed rules have been taken as indications that children explore writing and written texts as a problem space before they are able to read or write in adult ways. Do children impose similar constraints on numerals, or do they differentiate the two systems by applying different constraints?

Chapter 4 discussed how children relate to the different functions performed by numerals and how they progress from trying to map forms onto functions, to using numerals for different functions. It also pointed out that children are sensitive to relevant features of the written system of numeration and use these features to understand the functioning of the system. Specifically, they use the number of numerals in a string and the position of certain numerals as relevant cues for deciding which number is bigger. What cues are they going to use for distinguishing between writing and numerals?

My focus in this chapter is on children's early views of the relations between writing and numerals. Most of what I shall say is based on empirical studies in which toddlers and preschoolers were asked to compare graphic elements—letters and numerals—and to look at words, sentences, and multidigit ("big") numerals before having been formally taught at school. This approach to children's ideas about writing and numerals departs from the approach taken in other studies that have compared how children operate in the writing domain compared with how they operate in the number domain. For example, Munn and Scaffer (Munn, 1994; Munn & Scaffer, 1993) explored whether children believe that a story in a storybook is known from the pictures or from the text. Then they compared how children progress in this literacy activity and whether such progress is related to children's progress in the way in which they record numerosities. Whereas these researchers compared two developments and deduced links between them, the present approach questioned the child directly about the relation. Moreover, Munn and Scaffer's studies focused on children's reading and counting but not on children's ideas about the notational elements used to perform these activities. The reasoning underlying those studies was that through engagement in reading and counting, children will acquire an adult understanding of the notations.

In contrast, remember the constant interaction between knowledge obtained about notations from engagement in notational activities, and knowledge about the notations per se that orient children further in performing these activities. By participating in book reading or in a playful recording of quantities, children might very well learn about the features of letters, numerals, and their combinations. But, at the same time, their sensitivity to the formal differences between letters, numerals, and their combinations will guide them as to what sort of activity is likely to be connected with materials displaying letters and those displaying numerals.

The chapter first reviews the features that distinguish writing from numbers as notational systems from the perspective of literate adults. It then looks at children's ideas about these features. It becomes evident that from the earliest stages of notational development, numerals and writing are viewed as two distinct territories. Children apply different rules to each territory. Nevertheless, on some occasions, boundaries between territories are crossed due to the need to convey a message. When children want to reflect a certain content, to transmit how many or what kind of objects are shown on a card, they may engage every representational resource at their disposal. Thus, they may include drawings along with their writings or repeat a writing pattern many times to show that there are many cars on a card. But, even when children resort to another system to convey or to complete information, they always do it with attention to the formal constraints of each system. Furthermore, it seems that only when they are at least minimally aware of the formal features of each system are they able to manipulate these features to fulfill their representational needs. Where does this early differentiation between systems originate? Is it a consequence of environmental exposure and social interaction, or is it a result of direct instruction? The chapter attempts to address this issue by turning to the views of illiterate adults on the relation between writing and numerals. The ideas of illiterate adults will serve to highlight the role of environmental exposure, which is the main resource on which people deprived of formal instruction rely. Illiterate people have a clear idea of the differences between letters and numerals and the function each notational system performs.

I am convinced that differentiation between systems, both in the case of very young children and illiterate adults, is facilitated by the contexts in which writing and numerals usually appear, by the way people talk about letters and numerals, and by the activities people perform with the two systems. However, it is also apparently grounded in our biological endowment. For the purpose of providing some insights into the biological underpinning of notational differentiation I will consider some neuropsychological data related to the differentiation of letters and numerals in pathological states. Neurological studies with brain damaged patients show that there are specific neurological pathways that support handling of alphabetic materials that differ from those that serve to handle Hindu-Arabic numerals.

Initial differentiation between systems is indeed a favorable beginning because it guides children in the mass of notational input and in the attribution of meaning to the notational elements—sounds to letters and numerosity to numerals. Nevertheless, mature uses of the systems require using letters and numerals for multiple functions. It seems then that as children learn to differentiate between the systems, they must also learn when to blur these distinctions.

SIMILARITIES AND DIFFERENCES BETWEEN ALPHABETIC WRITING AND NUMERALS

For every literate adult, it is obvious that writing is reserved for the domain of language, and numerals are used for that of numbers and arithmetic. But, reflecting on this for a moment, it becomes evident that letters perform many other functions: In the context of algebra they represent variables, in the context of a bibliographic catalog they indicate location, and so on. Nevertheless, people still tend to associate them initially with language. Similarly, even though numerals perform many functions, they tend to be associated initially with numerosity and arithmetic.

When confronted with letters in isolation, people might think or say their name, and if prompted, they might provide their likely sound. Letter names, however, can either coincide with or differ from their sound. Although the name of the letter A is /ey/, its sound differs when it appears at the beginning of the following two words: *America aims*. People clearly distinguish between the sound of the letters in isolation and the lexical meaning of a combination of letters. For certain combinations of letters, those that form frequently used words, the lexical meaning is immediately activated. For other less frequent combinations, it may take some time, and for yet others (e.g., strock), no lexical meaning is activated, even though the combination is recognized as possible in our language.

In short, letters have names and represent a finite range of phonological segments that combine to form words. Not every combination of letters forms meaningful words: Some are valid but not meaningful, others are both valid and meaningful, and others are neither valid nor meaningful. The validity and meaningfulness of a combination is not embedded in the script but in the language. The same combination of letters that in English is valid but not meaningful (strock) is neither valid nor meaningful in Spanish because in this language a three-consonant cluster in word initial position is impossible. Obviously, every word in a language consists of a valid combination of letters, but not every valid combination of letters is a word.

When confronted with numerals in isolation, we might think or say their name. But, unlike letters, the name of a numeral is indistinguishable from its numerical meaning. For example, the name of the numeral 3 is always *three*, although the meaning 'three' can differ depending on whether we are talking about prices or phone numbers. The name of a numeral might be pronounced differently in different languages, but the numerical meaning is independent of pronunciation. Thus, numerical meaning is embedded in the system of numerals independent of language. Also, unlike letters, in the domain of numbers *any* combination of numerals will be both valid and meaningful. It is impossible to create a combination of numerals that denotes a nonexistent number analogous to a valid (but meaningless) string in writing.

Letters and numerals belong to different notational inventories, each having an internal order. The alphabetic order to which letters belong is unrelated to the sound or meaning of individual letters. Nevertheless, alphabetic order is a strong cultural ritual and is used to organize many things. However, the situation is more complex with numerals. Numeration systems are series ordered by the conceptual meaning of number, but numerals also have an internal order distinct from the conceptual meaning of number. An example may serve to clarify this somewhat complex issue. A binary system is a base 2 system (see chapter 2 for the notion of base), which works with only two notational elements (0 and 1). In a binary system, 1 is written 1, 2 is written 10, 3 is written 11, and so on. These notational elements (0 and 1) were selected because of the internal order of the notation and not for their numerical meaning. They were selected because they are the first two, not because they *mean* 'zero' and 'one.' In principle, any element could have been chosen for the binary system. It could have been 1 and 2, or even 5 and 6, but it would have been very strange to select 8 and 2, because they do not follow the internal order of the notation.

Another similarity between letters and numerals is that both can be identified by their outward shape. But, as was discussed in chapter 1, identification is simply a matter of cultural stipulation and familiarity. There is nothing intrinsic in the shape that makes them distinguishable one from the other. Letters are neither more rounded nor squarer than numerals, nor do they have a different symmetry. Strictly speaking, it is difficult to point to any distinguishing feature if the shape of isolated elements, such as l and **1,** is compared. It would be difficult to decide which one belongs to the inventory of letters and which to the inventory of numbers, but it would be less troublesome to compare them in the context of other elements:

lol   101

And it would be even less problematic if they were viewed in natural contexts of use. If people see someone looking at a sheet of paper and talking, they make the assumption that the person is reading a written text. They do this without even hearing what the person is saying and without seeing what is written on the sheet of paper, and they would be surprised were they to see just numerals.[24] Similarly, if someone is looking at a small strip of paper and speaking to a cashier in a supermarket, then the assumption would be that there are numbers on that strip of paper. Context, circumstances, types of object, and gestures provide clues as to the graphic elements that are expected in a certain display. Based on these expectations, people look for distinctive visual features and they are surprised if they do not find the expected elements—they assume that something is wrong, or that a typographical error has been made.

---

[24] This brings to mind the fact that according to the chronicles of the South American aborigine population, the Spanish conquerors were known by the indigenous populations as: "Those barbed men that move sheets while talking."

The entities in each notation (letters and numerals) also differ in the degree to which their aspect may vary. Sometimes "letter" applies to a family of graphic variations (e.g., the letter b means Capital **B**, italic *B*, script b), each of which is an allograph of the letter b. However, in certain contexts, b and B are not interchangeable. The reading of *buenos aires* and *Buenos Aires* is identical but, according to the orthographic conventions of Spanish, the first means good winds and only the second means the capital city of Argentina because proper names must be written with capitals. In proofreading, one must relate to b, **B,** and *B* differently. Numerals, on the other hand, have no allographs within a given notational system (e.g., Hindu-Arabic).

Consider the account balance sheet in Fig. 5.1 and observe that it includes both written and numerical texts. Do not read it, but rather examine the texts for their formal features. It is difficult; refraining from reading requires an effort for literate people. Examining the text from a formal perspective, notice that both types of notation are linearly arranged and have different levels of grouping. In the written text, however, no more than two identical letters ever appear in adjacent position, whereas in the numerical output there are many instances of more than two identical numerals appearing alongside each other. Note also that no element of the written text appears in isolation, whereas in the numerical texts there are many types of elements that appear in isolation. Written texts are more constrained than numerical texts in terms of number and variety of elements included in a string.

Pirincho Bank Co.
2 Vibero Road
Herethere   *ACCOUNT STATEMENT*

Titular: Rudolph Staircase   **Account N°** 1244 4440 0124

Page 1

Date	Activity	Amount	Balance
2.2.98	Previous Balance		2.324.00
7.2.98	Commission Charges	-5.52	2.318.48
10.2.98	Deposit of third party values	325.00	2.643.48
25.2.98	Transfer to other internal accounts	-1.000.00	1.643.48
28.2.98	Balance of this Statement		1.643.48

If no notice is received during the next 7 days we will assume this statement is correct. Our office hours are 9 AM to 5 PM, Monday through Friday.

FIG. 5.1.   A balance sheet including both written and numeric texts.

I started the comparison of the writing and numbers by analyzing the meaning of the elements and the functions they perform. That is, I made a *functional differentiation* between systems, and only then did I look at the formal features to attempt a *formal differentiation* between them. But, for the developing child, does *functional differentiation* precede *formal differentiation* or vice versa? That is, do children realize that (for example) MSCL does not exist in English because they know it has no meaning, or because they sense that this combination of letters never appears (and hence cannot have meaning)? Do they understand the meaning of 8999999765 and then accept its existence? Or, irrespective of wondering about meaning, do they know it is valid? One possibility is that sensitivity to the formal differences develops as a result of understanding the different functions of letters and numbers. An alternative possibility is that an awareness of formal differences *precede* children's understanding of the meaning and function of notations. It might be that formal features are what children initially perceive. And, in any case, how do children handle the information provided by the notational environment, pervaded as it is with such a variety of representational means?

Kamii (1986), for example, suggested that it might be problematic to expose children to two systems based on such different principles, and claimed that children may be confused and attempt to interpret numerals on the basis of writing or vice versa. Even if there is no agreement that such confusion may exist, it seems reasonable to assume that children who begin formal instruction with the two systems well and truly differentiated will be in a better position as they make progress toward literacy and numeracy.

THE CHILD'S VIEW OF WRITING AND NUMERALS BEFORE SCHOOLING

Most studies of the development of writing and number notations have concentrated on children's ability to use them to interpret or express meanings in the context of observational studies at home, or in the context of kindergarten activities in which children are encouraged to write stories, recipes, letters, or invitations (Bialystok, 1992; McLane & McNamee, 1990; Wolf & Gardner, 1983). The fact that children add drawing to their texts, and sometimes superimpose letters and numerals in the same graphic space, has created the impression that children confuse notational systems. Contrary to this impression, I have tried to show, in chapter 3, how early children differentiate drawing and writing. Yet, just how do children view the relations between writing and numbers?

Formal Differentiation Between Writing and Numerals

In a study I carried out with Annette Karmiloff-Smith (Tolchinsky-Landsmann & Karmiloff-Smith, 1992), we sought to determine whether children were sensitive to the different constraints inherent in the two systems of writing and numerals, or whether they considered both to be simply drawings. In other words, we wished to examine the extent to which they were sensitive to the similarities and differences in form and function between the two systems I presented at the beginning of this chapter. The participants—children between 3 years, 8 months and 6 years, 6 months who were recruited from a lower middle-class neighborhood of Barcelona—were asked to sort cards. The task was very simple: Two sets of cards were used, one set for the *writing domain task* and the other for the *numbers domain task*. For each set of cards, the children were asked to say *which cards were not good for writing* or *not good for counting*.[25] I will explain why we used such a question, asking for cards that were *not* good for a certain domain, but first let's consider the criteria used for selecting the cards.

The cards varied according to the following features: iconicity, linearity, identical elements, length of the string, conventionality of elements, and pronounceability of the string. The same features were used in designing cards for the numbers domain and for the writing domain: Some cards had figurative drawings, others had abstract schematic drawings, and still others had conventional letters or numerals. There were cards with strings of the same letter (or the same numeral) repeated many times, others including all different letters (or all different numerals), and still others with some letters repeated and some different. Some cards contained a single letter (or a single numeral) and others contained between two and eight letters (or numerals). Finally, there were cards containing obviously pronounceable words, and others consisting solely of consonants (and hence unpronounceable).

The intention was to determine whether the criteria children applied in admitting a card to one territory were similar to those they applied in admitting a card to the other territory. If they decided, for example, that a card containing the same repeated letter was *not* good for writing and similarly that a card containing the same repeated numeral was *not* good for counting, then it could be concluded that the same criterion—"avoid repetition"—was imposed on both writing and numerals. If, on the other hand, repetition was accepted in one domain but rejected in the other, then this would imply that children were applying a different criterion to each domain.

---

[25]The instructions were selected based on the results of a pilot study aimed at finding the expression children usually use to distinguish between elements.

Why did we ask for a card that *"is not good for writing (or counting)"*? By asking in that way, we were asking the children to choose a *negative* exemplar, that is, an exemplar that either lacked the features required to be part of the set or had some particular feature that prevented it from being part of the domain. We assumed that selection of negative exemplars would require more careful analyses of the cards than selection of positive exemplars. The reasoning was that for selecting exemplars that were part of the domain the children would only have to identify prototypes. On the other hand, in order to decide which cards did not belong to the domain, they would be required to analyze the features, as the selection could not be based on mere identification of prototypical entities. The purpose was then to discover whether the features that lead children to select negative exemplars in the domain of writing are the same as those that lead them to select negative exemplars in the domain of numerals.

The results of the sorting task demonstrated that over 95% of the children at all ages clearly separated between exemplars belonging to writing or numerals and those belonging to drawing.[26] They overwhelmingly concluded that cards containing drawings were good for neither writing nor numerals. Mixtures of elements from different domains [$M#&©] were also clearly rejected by 85% of the children as not being good exemplars of either domain.

However, the most revealing result was that the children drew a clear distinction between writing and number notation. Eighty percent of the subjects at all ages identified strings with repeated identical letters as not being good for writing, although they did not do so for number notation with respect to strings of identical numerals. They clearly imposed a constraint on writing that stipulates that strings must include a variety of different elements, while realizing that for number notation such a constraint does not hold. Moreover, they chose a card containing linked numerals imitating cursive writing as a bad exemplar of number notation, but accepted cursive writing for written notation. Table 5.1 summarizes the accepted features for numerals and writing.

Drawing and the mixture of characters do not appear in the table because they were rejected for both writing and numerals. Single elements, repetition of elements, and very many elements were accepted for numerals but rejected for writing, whereas linkage was accepted for writing but rejected for numerals. In the context of this task, 4-year-olds were clear about formal distinctions between writing and numerals. This sorting behavior did not present significant differences as a function of age except for two cards: The card showing a single

---

[26]Analyses were initially conducted separately for each card, but because no significant differences were found in the distribution of categories, the category most frequently used across cards was selected. A chi-square analysis of these categories and age showed that the differences found in the frequency of use of these categories in the different age groups were not significant.

TABLE 5.1

Accepted Features for Numerals and Writing

Feature	Numerals	Writing
Single elements	Yes	No
Repetition of identical elements	Yes	No
Limited range for length of string	Yes	No
Linkage between elements	No	Yes

letter $\boxed{\text{P}}$ and the card showing an unpronounceable string of consonants $\boxed{prlcst}$. The single letter was selected as not being good for writing by over half of the 4-year-olds and by almost all of the 5- and 6-year-olds. The children's increasing rejection of the single letter can be interpreted as being related to their increasing perception of writing in terms of readable strings. Initially, recognizing a single letter suffices to allow children to accept that a card contains writing, but later on, additional legibility criteria are imposed and isolated letters are rejected.

As for the string of consonants, at age 4, very few children considered it not good for writing, whereas by ages 5 and 6 over half the children decided that this card was not good for writing. For most of the youngest subjects, it was sufficient that the string of consonants obeyed the constraint of variety of adjacent elements in a string, whereas slightly older children were already sensitive to the lack of vowel/consonant alternation. Thus, another card displaying the Spanish word $\boxed{\text{OBOLO}}$, which is not in frequent use, was rarely selected as not being good for writing.

This shows how successful young children are at distinguishing drawing from either writing or number notation and at using different formal constraints to distinguish the domain of writing from that of number notation. However, whereas 4-year-olds consider strings to be appropriate for writing if they obey the aforementioned constraints, 5- to 6-year-olds impose a further constraint—that strings should obey the vowel/consonant regularities of conventional orthography.

A similar forced-choice task was used by Myriam Nemirovsky (1995), although with a slightly different rationale. Her aim was to determine whether the choices made by children were more strongly influenced by the shape of elements, their spatial orientation, or the way in which they were combined. In our study, the repetition of the same letter caused children to reject the string as being inadequate for writing even though it consisted of letters. This means that the constraint governing how letters should be combined was more decisive in determining whether a string belonged to the domain of writing than the fact

FIG. 5.2.   Cards used in a forced-choice task. From *Más allá de la alfabetización* [Beyond Literacy] (p. 225), edited by A. Teberosky and L. Tolchinsky, 1995, Buenos Aires, Argentina: Ediciones Santillana. Reprinted with permission.

that they were letters. That is, the combination of elements rather than the identity of the elements determined their decision. Nemirovsky systematically contrasted combinatorial constraints with graphic variation in shape and orientation of individual elements. The combinatorial constraints included oneness, mixture of elements, repetition, and linkage, and the graphic variation of the elements included inversion and rotation. The set of cards used in this study is shown in Fig. 5.2.

Children were asked to *put on one side the cards with letters and on the other side the cards with numbers.*[27] Unlike the study where the instruction oriented children to select cards that did or did not serve to perform a certain activity (writing or counting), this instruction oriented children to a closer examination of the elements.

The results showed that children only had problems in deciding whether the elements were letters or numerals when the elements were presented (a) mixed with elements of other domains, (b) affected by a feature typical of the other domain, or (c) presented in nonconventional orientation. Table 5.2 displays the percentage of children choosing letters, numerals, or neither for each card in the forced-choice task.

---

[27]These tasks were preceded by a sorting task very similar to that described earlier to find out what terms children use to denominate each of the domains. This group of children gave priority to the denomination *de letras* ('of letters') for the domain of writing and *de numero* ('of numbers') for the domain of numbers, which is the reason Nemirovsky (1995) utilized the aforementioned instruction.

TABLE 5.2
Percentage of Children Choosing Exemplars of Letters and Numbers by Card

Cards	*Letters*	*Numbers*	*Neither*
3584	0	100	0
1234	0	100	0
1234	52.7	47.3	0
2222	19.4	80.6	0
2	13.8	86.2	0
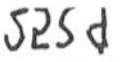	13.8	86.2	0
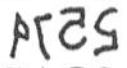	13.8	86.2	0
7AG2	83.4	13.8	02.7
A72G	13.8	83.4	02.7
MESA	100	0	0
TIZA	100	0	0
saco	100	0	0
RRRR	100	0	0
R	100	0	0
	100	0	0
	100	0	0

Only one child was bold enough to create three groups of cards: one for letters, one for numbers, and a third for the outsiders. This strategy would seem to be an artifact of classificatory difficulties. For other children, the first element (either numeral or letter) provided the key to their decision making. *Linkage* was clearly perceived as being related to writing rather than to numerals and thus cards in which the elements were linked were identified as letters. Just the opposite occurred for *oneness* and *repetition of identical elements*. These features were perceived as being more closely related to numerals than to writing. The only cases in which cards with letters were included in the group of cards "with numbers" were those containing isolated or repeated letters. In the case of *rotation*, children only had doubts with numerals and opted to include them with letters. This finding, together with the fact that rotated or inverted letters were usually sorted as letters, suggests a greater toleration of graphic variations in the domain of writing than in that of numbers. Despite the fact that the instruction placed the focus on elements, syntactic constraints still came into play.

The results of sorting tasks show that, from a very early age, the constraints children impose on notational forms are domain specific. The rules for entering the territory of writing are not the same as those for entering the territory of numbers. Children do not treat notations as a single general domain of knowledge, nor do they confuse number notation or writing with drawing. Rather, each system is explored according to its own particular constraints. When children's attention is directed to the activity to be performed (i.e., writing or counting), as in the 1992 study, they seem to be more tolerant in the domain of numbers and particularly careful about the combinatorial constraints that must be fulfilled in order to perform a given activity. When they are oriented toward the elements, as in Nemirovsky's study, they seem to show greater tolerance of variation in the domain of writing.

But, how does this finding fit with the observation that 4- and even 5-year-olds mix letters and numerals? Is it that differences arise when a child has to produce rather than interpret, so that the formal knowledge children put into practice when sorting cards is not shown when they have to create their own notations? An additional study (Tolchinsky-Landsmann & Karmiloff-Smith, 1993) was carried out to address the question of whether, and how, the formal distinctions that children show when asked to judge notations per se are put into practice when they are required to create notations and when these notations must convey certain information.

Functional Differentiation Between Writing and Numerals

Only toddlers, preschoolers, and first graders who knew how to write their names as well as some letters and numerals participated in the study. The mean age of each group was 4 years, 4 months; 5 years, 6 months; and 6 years, 6 months, respectively. The idea was to explore how children use their knowledge of formal constraints for communicative purposes. The task was very simple. We presented each child with a pair of cards and explained that because the cards would be put inside an envelope, they should write on the envelope *what* was depicted on the cards and *how many* objects were on each card so as to *remember exactly what is inside the envelope*. Because there is no specific verb for writing numerals in Spanish, the more general Spanish expression *poner cuantos hay* 'put how many are there' was used. Four pairs of cards were used: three pairs displaying the same objects but in different quantities (e.g., a picture of three wheels on one card, and a picture of five on the other; a picture of one car on one card and five cars on another card) and one pair of cards displaying different objects in the same numerosity (e.g., three trucks on one card and three police officers on the other). This material made it possible to determine whether and how children's recording of the type of object displayed on the cards differed from the recording of the numerosity of objects.

This task differed from the sorting tasks in two ways. First, it had a clear communicative purpose, whereas the sorting tasks were decontextualized and had no specific communicative purpose. Second, the children had to create a message, whereas for the sorting task they had to identify elements and strings as pertaining to different domains. Although our focus was on the functional use of notation, we first compared the children's graphics for the formal features to see whether the constraints of number of elements, intra-string variety and linkage, which were employed in the sorting tasks, appeared when children had to express the content of the cards.

Three important findings were as follows:

- Only two children used a single element for writing the names of the objects. The majority produced strings containing more than one but less than nine elements. In contrast, all the children, except two, used single elements, numerals, or simile numerals for recording numerosity.
- The children tended to repeat adjacent elements for recording numerosity but not for writing the names of the objects.
- Finally, half the children at age 4 used linked writing when recording the names of the objects. This percentage increased up to 93% at age 6. In contrast, only 20% at age 4 used linked strings for numerosity, and this use virtually disappeared by age 6. Some children, however, who already knew how to write conventionally, preferred to write the number-words rather than use numerals, or they did both.

In conclusion, from the perspective of their elements and formal constraints, children's graphic productions showed a clear differentiation between writing and numerals (for details see Tolchinsky-Landsmann & Karmiloff-Smith, 1993). However, despite the clear differentiation between systems, which adds weight to the results of the sorting task, there were three surprising findings:

- A significant number of children resorted to drawings. Almost 25% of the children's graphic output in each age group included drawings (25% at age 4, 23.7% at age 5, and 25% at age 6). The children used drawings either with writing (20% at age 4, 4.7% at age 5, and 12.5% at age 6) or to accompany writing and numerals (5% at age 4, 19% at age 5, and 12.5% at age 6).
- Some children (25% at age 4 and 18% at age 6) produced writing when numerals were needed.
- A significant number of children did not use letters and numerals for recording purposes despite the fact that knowledge of letters and numerals was a condition for participation in the study. No child used conventional letters at age 4, 60% did so at age 5, whereas all of the children at age 6 did so. The use of conventional numerals for quantitative information appeared earlier and more frequently. Only 39% of

4-year-olds, but 95% of 5-year-olds, used conventional numerals. There was a slight decrease at age 6 because some children decided to write the number-words.

Two conclusions can be drawn. First, children's knowledge of the formal differences between systems does not preclude their crossing the frontiers of the respective territories—using drawing, writing, and numerals—to fulfill communicative purposes. Second, children's knowledge of the formal features of letters and numerals does not guarantee their use for communicative purposes. Four examples of "notational solutions" that children used when recording the same qualitative and quantitative information may serve to clarify these conclusions (see Fig. 5.3).

José Manuel, a 4-year-old who participated in the study, exemplified a highly communicative solution. By examining what he produced, we can see the wheels and cars displayed on the cards and realize that the same objects ap-

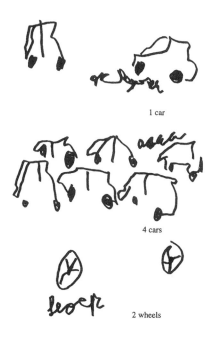

1 car

4 cars

2 wheels

5 wheels

FIG. 5.3. A notational solution for recording qualitative and quantitative information. From "Las restricciones del conocimiento notacional" [Constraints on notational knowledge] by L. Tolchinsky and A. Karmiloff-Smith, 1993, *Infancia y Aprendizaje* 62–63 (p. 43). Reprinted with permission.

peared on one pair of cards while different objects appeared on the other pair. We can also appreciate the number of wheels and cars on each card. In other words, both the quality and numerosity of objects displayed on the cards can be recovered from his inscriptions. This information is not provided by the writing—the pattern of which is virtually identical for each card—but by the drawings that show the shape and numerosity of the objects. Numerosity is not represented independently from the objects. We reencounter here a phenomenon already commented on in chapter 4: Numerosity is still attached to the enumerated objects.

Now, if the drawings depict the objects and their numerosity, then what does the writing pattern stand for? José Manuel's interpretation may help to answer this question. The following is a short extract from the interview in which the investigator asked him to interpret what he had written:

> Investigator: What does it say here? (pointing at the wheel drawing)
>
> José Manuel: That there are two wheels.
>
> Investigator: And here? (pointing at the writing-pattern)
>
> José Manuel: Here it says the name.
>
> Investigator: What name?
>
> José Manuel: The name.
>
> Investigator: The wheel's 'name'?
>
> José Manuel: (nodding, but without too much conviction)

When analyzing the development of writing in chapter 3 we noted that at the earliest stages of development, *names* is what some children call the written word, which does not yet fulfill any communicative-referential function; when writing is just writing, what is written is called *names*. Only drawing communicates in José Manuel's notational solution. Writing is present as writing, as a particular kind of object called *names*. It *is* formally differentiated from numerals but not yet communicative.

The second example, from a 4-year-old girl, offers a less communicative solution (see Fig. 5.4). Here, there are two different kinds of inscription: One looks like quick writing, the other like a sort of token-iterative device, with one mark for each object, no matter whether they are cars or wheels.

This type of notational strategy is already familiar; remember the case when children were asked to invent notations or to fill in the *identity card* (chap. 4). Just by looking at the girl's productions, it is possible to guess that the number of something changes from card to card, and there are changes in quantity both in what looks like a writing pattern and in what looks like an iterative device.

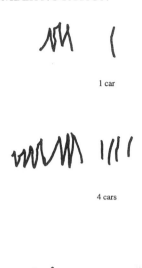

FIG. 5.4. A notational solution for recording only quantitative information. From "Las restricciones del conocimiento notacional" [Constraints on notational knowledge] by L. Tolchinsky and A. Karmiloff-Smith, 1993, *Infancia y Aprendizaje* 62–63 (p. 43). Reprinted with permission.

There is no way, however, to know what it is that increases or decreases in number because the same *undifferentiated* pattern was used both for cards depicting the same object and for cards depicting different objects; the girl reiterates the same writing pattern irrespective of the referents. That is, by examining her inscriptions we can recover quantitative information both from her writing and her purported number notation, but no qualitative information. Certainly this notational solution has lost communicative force, although in some respects it shows important progress compared to the previous solution: Numerosity has been detached from the objects and a similar device is used for the notation of different objects. However, both writing and number notation have been recruited for representing quantity! Again, as in the previous example, frontiers between systems are being crossed to convey a message. In the previous example, the frontiers were between drawing and writing, whereas in the present one they correspond to the the functional boundaries between writing and number notations, which are both used for representing quantity. The example in Fig. 5.5, from a 6-year-old girl, presents a rather different strategy.

The clearly differentiated use of conventional letters and numerals is immediately noticeable. The letters are completely unrelated to the objects the girl is trying to represent (for writing the Catalan word *roda* 'wheel,' she wrote *TROCNILI*, a nonword). But, in contrast to the previous example, something is repeated in the first two cards but not in the following two. As for the numerals, they are indeed conventional numerals but used in nonconventional ways; the girl iterated as many numerals as there were objects to be depicted. As discussed in chapter 4, the need to reflect multiplicity in a direct way, not compiled in a single numeral, motivates children to iterate numerals. This girl, like many other children, was adapting the conventional forms to her representational needs. Compared with the previous example, there is functional differentiation between writing and number notation; writing reflects things that are alike versus things that vary, and it reflects qualitative rather than quantitative relations, as in the previous case. Number notation, in

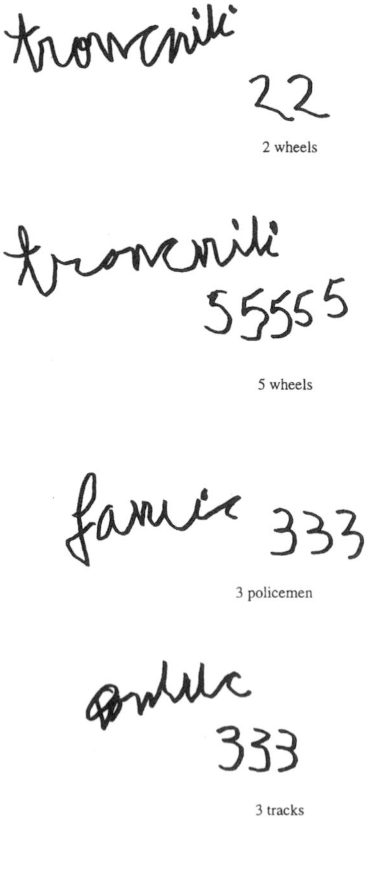

2 wheels

5 wheels

3 policemen

3 tracks

FIG. 5.5. Recording of quantitative information using conventional elements based on unconventional principles. From "Las restricciones del conocimiento notacional" [Constraints on notational knowledge] by L. Tolchinsky and A. Karmiloff-Smith, 1993, *Infancia y Aprendizaje 62–63* (p. 44). Reprinted with permission.

contrast, reflects contrasting numerosities very explicitly. It is important to note that, for this purpose, she reiterates identical elements within the same string, a resource she will never use for writing. In this way, she is both respectful of the formal constraints of each system and fulfilling her representational needs. As we shall see in the next example, however, the need to be explicit about the meaning of numerosities may lead children to exceed the boundaries of number notation despite having the meaning of letters clear.

Kalid, a 6-year-old boy, is already familiar with letter-to-sound correspondences. For *roda* 'wheel,' he wrote OA (see Fig. 5.6); for the word *policia* 'policeman,' he wrote OIIA. That is, for each syllable, Kalid wrote only the vowel in a clear-cut case of syllabic correspondence. No doubt Kalid was already aware that writing relates to phonological segments. Despite this, he was also using writing to show differences in numerosity by repeating the same written string

2 wheels

5 wheels

3 policemen

3 tracks

FIG. 5.6.   Recording of qualitative and quantitative information using conventional elements based on unconventional principles. From "Las restricciones del conocimiento notacional" [Constraints on notational knowledge] by L. Tolchinsky and A. Karmiloff-Smith, 1993, *Infancia y Aprendizaje* 62–63 (p. 44). Reprinted with permission.

as many times as there were objects on the cards. Note that, in the previous example, explicit depiction of numerosity was attained by repeating the same numeral (the same element within a single string), but in this case it was attained by reiterating the same string. Why is it important to highlight this? Because this shows that even without a clear functional differentiation (information about numerosity was provided in the previous example by numerals and in this case by writing and by numerals), care is taken to differentiate formal constraints. In the last three examples, the children are providing information about qualitative similarities and quantitative differences, not by iconic means as in the first example, but through the constraints of each system (although they are also assimilating conventional means to their representational needs).[28]

When communication of a message is the target, children resort to whatever representational means they have to achieve this end, even if it entails a transgression of the relative closure of domains by using drawing for writing or writing for numerals. So, in sorting printed materials, children show no doubt about what is for reading and what for counting, and they are also very clear that drawing is good for neither reading nor counting. Certainly, the formal constraints of each system are guiding their sorting procedures—remember that repetition of identical elements and use of single elements is accepted for number notation while rejected for writing. But, the situation varies when children are attempting to communicate a message. When focusing on the instrumental use of symbolic means, they may disregard the formal constraints that separate systems and are already part of their knowledge. This does not mean, however, that children are confusing drawing, number notation, and writing.

Imagine a situation in which a young German-speaking teenager, Gretl, arrives in Barcelona without knowing a word of Spanish or Catalan. She enters a typical *Tapas Bar*, and to ask for a chicken sandwich has no better idea than to wave her arms in a flying motion (by the way, this is not an invented example, I watched the scene and still remember the face of the waiter trying to guess what the girl was asking for). Are we going to say that Gretl was confusing language and gesture? Rightly or wrongly, she was just seeking the best way to convey a message. Similarly, under communicative pressure, a child looks for explicit ways to convey a message. Therefore, if single numerals seem insufficient to show that there are many objects on the cards, he will reiterate them as many times as needed. And, why not also take advantage of the multiple elements of

---

[28]Two children used a "notational" solution that provides neither qualitative nor quantitative information. They used the same kind and number of letters in different combinations. Perhaps these children have started to grasp the idea that it is possible to create differences (to reflect the differences in the cards) not only by increasing or decreasing elements, but also by making variations within the string.

writing? Besides, children are also exploring the systems. They do not have so many opportunities to write and notate quantities, at least not in the schools at the time these data were gathered. Kindergarten teachers teach children letters or numerals, but they never ask them to write a message of any kind *in their own way* without providing a model. Thus, for many children, this might be an exceptional opportunity to explore the systems.

We began the discussion of the different studies to shed light on whether, for the developing child, *functional differentiation* precedes *formal differentiation* or vice versa. From what has been said so far, the knowledge children show of the formal constraints of writing and number, the knowledge they demonstrated in the sorting and production tasks, does not seem to be a consequence of an instrumental use of writing and numbers. It is not the case that after learning to use writing to convey verbal messages, and numbers to convey numerical messages, children then discover the formal features that differentiate between the systems (e.g., that some elements are used for writing and others for number, that repetition is "allowed" in numerals and not so much in writing). Rather, formal differentiation is already part of children's knowledge even before they are able to write messages, and it constrains children's use of the systems for communicative purposes. So, as has been pointed out, children may resort to drawing or to writing when numerals are required because the specific notational features of these systems fit their communicative purpose better. But, in each case, they show an awareness of the specific constraints of each system. Remember, for example, that they repeat the same numeral as many times as they need to convey numerosity. But, when they use writing for that same purpose, they repeat strings of letters, not the same letter many times. There may be a lack of functional specificity (e.g., using writing to represent numerosity), but the formal constraints of each system are respected.

From the examples just discussed, it is clear that children are sensitive to the formal features and very early start using letters and numerals. They are not just incorporating this social information, but rather exploring possibilities and, most important, making use of them to fill a representational need. They use drawing when they need to make the meaning of a writing pattern explicit, and iterated numerals or strings of letters to make explicit the numerosity of a set. In other words, the need to show explicitly what is meant by the notation seems to function as a strong motivation for crossing boundaries. But, along with fulfilling a representational need, children are learning from their own external representation. They are learning to accept the implicit and arbitrary meaning of notations. It is as though the analogical means of representation they explore become internalized to provide a semantic interpretation to notations. Once the meaning is made explicit via external analogical representations, arbitrary forms (letters and numerals) gain referential meaning and the two systems become functionally differentiated. This is the transition I will elaborate in the next section.

Explicit Differentiation Between Writing and Numerals

The results of the sorting tasks show that children do not confuse numbers with writing or with drawing. Rather, each specific manifestation of notational systems is explored according to its own particular constraints. For example, *repetition* and *oneness* were rejected for writing but not for numerals. Surely, 4- and 5-year-olds would be hard put to explain verbally the differences between writing and numbers, and yet when they were asked to justify why a particular card was not good for writing, some of them could say things such as *because it says the same thing all the time*. So, are the constraints that serve to sort out the cards embedded in the sorting procedure? Or are they explicitly represented at some level in the child's mind? More generally, how is the knowledge that serves to make sense of external representations internally represented? If it is implicit knowledge, embedded in the sorting procedure, then it should be automatic, difficult to access and to change. If, on the other hand, children have some internal access to this knowledge, then they should be able to manipulate it and adapt it to different situations.

Indeed, as noted in chapter 4, there are many levels at which people can say they know something. Surely traditional dichotomies in terms of implicit versus explicit knowledge are not enough to illustrate these multiple levels. For this reason, the question of levels of knowledge about notation has been framed in Karmiloff-Smith's (1986, 1992) model of cognitive change.[29] I have chosen this model because it distinguishes several levels of representation and accessibility of knowledge; it distinguishes different levels at which knowledge can be explicitly represented. It also provides a methodological approach to tap intermediate levels of knowledge, neither completely implicit nor completely explicit. I will

---

[29]The model involves three phases that recur whenever children are in the process of acquiring new knowledge. During the first phase, the child focuses predominately on information obtained by interaction with the external environment. But the initial representations neither alter the existing representations nor are they brought into relation with them. New representations are simply added and independently stored. Phase 1 culminates in a consistently successful performance on whatever micro-domain acquisition of knowledge is going on. Phase 1 is followed by a Phase 2, during which children do not focus on external data but on their own already stored representations. This temporary disregard may lead to mistakes, which very frequently demonstrate children working on internal representations that, up to that point, had been juxtaposed. Finally, during Phase 3, internal and external data are reconciled and there is a balance between internal and external control. The processes and the phases are the same for the different domains of knowledge, but the representation on which the model is initially dependent and further develops is domain specific.

go through them first in a very simplistic manner and then in of Karmiloff-Smith's way of putting it.

Note first that with the same successful behavior, there may be a different underlying representation. Consider, for example, how successful 4-year-old children may sound when reciting the alphabet or the series of digits, and yet this behavior is different, in its deep sense, from that displayed by an 8-year-old who can read, write, and use numerals in basic arithmetic. The external behavior at 8 years may resemble that at 4 years, but the underlying representation has suffered an internal reworking, and hence a representational change.

At the most implicit level, we simply do things; we react to environmental input (if using the computer metaphor, we run procedures), but we are not at all aware of what is being run in our cognitive system. At the next level, part of our cognitive system *knows*, but we are not completely aware of what we know. At the third level, we know what we know but we can barely explain it in words. Finally, we can explain verbally what we know.

Karmiloff-Smith called these levels Implicit (I), Explicit-1 (E1), Explicit-2 (E2), and Explicit-3 (E3). At Level I, representations are in the form of procedures for analyzing and responding to the external environment. A procedure as a whole is available as data to other operators, but its component parts are not. The information embedded in the procedures remains implicit. Specific inputs can be computed in a relatively effective and rapid way, but the procedure remains relatively inflexible. The model posits reiterated processes of *redescription*. The process of redescription is a recursive psychological process; it reappears each time the subject is involved in acquiring new knowledge. When procedures are redescribed, many of the initial details embedded in them are lost, but components of the procedure become available for internal scrutiny and open to the establishment of intra- and interdomain representational links. The process of redescription can occur online or offline as a result of the "internal dynamic" of the system. Level E1 involves explicitly defined representations that can be manipulated and related to each other. Once knowledge previously embedded in procedures is explicitly defined, the potential relations between procedural components can then be marked and represented internally. Although E1 representations are available as data to the system, they are not available to conscious access and verbal report, which are attained at Levels E2 and E3, respectively (Karmiloff-Smith, 1992, pp. 18–26).

In general, developmental theories do not distinguish between the diverse levels of explicitness, especially not between Level I and Level E1, which is explicit internally (to other parts of the cognitive system) but not verbally explicit. This level is important because it indicates the beginning of an internal analysis of procedures into component parts, an analysis necessary in order to attain further flexibility. This is precisely the level of representation that the "transgression technique" was planned to tap.

This technique was initially devised for a drawing study (Karmiloff Smith, 1990) that provided support for the notion of different levels of explicitness of children's representations. Children who could produce typical drawings of such things as houses, trees, humans, numerals, and so forth, participated in the study. Although they had attained behavioral mastery of the drawing procedure, the question concerned whether they could access the internal manipulation the procedure put into play when drawing. With this aim, the children were asked to draw "a house that does not exist" (and a tree that does not exist, and so on). Karmiloff-Smith assumed that to make figural changes in the drawing so as to transform houses that were houses into houses that did not exist, the children would have to access the components of a procedure that might have been running automatically. The study demonstrated that the drawings produced by some of the children of "houses that do not exist" did not show any radical difference when compared to those they produced for houses that do exist. That is, the children could not make any radical changes in any of the components of their "internal" houses in order to transform them into houses that did not exist. Other children, however, created transformations in their drawings, showing that they had accessed the different components of the procedure that serves to draw a house. These children were assumed to have knowledge regarding drawing in a different representational format.

Similar motivations explain the application of this technique to the domain of writing and number. The children who participated in the study (Tolchinsky-Landsmann & Karmiloff Smith, 1992) were successful at the sorting task; on a procedural level their sorting behavior complied with a number of domain-specific constraints. We wished to determine whether those constraints could be accessed or whether they were implicitly represented. Children between ages 3½ and 6½ years were first asked to write down on a piece of paper their own name, other names, words, letters, and numbers that they knew. Irrespective of whether the children were able to write in a conventional way, they succeeded in writing letters, numbers, and what they considered to be words. We wished to see whether the knowledge they demonstrated for creating normal letters, words, or numbers was implicitly embedded in writing and number procedures or whether it could be accessed and manipulated. To test this, the investigator pointed to one of the child's productions, for example a number, and said: *Here you have put a number, now put a number that doesn't exist.* The same process was repeated with the children's productions of words and letters.[30] The following description details the findings.

Some 4-year-olds produced exemplars for nonexistent numbers, letters, and words that were barely distinguishable from those they produced for existent ones. From this behavior it was deduced that they could not yet purposefully manipulate the procedures they used for sorting and for writing "normally." These children displayed no capacity to produce nonexistent exemplars; nonetheless, they clearly distinguished between notational domains in their productions. For written notation they used, for example, a form that looked like writing, although it was not conventional writing, and ill- or well-formed numerals for the number domain. But their knowledge was still at Level I, inaccessible to internal scrutiny. However, a few other 4-year-olds and the majority of the 5- and 6-year-olds were capable of transgressing certain constraints on writing and number notation. The representations sustaining their sorting behavior had already been redescribed into E1 format. Some of them transgressed the intersystem boundaries and produced iconic elements to make nonletters, nonnumbers, and nonwords. They also used elements of the number system to make nonwords and nonletters, and vice versa. They transgressed the relative closure of each domain. Other children transgressed the constraints on elements and strings in a particular notational system. Thus, if they had produced a string of different letters for a real word, following their own imposed constraint of intra-string variety, they used a string of repeated identical letters for a nonword, violating the same constraint. For nonnumbers, they deformed the shape, or if they had produced a single numeral for a real number, they offered a very lengthy string of numbers for a number that does not exist, violating the constraint of oneness. For nonletters, they usually manipulated the shape or the quality of the trace. They deformed the graphic shape by duplicating parts or changing the contour. A few children blurred the boundaries between elements and invented new units by amalgamating two letters or two numerals to produce nonletters and nonnumbers. Finally, there were children who focused on the function of notations as referential-communicative tools. Thus, for nonwords, they announced that they would write "words that cannot be said"

---

[30]Several different expressions were used to ensure that children understood the instructions: "an X (number, letter, word) that doesn't exist," "an X that you invent," "an X that no-one has ever seen before," and so forth. When the instruction was given to produce a letter or a word that does not exist, the experimenter used the verb "to write." However, when it concerned a number that does not exist, the experimenter used the expressions "to make a number that doesn't exist" or "to put here a number that doesn't exist" in order to avoid actually suggesting the use of elements from the written system. For the word category, the term "name" was sometimes used because, as seen before, this term is frequently used to refer to written words. This was meant to convey to the children that they should violate the constraints that, in their view, define normal writing.

(sometimes, by this, they meant words that were unpronounceable but, at other times, they meant words that cannot be said "in public" and wrote 'pipi' and 'caca' or "words that aren't anything."). For nonnumbers, they announced that they would produce "numbers so large that they couldn't possibly exist," or that contained multiple zeros. Others suggested writing zero, because, as they explained, "zero is not a number."

Figures 5.7, 5.8, and 5.9 provide an illustration of the four types of transgression for words, letters, and numbers. Figure 5.7 shows pairs of productions for a word and for a nonword. The example at the top displays no transgression, while immediately below, for a word, the girl proposed a personal version of her name (Neus, which in cursive writing looks very similar to what she actually produced) but proposed a drawing for a nonword, and in doing so transgressed the constraint of relative closure. In the next example, the girl broke the con-

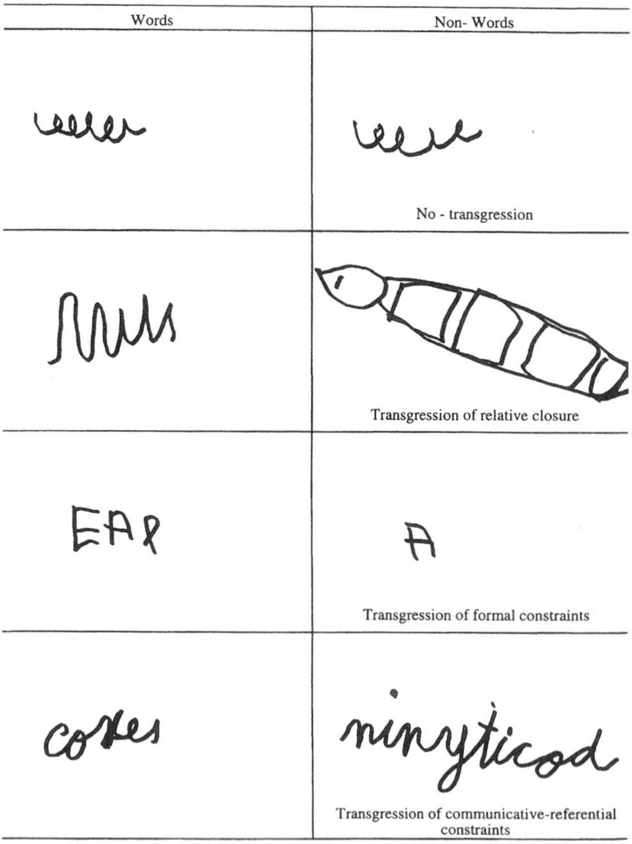

Words	Non- Words
	No - transgression
	Transgression of relative closure
	Transgression of formal constraints
	Transgression of communicative-referential constraints

FIG. 5.7.   Types of transgression for writing words and nonwords.

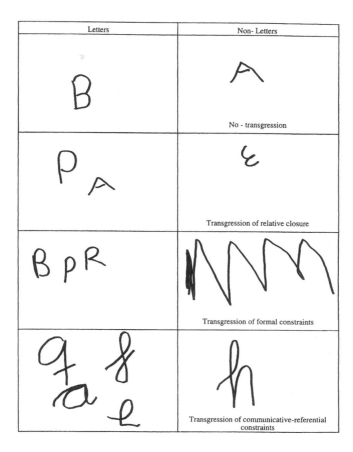

FIG. 5.8.   Types of transgression for writing letters and nonletters.

straint of minimal number of elements by producing a single letter for a nonword. In the last example, another girl produced the word *coxe* 'car' in Catalan, and an unpronounceable string of letters, which is an example of the violation of the referential-communicative constraints. These children were already working on the referential meaning of writing.

Figure 5.8 gives examples of the four types of transgression for writing letters and nonletters. In the top row, the example shows conventional letters used for both letters and nonletters. In the second row, the girl produced a number for a nonletter, and she clarified: *If it is a number, it is not a letter.* This is a clear example of violation of system boundaries. In the third row, there is an example of a transgression of oneness: The child produced a pattern that is similar to writing but in which no letter can be distinguished. The last transgression, in the bottom row, is particularly interesting. Here the child produced 14 letters of the alphabet as examples of letters (only part of them are presented here), but as an example of a nonletter he produced an H (*aitch*). This is called the silent letter by many teachers, because it represents phoneme 0 in Spanish. Surprisingly, two other children offered the same solution. Unfortunately, I could not obtain any verbal explanation from the boys, but I am convinced that the particular referential features of the H makes it almost a nonletter. I guess that the child's reasoning was as follows: If the letter does not sound, then it has no reference (because letters refer to sound). Therefore, this letter H violates the referential constraints for letters.

   That is why children who resorted to this solution were considered to be violating referential constraints for letters. For most children, however, it proved very difficult to find examples of a nonletter that transgressed the referential-communicative constraint. This difficulty was expressed by a 6-year-old who explained *la forma [de una letra que no existe] la puedo inventar, lo que no*

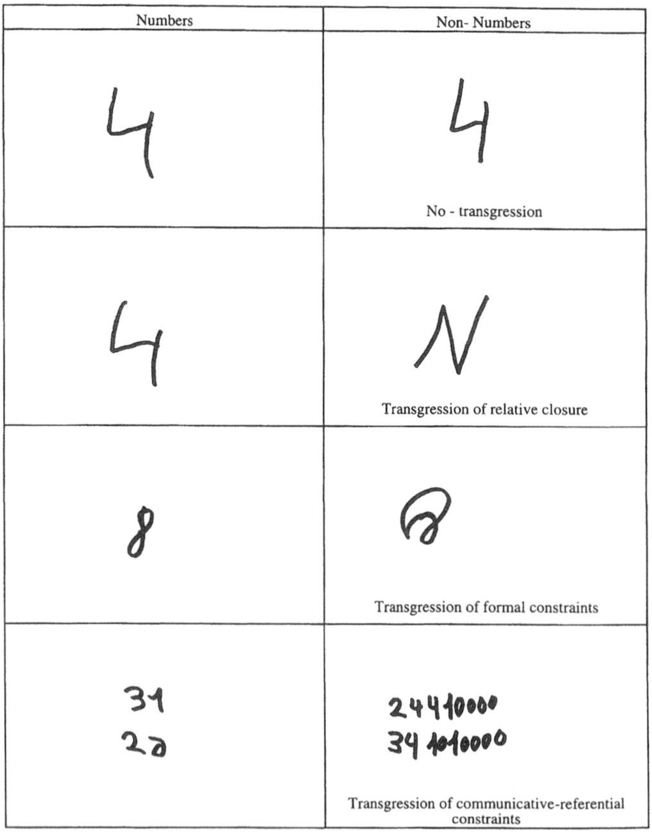

FIG. 5.9.   Types of transgression for writing numerals and nonnumerals.

puedo inventar es el sonido 'I can invent the shape [of a letter that does not exist] but what I can't invent is its sound.'

Finally, Fig. 5.9 provides several examples of the different types of transgression for writing numbers and nonnumbers. In the top row are examples of nontransgression; below this is an example of writing a letter for a nonnumber. In the third row, the shape of the numeral is deformed, whereas in the bottom row there is an example of the writing of a long number *porque con tantos ceros es infinito* 'because with so many zeros it is infinite.'

In general, the children progressed with age from nontransgression to transgression of elements/strings constraints, through transgression of referential-communicative constraints. Only at age 5 did children start to transgress the formal element/string constraint with a greater degree of consistency, and by age 6, 73% of children opted for this solution. Except for the referential-communicative constraint, the rest of the constraint responses were fairly evenly distributed across the remaining three categories at all ages.

Unlike the case of nonletters, as many as 74% of the 6-year-olds transgressed the referential-communicative constraint as a means of producing nonnumbers. Finally, for nonwords, 4- and 5-year-olds tended, in the main, to transgress the formal element/string constraint, whereas 87% of the 6-year-olds transgressed the referential-communicative constraint. At this age, elements and strings have referential meaning for the child, and therefore they can be transgressed.

In short, the purpose of this study was to find out how knowledge about numerals and writing is internally represented. Working with three age groups, it was assumed that there could be different levels at which this knowledge is represented. According to the reasoning, if the knowledge was completely implicit, embedded in sorting procedures that are triggered by particular material, or embedded in writing procedures, then children would be unable to create an example of an element that was *not* a letter or *not* a number, or a string that is *not* a word, and so on. This was based on the belief that in order to do this, children must know about elements and strings at a level that allows some analysis of their features and meaning. That is, only at a certain level of internal explicitness of knowledge could children violate the constraints they had shown themselves able to impose on each system. Using this approach, it was found that few children as young as age 4, but the majority of 5- and 6-year-olds, had explicit representations of the constraints they imposed on different notational systems. They were able purposefully to violate these constraints in order to produce nonexistent exemplars. Some transgressions were very global, the children simply produced for one domain an exemplar of another domain (e.g., a drawing for writing); others were subtler. These show that children were already analyzing notational features. They transgressed constraints of shape and quality of trace for letters and numbers, and constraints of variety and number of letters for words. Only later were they able to transgress referential-communicative constraints, producing letters that did not sound, words that did not mean, or *infinite numbers*.

What is the significance of the developmental order in the kind of transgressions children produced? At age 4, they rarely produced any transgression; but, with age, they moved to formal transgressions in each domain and finally to referential-communicative transgression. That is, the children first differentiated between systems by the formal constraints internal to each of them and then by the referential-communicative constraints. These findings confirm through a different approach that formal differentiation is a point of departure and constrains children's further experience with notations. Only after these features become relatively explicit for the subject can they manipulate them to create nonexisting exemplars and also very probably adapt these features to their representational needs. Indeed, the use of formal features of writing for representing quantities or conventional numerals as term-to-term devices occurs at the same age. These findings also demonstrate that internal explicitation of features might be a pre-condition for being able to work out the meaning of elements and strings.

In order to refine the view as to how children relate to the notational elements, consider the findings of another study. Nemirovsky (1995) asked 36 5- and 6-year-olds (all preschoolers) to write something *que esten bien para ser de letras* 'that are well done for letters,' *que esten mal para ser de letras* 'that are wrongly done for letters,' and *que no sean de letras* 'that aren't letters' and to jot down 'well done numbers,' 'wrongly done numbers,' and 'nonnumbers.' This study introduced an additional distinction between letter and nonletter: by asking children to produce letters that are not well done. The idea was to gain access to children's representations of problematic exemplars: letters or numerals that are not strictly drawn or interpreted according to the conventions of the system but are still letters or numbers. That is, they are within the boundaries of the system but without fitting all the adequacy requirements.

Out of 36 children, 91% (33) produced conventional letters for 'well done letters' and conventional numerals for 'well done numbers.' Only 3 children produced letters when asked to produce 'well done numbers.' None of the children used numerals when asked to produce 'well done letters.' Again the domain of letters appears more open than the domain of number. Despite the denomination utilized by the children ('for letters,' 'for numbers') they never produced single elements for the domain of writing but rather strings that ranged from 2 to 10 letters or traces that looked like letters but were not conventional letters. For the domain of numbers, 6% of the children produced one element and the rest produced strings of up to 10 elements. Most wrote either a partial (1 2 3 4) or a complete (1 2 3 4 5 6 7 8 9) series. For the domain of writing, the children were at different levels of development, but in no case did they violate the known constraints of the writing system (linearity, multiplicity of elements, and intra-string variety). The type of transgression the children carried out differed for each instruction. In order to produce 'not well done letters' (or numbers), an almost equal number of children either deformed the quality of the trace or changed the order of elements in the string. Therefore, for numbers, they usually obtained a disordered series or dispersed elements on the sheets of paper. Few children altered the strings by introducing elements foreign to the system and thus in violation of the relative closure of the domain (letters within the string of numbers, or numbers within the string of letters). Four children were unable to produce something they considered 'wrongly done.' No child, however, produced a drawing. A very different picture emerged when analyzing the productions for nonletters and nonnumbers. Here, most children (69%) produced drawings, a few produced exemplars of the other system, and even fewer altered the trace.

This study confirms that prior to formal instruction children have an explicit representation of the formal constraints of writing and number notation. They also know that the shape of individual elements and the order of elements in a string are conditions that influence the quality (well done or wrongly done) within a certain domain but do not necessarily exclude the elements or the strings from that particular domain. However, drawing is a totally different domain. *Drawing is not wrongly written writing but nonwriting.* Similarly for numbers, if the shape of the elements or the quality of the trace or the order within a string is altered, the result is wrongly written numbers—but, they are still numbers. On the other hand, a drawing is produced and boundaries are crossed, which takes things to semiotically different territory. These findings reassure us that if children are found to include drawings in their outputs, or even to use them with special communicative purposes, then it is done in order to take advantage of the characteristics of drawing, and not because they think drawing is interchangeable with either writing or number.

DIFFERENTIATION WITHOUT SCHOOLING

Throughout this chapter I have insisted on the distinctions children construct about the relations between writing and numbers. It is hard to believe that the constraints children impose on the systems or the precocious differentiation is an outcome of formal instruction. Most educators in nursery schools or kindergartens tend on the contrary to push in the opposite direction. Based on a very generalized assumption that drawing is easier and more primitive than writing and number notation, toddlers are usually encouraged to draw rather than to write or use numerals. Even when they play with letters, teachers accept and encourage the use of drawings. Despite this, children develop a tremendous sensitivity to the differences in graphic materials "simply by having plenty of graphic materials around to look at" (Gibson & Levin, 1975, p. 239). The necessity of exposure to written material for this discriminative learning to occur was apparent in the results obtained by Lavine (1972) when comparing two groups of children in Yucatan, Mexico. One was from a city enjoying a reasonable level of technological advancement (Merida) and the other was from a remote rural village where reading materials were very rare. Cultural setting proved to be at least as significant a variable as age. Children growing up in a rural environment "were by no means as knowledgeable about writing" (Gibson & Levin, 1975, p. 239) as those growing up in a city. However, "children from both environments distinguished pictures from writing at three years" (p. 239). A way to tease apart the influence of formal schooling from that of environmental exposure is by looking at illiterate adults' views on the relation between writing and numbers. This could be enlightening as to the source of children's early differentiation.

If we assume that the role of environmental notations and social interactions with notational artifacts is an important source of knowledge for toddlers and preschoolers, it is reasonable to explore what the effect of a similar environment would be on adults. Ferreiro (1983) carried out a study with 58 illiterate adults (31 men, 27 women) from Mexico to gain further insights into the knowledge illiterate adults have about writing. The adults participated in a number of tasks similar to those used with children: interpretation of written sentences, interpretation of short texts, sorting of cards displaying different writings, interpretation of reading and writing acts. The last two tasks are particularly relevant to discovering the views that illiterate adults have about the relation between writing and numbers. The purpose of the card sorting with the adults was to discover the criteria they use for defining the territory of writing. The purpose of the last task was to explore the physical acts that illiterate adults perceive as manifestations of people reading. Literate people are barely conscious of the movements and posture involved in the act of reading and writing, but these may function as relevant cues for illiterates.

Participants were asked to observe different actions undertaken by the interviewer and to say whether they believed she was reading. For example, the experimenter looked at a newspaper while moving pages but without pronouncing a word, or looked at a piece of paper and said a phone number in a loud voice pronouncing aloud each number in turn. A significant number of participants considered certain behaviors to be reading but others not. Most agreed that silent reading was reading and explained it using expressions such as 'you are reading in your thought,' 'in your mind.' But 40% of the participants refused to accept that saying number-names was reading. For them, the interviewer was *diciendo los numeros* 'saying numbers,' *viendo los numeros* 'looking at numbers,' or *contando los numeros* 'counting numbers,' but not reading. Numerals are not legible, they are not for reading; reading is used for defining the activity performed on letters that produces verbal utterances that are not number-words. For saying aloud phone numbers, the percentage of rejection was 39%. (These results are in line with those obtained for the sorting task in which 59% of the participants rejected a card containing '4' as good for reading and 48% rejected a card containing '193'). Participants were able to interpret the numerals (they said *it is four*), but they rejected that an act of reading was performed on numerals. Nonetheless, 100% of the participants accepted that *writing* numerals was an act of writing. Writing was perceived as being the most general activity, almost synonymous with leaving traces, be they numerals or letters, whereas reading was identified as a special-purpose activity related to linguistic utterances and performed on certain kinds of objects. Note that this is also the popular view and the one generally accepted in psychology. When psychologists speak about reading, it is usually assumed that they are referring to reading "letters." And, if numerals are involved, then it is usually clearly stated. Moreover, as pointed out at the beginning of the chapter, Munn and others also referred to reading and counting as the most transparent way of distinguishing between activities performed with letters and activities performed with numerals. It becomes evident that this association between certain notational marks and a certain activity may be the basis for one of the explanations for early differentiation between notational systems.

SOURCES OF EARLY DIFFERENTIATION

Very young children are sensitive to the differences between notational systems. Preschoolers can sort out written texts, numerals, and drawings in accordance with the different constraints operating on each system. Slightly older children are able purposely to violate the rules they have imposed on these systems when asked to write words and numbers that do not exist, and they adapt the features of the different notational systems to their representational needs. What is the origin of this sensitivity? Karmiloff-Smith argued that the distinctions between systems introduced in recent evolutionary time capitalized on distinctions particularly relevant to human attention and production mechanisms such as sequentiality, directionality, iconicity, and periodicity of movement: "Infants faced with various types of notational input would have a head start for attending to them differentially because their minds are structured such that sequentiality, directionality, iconicity, periodicity of movement are relevant to them" (Karmiloff-Smith 1992, p. 148). The problem, however, is that it is not very easy to distinguish between writing and number notation in these terms. In general, trying to explain differences between letters and numerals in terms of geometrical or topological features is an almost impossible task. There are no more symmetric letters than symmetric numerals, or more curvilinear letters than curvilinear numerals, and so on. Rather, there are exemplars of all of them in each notational system. Besides, there are multiple relations between forms and functions; the same notational forms may serve different purposes and fulfil different functions. The history of writing is full of examples of people that have used the same signs for writing and number notation (among them the Sumerians, the Hebrews, and the Greeks; see chap. 2). Neither can differentiation be explained either as a result of schooling; rather, as seen when discussing illiterate adults' ideas about letters and numerals, it is attained before and even without formal instruction. So, what explains the apparent universal early differentiation between writing and number notation? So far I have insisted on the facilitating role of natural contexts of use and on the activities yielded by each notational system as the main explicatory factors for differentiation. Nevertheless, remember that research on infancy demonstrates infants' capacity to discriminate and operate on small numerosities. Indeed, there appears to be an inborn sense that guides infants to attend to numerically relevant input. On the basis of this bias, children are able to map talk, gestures, and movement to what they perceive as numerical displays. Neuropsychological findings from brain damaged patients provide further evidence that biology might be a contributing factor supporting a differentiation between systems.

Brain lesions can destroy the most brilliant talents and provoke dramatic consequences in the lives of people who have suffered them; they serve, however, as *natural experiments* for studying the relations between abilities. Not only brain damage but also many disorders of genetic origin and other pathological states provide tools for formulating and testing hypotheses about possible relations between domains. For instance, when looking at the difficulty mentally retarded Down's syndrome children have in learning to use language rapidly or appropriately, the hypothesis of a necessary relation between general intelligence and language development may be advanced. But this hypothesis will have to be revised when confronted with children suffering from William's syndrome. These children have mastery of many syntactic constructions (passives, comparatives, and so on) whose acquisition is apparently independent of the ability to perform seriations, classifications, and the other cognitive tasks that these children consistently fail. The contrasting pictures of the relation between language and intelligence that emerge when comparing Down's syndrome children with William's syndrome children shows that selective specific impairments are the most revealing of the division of labor that characterizes the functioning of the brain.

Indeed, the key tool for evaluating the relations between mental abilities is that of *dissociation*, the preservation of one mental ability despite the loss of another. Remember Oliver Sacks' book *The Man Who Mistook His Wife for a Hat*? After suffering a cerebral lesion that affected his visual system, the eponymous man was unable to recognize even the most familiar faces, although he was able to identify people by their smell, voice, or touch, and his intelligence was intact. This man shows a *dissociation* between the preserved capacity to identify by smell/voice/touch and the affected capacity of face recognition. Interpreted by neuropsychologists, this would *hint* at a nonobligatory relation between these abilities and also at the possibility of different locations for the neuronal networks that handle these abilities in the brain. This is somewhat of an oversimplification for the sake of clarity; neuropsychologists must be very careful to consider other possible interpretations of apparent dissociation that might be related to differing difficulty of a task or with learned strategies after a certain injury has occurred. Having ruled out the other interpretations, however, *dissociation* is a reliable clue as to the links between abilities and cerebral localization.

It is even more reliable when there is a *double dissociation*, which means that a dissociation present in one patient is found in another patient but in a reverse sense. Steven Anderson, Antonio Damasio, and Hanna Damasio, for example, described a patient who, after a minuscule lesion that destroyed part of her left premotor cortex, could not read words or letters but could read Arabic numerals. When she was asked to write her name or the word *dog*, she could only produce scribbles. But she had no problem with reading or writing numerals (Anderson, A. Damasio, & H. Damasio, 1990). Being unable to read aloud letters and/or words while being able to read aloud numerals is actually an old finding in neuropsychology. Indeed, one of the first reports was made by Déjérine (1892). Until 1993, however, there was no evidence of the reverse pattern—that is, patients able to read aloud letters/and words but not numerals. In 1993, Lisa Cipolotti reported a case of a patient who had no problem reading letters (or number names written in alphabetic writing) but could not read aloud multidigit Hindu-Arabic numerals (Cipolotti, 1993; Cipolotti, Warrington, & Butterworth, 1995). Taken together, the two types of patient show a *double dissociation*, at least for multidigit numbers. That is, as a result of brain injury, there can be a loss of the ability to read and write alphabetic material but preserved ability to read numerals, and the reverse, loss of ability to read and write numerals but preserved ability to read alphabetic materials. This means that the reading mechanisms triggered by written words are supported by neural networks that can be distinguished (and therefore selectively damaged) from those that handle the reading of numerals. Cases of *double dissociation* are considered a strong indicator of differentiation of the two abilities—lack of a necessary obligatory link and evidence that each ability is supported by different specialized neural networks. They provide supporting evidence for a biological underpinning of the differentiation observed at a behavioral level.

SO WHERE DOES EARLY DIFFERENTIATION ORIGINATE?

We appear to be equipped at birth with at least two strong biases that channel our attention, one for language relevant input, the other for number-relevant input. Evidence for this is provided by the research on infancy reviewed in previous chapters. Very young infants discriminate linguistic from nonlinguistic noises, have a categorical perception of speech, and distinguish their mother tongue from other languages. Similar precocity was established for number-relevant input discrimination. Thus, if children very early on manage to relate verbal activities to certain forms, and number-related activities to other types of forms, then the way has been paved for a differentiation between the systems. It is evident in the words of very young children when sorting cards how they distinguish between those that are *good for reading* and those that are *good for counting*. Evidence has also been gathered for this primary distinction in illiterate adults who rejected saying numbers aloud as reading.

Obviously, exposure and successive interaction with notational input is *at least* a necessary condition for fulfilling the initial expectancies created by assigning forms to certain activities. If children's expectancy to have *a human voice saying things and moving* when looking at a set of marks is confirmed once and again, it will become reinforced. Formal differentiation is grounded in the activities for which the systems are used. Initial differentiation is only a point of departure that serves to discriminate various types of notational input. With this purpose, the features of notational systems are observed and obeyed, but the referential meaning of elements is not yet understood. Children may know the names of letters and numbers, and they may know how to draw their shapes as well as recognize the valid and invalid combinations, but they still do not know how the systems function to produce messages.

When children are asked to convey a message, however, a different situation emerges. Notations are no longer just problem spaces, or domains of knowledge. Rather, the requirement put children in a situation in which they needed to use notations as referential-communicative tools; they felt the communicative pressure to transmit information. Then, when communication was the target, formal distinctions were relaxed, boundaries between systems were opened; they had to find a way to convey a message. This was when writing was used to show quantitative features, and all kinds of referential hints appeared in writing (chap. 3). This was also the time in which differences in numerosities corresponded with term-to-term devices. Children repeated conventional numerals or strings of letters; exactly what they used was not crucial, the point was to use the features they already commanded to serve their communicative ends. Because of the main characteristics of external representation—permanence and detachment from the notator—children can look again at what they have done and learn from their work. They can learn from their externalized work. This is the effect of the use of analogical representation for the notation of small quantities: After the process of explicitation, children can turn to more hermetic use of conventional numerals. As an outcome of the transition through a process of explicitation, the notational elements become both arbitrary and meaningful according to the rules of the system.

In more mature uses of writing and numbers, the initial differentiation between systems will be overcome and users will use the same notational forms for a diversity of functions. Initial differentiation may serve only as a pivotal point for further functional diversity; this diversity rules the use of notations in daily communicational activities, science, mathematics, and computer writing.

NEW WRITING SPACES OR REDEFINING RELATIONS BETWEEN NOTATIONS

The assumption that different things are used for different activities provides many advantages for the systematic learning of literacy and numeracy. For example, it helps determine what type of notational input to look for in different contexts. Nevertheless, differentiation between systems and correspondence between forms and functions is the rule neither in more mature uses of writing and numbers nor in computer writing spaces. In literate uses of writing and numbers, the same notational forms are used to fulfil different functions and, many times, the same function is fulfilled by forms belonging to different systems (e.g., hierarchical categories can be expressed both by letters and numerals). Indeed, in the daily writing spaces of literate people, the distinctions between notational systems are becoming increasingly blurred.

Jay David Bolter used the expression *writing space* for the surface created by the computer for recording and presenting text together with techniques for organizing writing. The computer writing space resembles and differs from the space of the papyrus scroll, the codex, and the printed book. Certainly in all these spaces, numerals, letters, and images coexist. As expressed by Bolter (1991), "The development of phonetic writing ... did not eliminate pictures altogether from the writing space ... but it did create a dichotomy between image and the phonetic sign.... In electronic writing, pictures, and verbal text belong to the same space, and pictures may cross over and become textual symbols" (p. 72). In the computer space, iconicity and mixture of notational systems is the rule. E-mail addresses contain elements from different notations, tool bars are full of icons whose meanings have became conventionalized, electronic books use pictures and texts in complementary terms, and in chat messages (e.g., the one transcribed in Fig. 5.10), numerals and letters are not only mixed, but numerals are also interpreted in verbal terms.

The place 4 teens 2 talk to teens

u

any 1 want to talk with 14/f

how old r u

FIG. 5.10.   CHAT examples of mixture of notational means.

A mixture of notational forms in the same space does not only occur in electronic writing. Children's literature breaks down the borders between iconicity, numerals, and writing. Children today grow up in literate communities with an increasing diversity and multifunctionality of notational forms. They are confronted with a diversity of notational forms and a diversity of interpretations of the same forms. The initial differentiation between forms and functions may help them to find their way in the notational territories, to learn the meaning of elements in the different contexts of use and the functioning of each system. As in any other domain of development, however, the idea is to become increasingly flexible so as to master a creative use of the multiple functions that each notational system can fulfill.

The following are some key points in this chapter:

- Children begin their notational development with an implicit differentiation of two distinct territories: writing and numbers. They identify letters and numerals as belonging to one or the other, they use different conditions for judging a string of letters to be acceptable than for a string of numerals to be acceptable, and they associate each with different activities.

- Children's recognition of formal features is implicit in their sorting procedures and in the notations they produce. With time, this knowledge becomes more accessible so children can manipulate these features to serve their representational needs. Then, they may turn to writing to represent quantity or to drawing to convey a message.

- Children learn from their own external representations to accept the implicit and arbitrary meaning of notations. Indeed, after a phase of "crossing territories" and using analogical representations, children begin to use single digits for multiplicity, and discard the use of writing for quantity and the use of drawing to convey either a verbal or a numerical message. It is only among those children who show a clear functional differentiation between systems that researchers have found explicit manipulation of the referents of numerals and letters. Only these children suggested silent letters as nonletters or very *big* numbers as nonnumbers.

- Neuropsychological findings in brain damaged patients support the idea that specialized neuronal circuits underlie the differentiation between the reading and writing of alphabetic material and the reading and writing of numerals.

The last three chapters have been devoted to tracing the development of children's ideas about writing, numbers, and their relations. Despite the specificity of each development, there is a common developmental principle: Children notice the notational environment from very early on and they use this socially transmitted knowledge in unconventional ways as they come to understand its functioning. Up till now, I have been analyzing how children interact with notational systems in order to learn about them. The next and last chapters move on to discussing the consequences that learning to write has on the learners. It is a very complex issue indeed, because learning to write never comes alone, but always as part of institutional and social literacy.

6

The Effect of Writing
on Children and Grown-ups
Once It Has Been Learned

Psychologists have demonstrated that if native Chinese speakers are asked to say a sentence "bit by bit," they cut the sentence into syllables. Hebrew speakers, even literate adults, do the same to words but not to sentences: They cut words into syllables but sentences will be broken down into parts of speech or words. Yet, this form of segmenting words into syllables would rarely occur to an educated English speaker, who would probably rather segment words into individual sounds. The point is that the writing system people learn seems to be a determining factor in the way they analyze language. As discussed in the introduction, even infants are able to discriminate speech sounds and to combine them to form words. Long before learning to write, toddlers have already acquired the basic morphology and syntax of their language (Jusczyk, 1997; Mehler & Dupoux, 1990). But this knowledge that infants and toddlers have is implicit. As children interact with the specific characteristics of writing, this implicit knowledge undergoes a process of reorganization: It becomes increasingly accessible and is shaped by the specific features of the writing systems to which the children are exposed. Thus, people who become literate in different writing systems develop different segmentation abilities.

Learning to write with an alphabetic system seems to be critical for the development of an awareness of the individual sounds that make up a word, an ability that people who have been educated in nonalphabetic writing systems have more difficulty in acquiring. In addition to developing a particular awareness to the sound structure of language (i.e., a phonological awareness), there is increasing evidence that learning to spell with an alphabetic system facilitates an awareness of the internal structure of words (i.e., morphology)—for example, the extent to which words contain an /s/ for plural marking or an /ed/ for marking the past tense. Before learning to spell, children are barely aware of the common grammatical suffix included in *saved, played,* and *painted,* even though they can use all these verbs in the past tense when required. After a child learns to spell, grammatical markers have a graphic support that makes them more visible and, as a consequence, the internal structure of words becomes more accessible.

The process of becoming literate also seems to determine children's conception of words. Before learning to write, children find it difficult to accept that a word such as *the* or *a* is just as much a word as *girl* or *jumping*; they tend to believe that only words having independent meaning are "real" words and that the others do not count as words. Thus, when preliterate children are asked to count words in a sentence, they will usually count only content words like nouns, verbs, and adjectives, but not prepositions or conjunctions. Obviously, children include various kinds of words in their daily language use, but only after learning to write do they seem "to see" these words. Writing provides a graphic representation that makes the various categories of words more visible. In our writing system, words—whatever their category—are written as strings of letters with blanks on both sides (typically). This feature helps children access the internal structure of sentences and the status of any category of word as word.

In sum, children's implicit knowledge of the sound structure of language, the internal structure of words, and the relations between words all interact with the particular features of the writing system and become more explicit in a way that is shaped by the particular features of the writing system. Three features of alphabetic writing are particularly important in this process of growing awareness: (a) Letters in alphabetic writing graphically represent the sounds in a word, (b) grammatical suffixes are spelled in the same way independently of context and pronunciation, and (c) strings of letters separated by blanks represent words, irrespective of their category. The sound structure of words, the presence of grammatical suffixes, and the idea of what a word is are all very abstract notions, but the fact that such notions are graphically represented facilitates their recognition. In turn, this growing awareness of phonology and morphology must have consequences in the way people perceive and conceive of language. This brings up the claim that permeates the whole book: Knowledge of a particular domain is affected by learning the notational system of that domain.

But, is that all there is to the effect of literacy—an increasing awareness of the different levels of language shaped by the features of the writing system?

WRITING AND LANGUAGE

Alphabetical systems represent phonological (rather than semantic) units as the basic components of the writing system (Coulmas, 1990). In some languages, the links between the phonological units and the graphic units of the writing system (i.e., the letters) are more systematic, or *transparent,* than in others. For example, in English, the letter A corresponds to very different sounds when it appears in the words *at, car, pear, fear,* or *day.* But, in Spanish, the same letter A sounds the same in whichever word it appears. Thus, Spanish is said to have a more *transparent* orthography than English. It is in transparent orthographies where the link between phonology and alphabetic writing is most clearly seen. But, even in transparent orthographies, it cannot be said that the sounds of speech are directly transcribed in the orthography. If this were the case, there would be different spellings for different pronunciations and for every dialect, which is far from the case. With the exception of the initial stages of Greek alphabetic writing, during which dialects and changes in pronunciation were reflected in different spellings (see chap. 1), languages undergo different rates of change that are not reflected in their respective orthographies. Contemporary English spelling is based for the most part on that of the 15th century, but pronunciation has changed considerably since then, especially that of long vowels and diphthongs. The extensive change in the pronunciation of vowels, known as the Great Vowel Shift, which changed the whole vowel system of London English (e.g., /i:/ and /u:/ became dipthongized to /ai/ as in *bide* and /au/ as in *house*), left no trace in English spelling (Aronoff, 1994). The differing rates of change in the evolution of pronunciation and that of orthography will come as no surprise if one stops viewing writing as a reflection of speech and instead considers them as two systems each with its own dynamic (Vacheck, 1989).

   It is clear, however, that alphabetic systems do not relate to language only through the links between letters and sounds. Orthographies also directly reflect morphology (Chomsky & Halle, 1968; Blanche-Benveniste & Chervel, 1970). Thus, *helped* and *frightened* have an identically spelt *ed* ending despite their differing sounds, /t/ and /d/, respectively. Endings such as *ed* or *ing* have morphological meaning, as does the *s* on the end of nouns.

(continued)

These observations should convince anyone of the need to abandon the idea that alphabetic writing is a recording or transcription of spoken language. As Aronoff claimed (1994), orthography is a mnemonic device "for invoking rather than representing or recording language" (p. 71). Orthographies are tools that use different means of "conjuring up" instantiations of the reader's language. One of the means of conjuring up language is by writing lexical items in a constant way at the expense of letter-to-sound correspondence. In this way, despite differences in pronunciation, people can call on their lexical knowledge and interpret the meaning simply by looking at written words. This characterization of orthography is particularly suitable for English.

In addition to phonological and morphological information, for text management alphabetic orthographies include a system of punctuation to express supra-segmental, syntactic, semantic and pragmatic information in the form of nonalphanumeric devices (Nunberg, 1990). Punctuation is taken here in its broadest sense, including emphasis markers, conventions for word separation (i.e., blank spaces whose function is to mark the boundaries of these lexical items), and text layout (including blanks at the beginning and end of a line as well as those that produce paragraphs; Catach, 1989; Parkes, 1992). This rather heterogeneous set constitutes a notational system that complements the information provided by the alphabetic system.

There may be two different answers to this question. The first would claim that literacy has consequences far beyond the domain of language, whereas the second would be much more conservative as to a generalized effect of learning to write. According to the first view, literacy influences not only human perception and conception of language but transforms human life itself and brings about a qualitative change in human evolution. Literacy both amplifies cognitive powers and interpretational capacities (Bruner, 1966; Cole & Griffin, 1981; Goody, 1977; Olson, 1994; Serpell, 1993) and provides the basis for "theory building," a way of knowing qualitatively different from other preliterate ways of knowing (Donald, 1991). Within this view, however, it remains unclear whether it is the acquisition of the "techniques" of reading and writing as such that have these effects, or whether it is the social practices within which writing is learned, and the social meaning of writing that are responsible for these crucial consequences. This question, however, may well be unanswerable. The technological and ideological aspects of literacy are intertwined in such a way that it is difficult to evaluate their respective roles in the process and consequences of learning.

The second view warns against generalizing to other cognitive domains the effect of learning to read. This view is supported by a number of cases found in clinical experience showing that learning to write has no effect at all on general intelligence, or on specific cognitive abilities. For example, children who are affected by severe mental retardation may become fluent readers within a few months of starting school and without special teaching (Cossu, 1997, p. 246), but the acquired ability does not provoke any change in their general level of intelligence. This evidence forces serious reconsideration of the role of learning to write on cognition and language.

There are then two contradictory views as to the effects of writing as well as to the many facets, processes, and factors involved in literacy. It is not an easy task to isolate the effect of learning to write on children and grown-ups because literacy does not come alone; it is embedded in a net of social practices and supported on an ideological base. On the other hand, there is evidence as to the impenetrability of cognition to the effect of literacy. Given the conflicting panorama, this chapter analyzes each view separately, as far as that is possible. It first briefly reviews some of the purported effects of writing on perceiving language, and then considers the effects of writing beyond language. To that purpose, this chapter features a number of true stories—that is, stories of real people whose lives have been changed by literacy. I believe that in this way I can best illustrate the manner in which the technology of writing adapts to the social context, and how the personal history of individuals may have different outcomes despite acquiring the same technology. The third part of this chapter focuses on the biological aspect of literacy so as to illustrate the limitations of learning to write.

THE EFFECTS OF WRITING ON LANGUAGE

Phonological Awareness

For many years, educators and psychologists were convinced that a prerequisite for making sense of the alphabetical principle was learning to segment words explicitly, by which they meant phonemic segmentation, that is, the ability to detect the constituent phonemes of a word (Mattingly, 1972).[31] In the main, psychologists highlighted the importance of phonemic awareness for learning to

---

[31]The bulk of research on phonological awareness flourished after the publication of Chomsky and Halle's (1968) monumental study on the phonology of English. In this work, English orthography is described as reflecting the deep structure of English. Although highly speculative, it was then that the question was turned upside down. Instead of assuming that children first had to learn orthography to discover the deep structure of English (if indeed it is represented by orthography), psychologists began to work on the assumption that speakers must first become aware of the deep structure to gain access to orthography.

read but also stressed it as necessary for correct spelling (see Adams, 1991, for a complete review). This ability was supposed to be fully developed at age 6, when most children could successfully put together the segments provided by the investigator to form a word (e.g., the investigator said /c/.../a/.../t/ and the child *cat*), break the initial phoneme off a word and say what was left (e.g., the investigator said *feel* and the child *eel*), or find which word was different in a list presented to them (e.g., *pig, hill, pin*). Psychologists developed a diversity of creative tasks to explore phonemic awareness under the general supposition that this awareness is attained independently of learning to write through a process of maturation. Because most psychological studies showed a high correlation between phonemic awareness and learning to read (Goswami & Bryant, 1990), educators went to great lengths to improve children's phonemic awareness so that they would be better prepared when it came to learning how to read and write.[32] The conviction that phonemic awareness represents a maturational ability that develops with age and can be improved through training has remained strong, despite an increasing body of evidence against it.

The first strong evidence against this conviction was, in my view, a 1979 paper by José Morais and collaborators (Morais, Cary, Alegria, & Bertelson, 1979) in which they showed that illiterate adults could not perform most of the typical segmentation tasks. But, 6 or 7 months after learning to read, they could perform the tasks (Bertelson, Cary, & Alegria, 1986). If this is the case, phonemic awareness cannot be said to be a *maturational* ability; it does not develop with age, but rather requires learning to read with an alphabetic system. So phonemic awareness would be a consequence of literacy and not a prerequisite. Some forms of speech manipulation, such as rhyme recognition (recognizing that the sound of *mice* is similar to *ice*) and syllable segmentation (separating *pupil* into *pu#pil*), may develop spontaneously. Phonemic awareness, on the other hand, requires the intervention of the alphabetic system to make language visible at the phonemic level, altering children's perception of spoken language (Ehri, 1984, 1993; Scholes, 1993; Treiman, 1992; Treiman & Baron, 1981).

In addition, the kind of writing system that people learn influences phonemic awareness. Users of Chinese script tend to segment sentences into syllables (Read, Zhang, Nie, & Ding, 1986) instead of words. Further evidence comes from a group of researchers from the All India Institute of Speech and Hearing, who found that, in the early stages of acquisition of a semi-syllabic Indian writ-

---

[32]Kindergarten and preschool teachers were encouraged to play different games to enhance this "natural" development. For example, children were invited to build trains with one wagon for each sound and then add or delete wagons according to similar manipulations performed on the word, to walk one step "for each sound in your name" and then to compare who had gone furthest, to tap on a table with a wooden stick the number of phonemes in each syllable, and so on.

ing system, children performed well in rhyme recognition, but very poorly in phonemic awareness tasks, even after having learned to write. In contrast, Indian children who had also learned to write in English, that is children who were biliterate, performed equally well in both tasks (Prakash, Rekha, Nigam, & Karanth, 1993). Although Mann (1986) showed that Japanese children who had not been exposed to alphabetic writing could successfully perform phonemic segmentation tasks, they could only do so by the time they entered the fourth grade, due perhaps to an awareness of some phonemic features of Japanese writing (Morais, 1991).

One purpose of the comparative Hebrew/Spanish study (Tolchinsky & Teberosky, 1998), already discussed at length in chapter 3, was to explore the effect of writing system on word segmentation. Recall that Hebrew- and Spanish-speaking children from preschool through second grade were asked to write and to segment orally a number of words. For the writing task, a number of cognates was dictated (words that sound and mean the same in the two languages) and for the segmentation task they were asked to segment these words orally. We proceeded in this way: First, we showed them a picture, for example, a picture of a piece of chocolate, and asked them to say what they could see in the picture (no child was wrong, they all said *chocolate*). Then we asked them to say it again, but "bit by bit." Note that this was strictly a metalinguistic task: The children were required to imagine the word, analyze it into parts, and then say aloud the parts, whatever they were. They were required to work on an internal representation offline, after having said aloud the word. This ability to analyze words is also required to write words, especially if they are words the children are not familiar with and whose written form they have not memorized. This study had three goals: first, to see whether the development of writing is similar in the two languages; second, to see whether the segmentation of words is influenced by the different languages and writing systems; and third, to see whether being able to segment words explicitly is a prerequisite for writing the same words successfully.

As we mentioned in chapter 3, prior to formal instruction, preschoolers in both language groups displayed knowledge of the respective writing systems. Although they were not able to write in a conventional way, they did use the letters of the respective scripts. Later, when they started looking for some sort of letter-to-sound correspondence, the children made use of the orthographic options that were available in each language. The Hebrew-speaking children used consonants, whereas the Spanish-speaking children mainly used vowels. Most of the first graders and all of the second graders attained writing competence in both languages according to the conventions of their respective writing systems. But, did this script-specific knowledge affect their segmentation behavior?

In order to analyze the way in which children segment words, a scale measuring the unit of pronunciation was constructed. Those cases in which children were not able to analyze the words at all were assigned to this scale's lowest level. When they were asked to say the word again "bit by bit," they said it in one breath, without producing any pause between parts of the word (e.g., /salami/). The cases in which the children said the word in parts (e.g., /soko/ /late/) were assigned to the next level. Those cases in which the children segmented the words into syllables (e.g.,#so# #ko# #late#; sa#la#mi) were assigned to a higher point on the scale. Finally, the cases in which children were able to pronounce all the phonemes in the word (e.g., /s/ /o/ /k/ /o/ /l/ /a/ /t/) were assigned to the highest point on the scale. The distribution of the children's segmentation behavior according to this scale showed a very interesting path. Two findings were common to the two languages: the scarcity of phonemic segmentation and the popularity of syllabic segmentation. Very few children managed to say the all phonemes[33] in the word correctly: in the Spanish group, only one first grader and three second graders, and in the Hebrew group, only three second graders. Breaking the words up into syllables, however, was the most popular segmentation behavior in preschool and first grade in both languages, although significantly more popular in Spanish. The popularity of syllabic segmentation tended to decrease with grade, but even in the second grade it was employed by 35% of the Spanish-speaking children.

In What Ways Did the Two Languages Differ?

A large number of Spanish speakers, mainly first graders, did something we had not even considered when we constructed the scale for analyzing segmentation: instead of pronouncing the components of the word in one way or another, they said the names of the letters used for writing the word. That is, the children used the names of the letters to say the sounds of the words "bit by bit." We interpret this behavior to mean that they handled the sound structure of the spoken word through the imagined written word. However, this form of handling the segmentation task did not occur with the Hebrew-speaking children. Instead, another form of response occurred that was exclusive to Hebrew: children attempted to pronounce consonants in isolation. No Spanish speaker did anything similar. In sum, Spanish-speaking children provided a response, oral spelling, that was almost completely absent from the Hebrew speakers' repertoire of

---

[33]Phonemes are unpronounceable in isolation. What was meant by exhaustive segmentation in the study was that children would pause between subsyllabic units like /s/ /a/ /l/ /a/ /m/ /i/, but clearly making a sort of hissing sound to pronounce the consonants.

responses, whereas Hebrew-speaking children produced segmentation, pronunciation of consonants, that was almost completely absent from the Spanish speakers' repertoire of segmentation.

Looking at the development of both writing and segmentation, the interpretation of the general picture ran as follows. In preschool, when children's writing is still formally constrained or children use letters without conventional value—the syllable is the preferred unit of segmentation in both languages. This preference reflects not only the phonetic-acoustic similarities between the two languages but also the fact that syllables can be said in isolation; they are not an abstraction like phonemes are, therefore they function as a more natural unit of segmentation (Mehler et al., 1984; Treiman & Zukowski, 1988). At this level, both writing and segmentation are very similar in the two languages.

By first grade, however, to the extent that children become literate in the two languages, the discrepancies between the two groups increase, Spanish-speaking children resort to oral spelling and Hebrew-speaking children attempt to isolate consonants. Interestingly, the names of the letters is social knowledge and not so much school knowledge. This means that people tend to name the letters when they refer to them or if they need to spell something but, as a rule in school, teachers tend to sound words out rather than use the names of the letters (e.g., they say /s/ for S, not "la ese"). In the case of vowels, however, the sound coincides with the name of the letter, providing a strong clue for analyzing the word.

The situation is different in Hebrew. The names of the consonants do not provide strong clues for sounds (e.g., samex for /s/) and the names of the diacritics used for representing vowels is a rather specialized knowledge, rarely employed in conversations about writing. It seems that the features of the respective scripts influence the way people speak about the elements of writing and this in turn influences children's way of segmenting words. As to the fact that Hebrew-speaking children pronounce consonants in isolation, this finding is related to the role of consonant roots in Hebrew and the features of Hebrew writing. It could be argued that the script is mirroring the morphological structure of Hebrew and it influences children's segmentation behavior via this mirroring.

This picture of the development of word segmentation and word writing in Hebrew and Spanish illustrates the way in which writing systems shape native linguistic intuitions. Children approach the learning process with similar segmentation abilities but, as they become literate in their respective writing systems, scripts reinforce certain features of their segmentation abilities while neglecting and substituting others. Social knowledge, in particular the way people talk about the elements of writing, also has an important role in this development. In the case of Spanish, syllabic segmentation is increasingly substituted by letter naming for handling the sound structure of words. In the case of Hebrew, syllabic segmentation is instead diminished as children attempt to isolate consonants.

What about the relation between phonemic awareness and writing? In the context of the study, children did not *spontaneously* attain exhaustive phonemic segmentation in Spanish or in Hebrew. However, they could write all the words successfully. Being able to segment into phonemes in the context of a metalinguistic task was not a condition for knowing how to use this ability for writing words. Analyzing words for writing is a different task than analyzing words for looking at their components. In the context of a writing task, segmentation is a means to an end and is supported by the task itself; aural segmentation is monitored by letter writing. Although they are saying the parts of the word, they are writing the letters. But in the segmentation task, everything happens in their head without the help of a graphic support (Van Bon & Duighuisen, 1995). So, two conclusions can be drawn from these findings. First, knowing how to write in an alphabetic system does not provoke spontaneous use of phonemic segmentation for analyzing words; rather, words are viewed through the elements and features of the writing system itself. Second, phonemic segmentation, as measured by strictly metalinguistic tasks, is not a requirement for writing alphabetically.

Morphological Awareness

As mentioned earlier, alphabetic systems also represent morphological units and certain spelling decisions are grounded in morphology rather than phonology. In English, for example, the words *box* and *socks* end with the same consonantal cluster, but *box* is written with a final *x* whereas *socks* is written with a final *s*. The reason for this difference is not phonetic but morphologic because, being plural, *socks* must end with an *s*. In the case of pairs of words such as *medicine* and *medical*, their similar spelling can be explained by the fact that they share the same stem, although the *c* in *medicine* is pronounced /c/ and in *medical* it is pronounced /k/.

If words are spelled in a certain way for morphological rather than for phonetic reasons, do children need to be aware of the morphological marking of words in order to spell them correctly? Or does children's awareness of the morphological marking result from learning the written representation of morphology? The link between spelling and morphology is only a relatively recent concern in the study of children's writing and no definitive answers have as yet been found.

Nunes et al. (1997) followed schoolchildren for a 3-year period, testing at intervals their spelling of the *ed* past tense suffix of regular verbs (e.g., kissed), irregular verbs whose endings are spelled phonetically (e.g., felt), and nonverbs with phonetically similar endings (e.g., belt). They proposed a four-stage developmental model in which children are first unaware of the grammatical function of the verb suffix, then overgeneralize its use to other categories, including nonverbs with phonetically similar endings, then restrict its use to the regular and irregular verbs, and finally achieve conventional spelling only when required for regular verbs. They found that an increasing command of spelling improved children's morphological awareness, and this in turn improved children's spelling.

Levin, Ravid, and Rapaport (1997) arrived at similar conclusions in a study with a longitudinal design that examined Hebrew children's invented spelling and morphological knowledge, from kindergarten to first grade. These authors found that spoken morphology and writing were correlated concurrently in both kindergarten and in first grade, and predictively from kindergarten to first grade. Although different explanations might be advanced for this finding, the authors insist on the role of orthography: "Since orthography reflects morphological structures, becoming aware of spelling can enhance morphological awareness" (Levin et al., 1997, p. 21).

Although much more work is needed, the evidence gathered to date indicates that, as was the case for phonological awareness, orthography functions as a tangible means of handling grammatical relations. Therefore, *awareness* of these relations may be a consequence of literacy.

Judgments of Grammaticality

Learning to write may not only alter phonetic and morphological intuitions, but also shape intuitive judgments of grammaticality. In 1957, Noam Chomsky insisted that every speaker of English recognized the differences between sentences that were grammatical and those that are not. The following two sentences, probably the most quoted in the linguistic literature, are equally absurd. Nevertheless, according to Chomsky, English speakers will undoubtedly recognize that the first is well-formed and the second is just absurd:

> *Colorless green ideas sleep furiously*
>
> *Furiously sleep ideas green colorless*

Some years later, Lila Gleitman (1970) admitted that if the average taxi driver were asked, "Is the following a grammatical sentence in your dialect: Colorless green ideas sleep furiously?", the reply would probably be one that no one would dare set down in print, but surely it would not throw any light on the driver's linguistic intuitions.

Many studies in linguistics during the 1970s were based on the naïve native speaker's purported capacity to judge whether sentences were grammatically well-formed and semantically coherent (L. R. Gleitman & H. Gleitman, 1979). After a period of optimism, linguists realized that the issue was more complex than expected. Quite a few well-educated adults were ready to accept that sequences as bizarre as *I saw a fragile of* were grammatical (Hill, quoted in L. R. Gleitman & H. Gleitman, 1979). However, very young children demonstrated that they were able to perceive the difference between grammatical and nongrammatical sequences. Shipley, Smith, and Gleitman (1969) asked mothers to present commands to their children that varied in structure but not in meaning. For example, "Talk telephone!" and "Talk on the telephone!" These researchers found that children responded most readily to well-formed commands and less readily to the rudimentary forms that they themselves used in their speech.

Over the years, accumulating evidence shows that the acquisition of grammatical judgment is a gradual process with certain qualitative shifts. Children between ages 2 and 3 base their judgments on comprehension: If they understand a sequence, then they accept it as grammatical. Between ages 4 and 5, children base their judgment on semantic reasoning; they reject a sequence as well-formed if they find something bizarre in the content. Only after age 6 are children capable of supporting their judgment on grammatical reasoning and then differentiating between those sentences that are understood, those that are not true, and those that are ill-formed. These findings are explained in terms of the development of metalinguistic ability considered as a developmental capacity—knowledge that grows with age (Tunmer, Pratt, & Harriman, 1984).

The group of researchers from the All India Institute of Speech and Hearing were also interested in issues of grammaticality. They were convinced that children's increasing ability to rely on syntactic structure for classifying sequences as grammatical might not be an ability that simply grows with age. This was due to the fact that they had also found *adults* with difficulties similar to those encountered by children; the adults, however, were illiterate. On this basis, they formulated the hypothesis that judgments of grammaticality might be related to literacy, and not just to age. Karanth and his associates (Karanth & Suchitra, 1993) performed a study among 100 Kannada-speaking adults, 67 literate and 33 illiterate, in the city of Mysore, South India. Kannada is a widely spoken Indian language, prevalent in Southern India. They were particularly interested in obtaining a measure of the syntactic competence of children and adults and they used a standardized test for that purpose. Among the tasks in the test, there was one that required the participants to judge the grammaticality of sentences that were orally presented. The literate adults performed satisfactorily, with no one performing at chance level. Among the illiterate adults, however, quite a few could not perform the task or responded indiscriminately. The rest performed uniformly poorly in the different categories of the test. The study was replicated in Hindi, an Indian language prevalent in Northern India, in a city located 2,000 miles from Mysore. The results were identical: The difference between literate and illiterate adults was dramatic. The findings of these and other related studies provide strong evidence that the metalinguistic ability to deal with the grammatical form of sentences might well be an outcome of learning to write and not a developmental acquisition.

Conceptualization of Words

People do not speak "in words"; only teachers when dictating to their pupils are very careful to pronounce each word in a sentence separately. In normal speech, words are joined in intonational phrases and these rarely coincide with words (Nespor & Vogel, 1986). Nevertheless, there is no doubt that children have an implicit knowledge of words. Without this knowledge they would be unable to combine words to produce different utterances, something children do from very early on. Following are four examples of utterances produced by a Catalan child age 2 years, 2 months (Serra, Serrat, Solé, Bel, & Aparici, 2000):

1. *Este un xino* 'This a chinese'
2. *Pol aquí* 'Pol here'
3. *Aquest un xino* 'That a chinese'
4. *Una coseta aquí* 'A little thing here'

Note that the word *xino* 'Chinese' and the word *aquí* 'here' appear in different combinations, The first time (1) preceded by *este* 'this' and the second time (3) by *aquest* 'that.' Similarly, the first time the word *aquí* 'here' appears (2), it is preceded by Pol (a proper name); the second time it appears (4), it is preceded by *Una coseta* 'a little thing.' If the child were not able to single out words, then he would not have been able to use the same word in different positions.

At the same age, children consistently produce both open-class or content words like *girl, house, nice, eat,* and closed-class or function words like *a, to, in, the* in different contexts and in multiple combinations (Bottari, Cipriani, & Chilosi, 1993/1994; Jakubowicz, 1997). Nevertheless, when young children are questioned explicitly about words, not every lexical item counts for them as a word. If asked directly whether *house* is a word, they will respond without hesitation but will be reluctant to say that *the* is a word. Ioanna Berthoud-Papandropoulou (1980) showed that before age 6, most children "confuse" content with form so *strawberry* is said to be a short word and *train* is said to be a long word. Whereas the researcher is focusing on the acoustic length, children base their answer on the size of the referent. It is not until about age 6 that children consider both open-class and closed-class items as words. A similar process was found when children were asked to count the words in a given sentence. The youngest children (4-years-old) focused on the situation being described in the sentence. For a sentence such as *Six children play*, they said it contained six words. Five-year-olds divided it into constituents so that the same sentence was considered to have two words (i.e., *there are six children* and *they play*). It is only after age 6 or 7 that children count both function and content items as words. These findings are in line with those reported by Karpova (1955) in a seminal study in Russian, and by E. V. Clark (1978) and Tunmer, Bowey, and Grieve (1983) in English. Based on these findings, researchers concluded that children younger than age 6 are not able to focus on linguistic form, thus, only elements with independent meaning, such as content-words, are viewed as words. That is, before age 6, children do not identify words as linguistic elements.

Karmiloff-Smith (1992) argued, however, that the kind of questioning used by researchers on children's conceptualization of words is misleading as to the state of children's knowledge. She claimed that this questioning is overly metalinguistic and, therefore, not really suitable for determining young children's knowledge about words. Based on her model of psychological development (see chap. 5), she predicted that there must be a level of representation between the implicit knowledge children show in their current use of language and the level of explicit knowledge about words that is required to answer the metalinguistic questioning about words (Karmiloff-Smith, Grant, Sims, Jones, & Cuckle, 1996). This intermediate level would be accessible to certain tasks outside the normal use of language but not yet to metalinguistic explanations. Karmiloff-Smith tested this prediction in a study in which she compared the performance of 3- to 7-year-olds on two tasks. In one task, children had to help a teddy bear find out what counts as a word. It was a strictly metalinguistic task; children had to reflect on an utterance after it had been produced. In the other task, children had to listen to a story in which the narrator paused repeatedly on open-class or closed-class vocabulary elements and they were asked to repeat "the last word" said by the narrator. This task was much closer to online normal language use and required less reflection on the part of the children. Results showed that some of the children as young as age 4½ and the majority from age 5 on, were able to repeat the last word produced by the narrator, regardless of whether it was an open- or a closed-class word. These same children, however, were significantly worse at the metalinguistic task.

These studies indicate that young children do not have any trouble isolating and combining both categories of word in their normal use of language. There is no doubt about their implicit knowledge of words and about their ability to access this knowledge to solve tasks that are close to online communication, as in the narrator task. Beyond age 5 or 6, however, there seems to be a qualitative shift in children's conceptualization of words, as shown in the way they solve metalinguistic tasks in which they are asked to isolate words in sentences or to define words. It is from this age that formal instruction in reading and writing usually starts. Thus, it is not unreasonable to suggest that this qualitative shift in children's conceptualization of words might be influenced by literacy. In the written modality, words have a permanent existence; it is possible to look at them, unlike in the spoken modality where words disappear after they have been pronounced. Moreover, words have a clear spatial definition in writing, independent of their category: Both open- and closed-class items are separated by blanks on both sides. Indeed, many 6-year-olds in Berthoud-Papandropoulou's study (1980), when asked to explain what a word is, said that words were strings of letters. Again, as in the case of grasping the sound structure of words, the written representation provides concrete support for such abstract notions as the notion of word.

Learning the conventions of writing helps children to conceptualize words as linguistic elements. Furthermore, similar to what has been said in connection with the process of grasping the sound structure or the morphological marking of words, there is an interaction between children's linguistic intuitions and the features of writing, in this case, the way alphabetic systems represent words. So, how do children interpret blanks between strings of letters? How do they use them in their written production, if at all?

Rosa Clemente (1984) asked Spanish-speaking children between ages 5 and 11 to write short stories and then to split them into "the smallest possible parts." Children from ages 5 to 7, who were just starting to learn how to read and write, tried to divide the stories into words. However, they did not produce any blank spaces within the string *AVIAUNAVEZ*, which should be written with two gaps (and with an *hi* and a *be*, in correct spelling): *HABÍA UNA VEZ*, 'once upon a time,' or in *SUPERRITO*, which should be written *SU PERRITO* 'his little dog.' That is, children had difficulties in separating function words (auxiliary verbs, articles, and possessives) from content words (nouns and verbs). They reflected in their use of blanks a similar approach to that in the metalinguistic tasks: Words that were not conceived of as words were not represented separately, but stayed attached to those that were "real words." After the age of 7 (i.e., after children learn to read and write), conventional spacing between words is achieved.

Using a different task, Ferreiro and Teberosky (1979) arrived at similar results. The investigators wrote a sentence in front of the child (e.g., *Papa patea la pelota* 'father kicks the ball') and read it aloud. Then they asked the children to show where each word was written ("Where is *Papa* ['father'] written?, and *la* ['the']?"). Children of different ages had different expectations as to what words should actually be in the written sentence. The youngest did not expect to find in the written sentence all the words that the investigator had said when reading the same sentence aloud. At age 4 to 5, only nouns were expected to appear in the written sentence; thus, children would say that there was no *la* 'the' actually written in the sentence. Later on, they expected nouns and verbs to be written, and finally, after age 7, they expected every category of word, including articles. Clearly, children only gradually come to accept that all the words that are said, including closed class function words, should appear in the written form, and that every word deserves independent representation.

Ferreiro and Pontecorvo explored the way second and third graders separate words when asked to write a well-known fairy tale. The same study was replicated in three different languages: Italian, Spanish, and Portuguese (Ferreiro, Pontecorvo, Ribeiro Moreira, & Garcia Hidalgo, 1996). Irrespective of the different languages in which the study was carried out, children had problems with the same kinds of elements. Closed-class words like prepositions (to, at), articles (the, a), and conjunctions (and) were usually written joined to the following word (usually a noun, verb, or adjective). Thus, constructions such as *a llamar* 'to call' were written altogether, without a blank space separating the first and the second word. Running words together, without creating blanks between words that should be written separately, was always more frequent than creating blanks within words. Interestingly enough, when children created blanks within a word, the resulting strings of elements usually corresponded to possible written words in the respective languages. For example, they hypersegmented *bosque* 'forest' producing *BOS QUE*, where the second part *QUE* 'what' is a very frequent written word.

All studies agree that the likelihood of creating blank spaces on both sides of a string of letters is related to whether children regard the letters as standing for what they conceive as an autonomous word. But, it is apparent that children do not consider every category of word as being equal; they seem to consider open-class, content words as "better words" than closed-class, function words. As children are learning to write, the effect of word category decreases so that they increasingly adapt to the conventions of the writing systems to which they are exposed. Learning the conventional separations between words is a long process and some difficult cases sometimes remain problematic, at least in Spanish, until high school or even later.[34] Such cases usually include prepositional constructions (e.g., *a pesar* 'in spite'), auxiliary verbs, or other clitics. All these are "small words" that, although very important in building discourse, are not conceived of as having independent meaning. Despite these exceptions, however, there is no doubt that children's initial conceptions as to what constitutes a word become transformed through literacy. The notion of graphic word, the word as it is spatially defined in the writing system, substitutes for children's previous notion of words.

To sum up, there is convincing evidence that learning to read and write affects individuals' way of perceiving and thinking about language. Awareness of the sound structures of words, the morphological markings of words, and the definitions of words are all shaped by literacy rather than being acquired outside the written system and subsequently applied when learning to read. As pointed out in the next section, literacy seems to affect not only ways of thinking about language but also ways of being.

THE EFFECT OF WRITING ON LIFE

When Goody (1977) suggested that literacy domesticates the savage mind, he was thinking about consequences that lie beyond changes in people's perception or conceptualization of language. Goody was not alone in this idea; many other anthropologists, historians, and psychologists claim that beyond providing a "model of speech" (Olson, 1994), writing is responsible for creating the form of consciousness found in Western thought (Havelock, 1996; McLuhan, 1962). The fact that writing serves to store mundane information and expand memory has played a critical role in the development of meta-activities of all kinds, and it represents the chief contribution of written representation to the development of theory building (Halliday, 1987). As explained by Olson (1994), "What literacy contributes to thought is that it turns the thoughts themselves into worthy objects of contemplation" (p. 277). In this view, the development of new representational systems provoked a qualitative change in people's ways of knowing (Donald, 1991). As pointed out by Street (1984), however, writing might be a necessary condition for certain intellectual achievements, but not a sufficient condition. Any consideration of the consequences of literacy should take into account the sociohistorical circumstances of acquisition. Writing is not a neutral technology; even its most technical aspects—for example, directionality (writing from right to left or from left to

---

[34]Initial research findings conducted with a pathological population show that separation between words is one of the most difficult aspects of writing to acquire, even for those children who have full command of the alphabetic principle.

right) or the rules of spelling—are concomitant with the incorporation or rejection of ideologies, aesthetics, and often language (Sirat, 1994, p. 389).

In the 1940s, when Ataturk, the Turkish leader, decided to abandon the Arabic abjad in favor of the Latin alphabet, it was not merely a technical decision; it implied concomitantly accepting the Western mentality associated with it. Likewise, when Felix UFVE BUANY decided to spell his name HOUPHUER BOIGNY, this was not a technical decision. Born in the Ivory Coast, then a French colony on the Atlantic coast of Africa, Felix was one of the main instigators of independence when the country became a free republic in 1960. In common with other members of a comfortably well-off minority, he was educated in France. And when it came to spelling his name, he insisted on following the rules of French, which has one of the least transparent orthographic systems. Spelling his name in French was far more prestigious than spelling it according to the rules of the local language, which offered a much more functional option (Cardona, 1994). The rules of spelling are not just conventional norms people must acquire to be understood; they convey social status. In the cultural representation of educated adults, spelling mistakes are not merely associated with lack of knowledge or attention, but with social deprivation.

Most reflections on the consequences of learning to write emphasize the functional benefits that society and the individual have gained from this highly efficient recording technology. There is no doubt that the mere possibility of preserving and therefore accumulating knowledge is revolutionary (Donald, 1991). But, the ideological aspects associated with those of a more technological nature are the features that bring about dramatic changes in the lives of individuals. Therefore, the next section describes several cases, personal stories, in order to examine the effects of becoming literate on the lives of a number of individuals.

Valentin Jamerey-Duval: Acquiring Technology and the Prevailing Ideology

Valentin Jamerey-Duval was born in 1695 in Arthonay, a small village in France. He was the son of a carriage maker who died when Valentin was only 5 years old. At the age of 13 he ran away from a life full of misery and cruelty to seek his fortune in Paris. When he died, he had found it. Indeed, he was the director of the Imperial Cabinet of Coins and Medals. The acquisition of the technology of writing transformed Jamerey-Duval's life. Let's examine the circumstances that apparently led him to literacy.[35]

---

[35]The process by which Jamerey-Duval taught himself to read is documented in a marvelous book written by Jean Hébrard (1993).

An apparently crucial circumstance was the presence in his life of an "older, wiser man" who served as an intermediary between Jamerey-Duval's ignorance and a relatively more cultivated environment. This man was an elderly surgeon whom Valentin met by chance and who was prepared to answer Valentin's questions and teach him the alphabet. Their meeting might have been a chance encounter, but Valentin, still only a young boy, wanted to learn from him, and the man was willing to teach. A second circumstance was the contradictory literacy practices to which Valentin was exposed. On Sundays, at the church, he would have listened to the Bible being read aloud interspersed with spoken comments. In day-to day life, he would have been familiar with the circulation of all kinds of written lampoons from the "Biblioteque Blue," a very popular book series at the time. French society was undergoing a process of increasing literacy, although there were probably no modern schools. At least, Jamerey-Duval never mentioned any in his subsequent writings.

Valentin lived in a diglossic situation, immersed in overlapping languages: "My instruction consisted in learning by heart the Sunday sermon given in Latin and bad French and many other plagiaries that were carefully explained to me in different versions of an elegant patois" (Hébrard, 1993, p. 45, my translation). He learned to read before learning the alphabet. He knew some passages by heart, from listening to them many times, and looked for them in the written texts. The discrepancies between the sermons and the written texts enhanced a metalinguistic manipulation of language that seems to have been fundamental in his becoming literate. By comparing different versions in different registers and languages, and by looking for correspondences between spoken French and written Latin, Jamerey-Duval introduced segmentation into his stream of speech in order to find the correspondences. This comparison between parts of the spoken and written texts surely augmented his phonological and morphological awareness (Hébrard, 1993, pp. 46–47). *"Sans avoir la moindre notion de cet art divin qui apprend à fixer la parole et a peindre la pensée […] je m'engageay mes confrères dans la vie bucolique a m'apprendre a lire"* 'Without the least idea of this divine art that teaches to fix words and to depict thought, I engaged my comrades in this bucolic life in teaching me how to read' (Hébrard, 1993, p. 56). The participation of his comrades was essential to the autodidactic process. Another key factor was distancing himself from his previous cultural referents. By participating in literacy practices before he became fully literate, Valentin had broken ties with his original group of reference and his cultural origins. There was no turning back, and he had to create new affective links. The fact that he was an illiterate foreigner in a literate territory made him susceptible to adoption by new cultural referents. Last but not least, he realized the divergences between his own reading of the texts and the official interpretations of the same texts.

Therefore, he turned to those he recognized as the official representatives of the allowed interpretations, the parish priest and the teacher, seeking validation from them. Indeed, he put himself in the intellectual custody of these people so that he could learn from them not only how to decode, but also how to interpret the texts. He made his own the ideological correlates of writing "technology."

The process of becoming literate produced a profound change in the life of Jamerey-Duval. Although he was born into a situation that nearly ensured a life of poverty, he managed to find considerable material (and cultural) success. It seems almost certain that he was successful because he was able to apply his newly acquired technological skills in the context of the literate practices of the dominant culture at that time and place.

In contrast, the autodidactic process of acquiring literacy might be harmful for other people in other circumstances. For example, it could result in the newly literate person becoming even further separated from the literate community. The next story, the story of Menocchio, shows how becoming literate may lead to a completely different outcome when the autodidact is unable to adapt his ways of reading to those of the dominant culture.

Writing in the Life of Domenicho Scandella: Incorporating Technology Into One's Own Ideology

Domenicho Scandella, better known as Menocchio, was born in Montereale, a small town in the Friuli region of Italy, in 1532.[36] He was a miller and the father of 11 children. On September 28, 1583, he was denounced before the tribunal of the Inquisition, accused of having uttered "heretical and most impious words" about Christ. The first trial started in 1584, the second followed 15 years later, and in 1601 he was burned at the stake by order of the Holy Office. Menocchio was burned because he was an "illegitimate" reader of "legitimate" materials. Instead of using the technology of reading in the service of the allowed interpretations, he developed his own interpretation attuned to his own cultural origins, probably without even being aware of the difference.

Menocchio developed a particular cosmogony, according to which God was not created by a special and distinct act of creation but out of a common mass of angels. He explained that "out of a bulk of earth, air, water and fire just as cheese is made out of milk and worms appeared in it ... a mass formed and these were the angels, and from the mass of angels God was created." He also put forward his ideas as to how the relation between the church and the people should be

---

[36]This story forms part of an outstanding historiographic study undertaken by Carlo Ginzburg (1982), who studied the records of the two trials, the documents left by Domenicho Scandella concerning his economic activities, the lives of his children, and a partial list of what he read. Through these documents, Ginzburg attempted to uncover the source of Menocchio's heretical ideas.

regulated. He denounced the speaking of Latin as a "betrayal of the poor" because they could not understand it, and he judged unfair that "everything belongs to the church" (Ginzburg, 1982, p. 9). It might be the case that Menocchio never understood why his interpretation of the texts irritated the established readers so much. He did not explicitly reject the ideas transmitted by the texts, but neither did he accept them as such; he used the words he found in the books to give legitimacy to his own interpretation.

What was the source of Menocchio's heretical ideas? They were not an outcome of reading forbidden books; the source of Menocchio's ideas was presumably his own way of reading the books that were allowed by the church. A list of the books he read was compiled based on his own declaration and an investigation during the Inquisition trials. Examination of this list shows that he had only ever read permitted books. However, after comparing the content of these books and the declarations that he made to the tribunals of the Inquisition, Ginzburg (1982) concluded that "the gulf between the texts read by Menocchio and the way in which he understood them and reported them to the inquisitors indicates that his ideas cannot be reduced or traced back to any particular book" (p. xxii). Menocchio was condemned because he did not reproduce the content of the texts. Instead of "discovering the truth" in the texts, he was led astray by detail and understood metaphoric language in its literal sense. He did not learn to read in the accepted fashion, but rather related the words in the texts with his own previous ideas, shared by many peasants at that time. By condemning Menocchio, the inquisitors were condemning the insertion of a peasant ideology into the values of the written culture (Hébrard, 1993).

Unlike Jamerey-Duval, Menocchio did not adapt his own reading to the legitimate culture but rather to his own cultural origins: "The roots of his utterances and aspirations were sunk in an obscure, almost unfathomable, layer of remote peasant traditions" (Ginzburg, 1982, p. 112). His cultural origins, founded in an oral tradition, acted as a filter that he placed between himself and the printed page. "More than the text, then, what is important is the key to his readings, a screen that he unconsciously placed between himself and the printed page.... This key to his reading, continually leads us back to a culture that is very different from the one expressed on the printed page—one based on an oral tradition" (p. 33). The texts were used to confirm his own ideas and provided him with the words and the courage to express them, and he was condemned for that.

The consequences of becoming literate differed greatly in the cases of Valentin and Menocchio. Both acquired the same technology, and the circumstances of acquisition did not differ so very greatly. Yet, in Valentin's case, there was a process of identification with the literate culture that enabled him to become a successful member of the dominant group; in contrast, Menocchio in-terpreted his readings in terms of the cultural references of his own origins, and because of that he was condemned.

The next story also establishes a conflict between cultural values. It illus-trates the unconscious rejection of the values embedded in the technology of writing, which are perceived as dangerous for the preservation of self-identity and belonging.

Writing in the Life of Latifa: Writing as Alienation

Latifa was born in France, in 1980,[37] one of eight children in an Algerian family living in Lyon. Her parents had been born into virtually illiterate peasant fami-lies; neither could speak fluent French or read or write in French. She lived with her family in a small apartment in a crowded tenement block in an outlying neighborhood and attended a state school in Lyon.

Latifa and her family knew that two people would be visiting their home to ask some questions. The appointment had been arranged over the phone by the school, and the family had also been sent a written note telling them of the visit. That same day, Latifa had been told at school about the visit. The inter-viewers arrived late. The whole family was there—the mother, the father, and seven of the eight children—but they were not expecting the visitors. The family had forgotten about the phone call and the written note was still in the child's satchel.

The interview took place against a background of constant noise with the children jumping on the table, touching the microphones, and attempting to untie the interviewer's shoelaces. Nobody was allowed to finish a sentence; they constantly interrupted each other. The father did not seem very happy when any of the children spoke; it was obvious that he preferred to be in control of the conversation.

The family was asked about the lists they usually made for shopping or the notes they kept of their expenses. Latifa's mother remarked, "We do not write

---

[37]I came to learn about Latifa and her family by reading Bernard Lahire's (1995) *Tableaux de Famille*. Lahire was looking for the roots of success or failure at school, which in French schools, as in any other state school in Western countries, is completely dependent on reading and writing. His belief was that the roots of success were in the home—more specifically in the relations between home literacy activities and attitudes toward literacy and school activities. The idea was not new; it had been widely argued pre-viously in the works of Heath (1983), for example. However, the approach was original. Lahire looked at those cases that confirm expectations and compared them with those that do not. Lahire dwelt heavily on those children who had been successful and sought to discover the key to their success. Latifa was not among them.

those things down," and went on to explain that this would mean showing a lack of confidence. She explained, "When we are together, we eat ... we take whatever we need ... perhaps 100 francs or 200 francs ... when it is finished, it is finished" (Lahire, 1995, p. 77). Besides, she added, "What's the point of writing? In any case, we are going to spend just the same."

The eldest brother, who did not live at home any more, was responsible for filling in the various official forms that had to be completed by anyone in the family. Latifa was not exposed in the home to any example of the ordinary uses of written culture. Neither magazines nor newspapers were read at home; the Koran, considered the source of all legitimate knowledge, was the only book the father read.

The family's message was very clear: The technology of writing and its functional uses are not of any use "to us"; writing might be useful "for them," meaning the strangers living outside their home. The family did not cultivate any of the ordinary uses of writing, such as shopping lists, the keeping of accounts, calendars, or notes. All such uses, which are encouraged at school during the initial stages of learning to read because they are considered meaningful contexts for engaging children in writing and reading activities, were completely foreign to Latifa's family. These ordinary uses of writing were not only unfamiliar, they were considered useless and offensive. For Latifa, using writing for such purposes would mean becoming alienated from her roots, from her own original cultural points of reference; it would endanger her basic self-identity and affective belonging. It seems that Latifa, like many other children, preferred to remain a foreigner in the school culture rather than become an outsider in her own home culture.

Whenever the consequences of literacy are discussed, it is somehow implied that they are positive. Thanks to literacy, people become more aware, more powerful, and better prepared for life. And yet, it seems that, for Latifa, literacy lacks the many positive connotations implied. The danger of alienation perceived by Latifa as one of the possible consequences of writing in many ways resembles what Fordham and Ogbu (1986) described as the fear some boys and girls of African American descent feel about "acting White." For these boys and girls, success in learning to write, as with any of the tasks set within the school curriculum, is undesirable because this could be interpreted by peers as "acting White." In their situation, literacy, especially school literacy, is not viewed as a positive asset (Ogbu, 1990). These boys and girls prefer to be rejected by the school rather than by their friends. Cases like these call for caution in evaluating the consequences of literacy. The next section refers to another case in which the benefits of literacy are questioned.

Writing on Writing

"TA is an 8.11-year-old, left-handed boy, from a family of low socioeconomic status in a small town in northern Sardinia (Italy)" (Cossu & Marshall, 1990, p. 23). This is part of the description of a case study carried out by Josep Cossu, from the University of Parma, Italy, and John C. Marshall from the Neuropsychology Unit at the Radcliffe Infirmary in Oxford, England, in a paper entitled "Are cognitive skills a pre-requisite for learning to read and write?" which appeared in *Cognitive Neuropsychology*.

TA is left-handed, and at birth he was diagnosed with a congenital cyanogenic heart disease and had surgery before the age of 6 months. It took him more than 4 years to pronounce two-word phrases, but then his language underwent what can only be termed an "explosion" and he started to talk. His phonology, morphology, and syntax were good, but his "verbal communication was a kind of free wheeling verbal association, only marginally related to the context; his answers to questions were seldom appropriate" (p. 23). His problems, however, were not confined to communicative inadequacy; his cognitive capacities were very low. On different tests used to measure intelligence, his performance was poor. For example, on the Wechsler Intelligence Scale for Children (WISC) he obtained a total IQ of 47. He was completely unable to reproduce hand movements, to copy line drawings, or to reproduce simple geometric figures using short sticks. The degree of TA's difficulty is shown in Fig. 6.1.

Moreover, at the time that TA was referred to the Institute of Child Neuropsychiatry in Sardinia, he still had considerable difficulty tying his shoelaces and could not dress himself; he was unable to understand elementary rules in a game, and he could not determine in which direction to kick a ball. Up to this point, everything fit together logically enough; TA was suffering from gross impairment in any activity requiring cognitive, practical, or motor abilities. To the authors' surprise, however, and despite his extreme difficulties, TA showed a reading ability. He showed that he was able to recognize and decode both words and nonwords without any problem, no matter how complex or irregular. The same words and nonwords were dictated to him and again he made no mistakes. In fact, TA's reading and writing skills were so good that his teacher considered him to be the best reader in the class. In addition, he could copy letters, words, and sentences correctly, although only in cursive writing, despite his severe difficulties with drawing and geometric figures. As Cossu and Marshall noted, the "dissociation between TA's ability to copy letters and his complete failure to copy simple geometric figures or drawings" (p. 32) was especially remarkable.

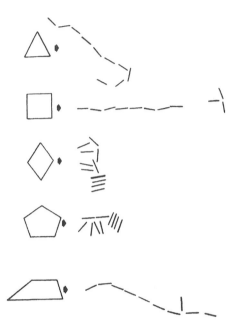

FIG. 6.1.   Examples of TA reproducing simple geometric shapes with sticks. From "Are cognitive skills a prerequisite for learning to read and write?" by G. Cossu and J. C. Marshall, 1990, *Cognitive Neuropsychology, 7* (p. 26). Reprinted with permission.

The boy was hyperlexic: He had a capacity to read far beyond what could be expected from his other cognitive, linguistic, and motor capacities. Unlike other hyperlexic children, he was not a compulsive reader, although he really enjoyed reading and writing. Indeed, he was always anxious to demonstrate his reading and writing abilities in class.

Was TA at least "aware" of the kind of units he was using to map to letters when decoding? As pointed out at the beginning of this chapter, phonological awareness is considered by some authors to be a prerequisite for acquiring reading. However, when TA was presented with four different metalinguistic tasks, he was not able to understand what was required of him. In a typical "tapping task" in which he was asked to tap the number of sounds in each word, he was only able to tap the correct number of sounds for 5 out of 45 words. In contrast, a group of 8- to 9-year-old third graders tested on the same task were able to do it for a mean of 43 out of 45 words. Similar differences were found for a deletion task in which children must say what word remains after taking out a phoneme. Evidently, TA was able to segment words for decoding without the least awareness of what he was doing.

What about his reading comprehension? Here, too, a dramatic dissociation was found. Although he was perfectly able to translate letters to sounds and sound to letters without difficulty, his comprehension abilities were almost null. He understood fewer than half of the words that he could correctly read, and fewer than 30% of the sentences that he correctly read were correctly acted out with toys.

So what were the effects of reading and writing as such on TA's cognitive functioning, linguistic development, and symbolic drawing? TA's ability to translate letters into sounds or sounds into letters did not have any consequence on his understanding of language, or any of his cognitive, practical, or motor capacities. His decoding and spelling abilities showed themselves to be independent from his other cognitive capacities. His ability to copy and to produce letters and words was completely unrelated to his ability to draw or to copy drawings or geometric figures. Why are other cognitive functions not affected by knowing how to read and write?

Cossu and Marshall (1990) analyzed the meaning of these findings not from the perspective of the lack of effect of this form of literacy on other cognitive domains, but rather from the perspective of the lack of cognitive prerequisites for acquiring this form of literacy. The two perspectives are complementary. The findings were that TA could learn to decode and to write words to dictation, apparently with relative ease and without any particular help, and on the basis of standard Italian methods of teaching. Further, he was able to acquire this ability despite his general linguistic and cognitive retardation, his lack of metaphonological awareness, and his difficulties in short memory. None of the commonly argued prerequisites for acquiring literacy—metaphonological ability, minimal level of IQ, or short-term memory span—could account for TA's decoding abilities: Therefore, the authors concluded, these things cannot be considered prerequisites for learning to read and write. Against a background of impaired cognition, the phonological, morphological, and syntactic aspects of language were preserved despite semantic and pragmatic difficulties; the "transcoding skills" were preserved despite lack of understanding. Thus, for these abilities that are subcomponents of language and reading, respectively, it is possible to postulate an autonomy from other cognitive abilities. That is, language has a phonological, a morphological, a syntactic, and a pragmatic component that can be separated so that one or many of the components can be damaged or preserved. In the case of TA, the first three components were relatively preserved, whereas the pragmatic component was damaged. For the preserved components, it was evident that they did not depend on general cognitive abilities, which the boy lacked.

As for reading, it seems clear that segmenting a visual pattern into the elements that are relevant in the particular writing system the child is exposed to (characters, letters), and attributing phonological segments to these elements according to mapping rules that are specific to this writing system, is only part of the reading process. The semantic interpretation of these mappings between segmented visual and phonological representations is another part. The first part was preserved in TA, but not the other. Cossu and Marshall (1990) conjectured that this first part is "encapsulated" in acquisition. By that they mean that if the learner is exposed to written words that are paired with spoken interpretation—the usual thing teachers do whenever they teach words—the mapping is produced "automatically," without influence from other knowledge or ability (p. 53).

Many of the studies discussed (e.g., Bertelson et al., 1986; Read, Zhang, Nie, & Ding, 1986; Tolchinsky & Teberosky, 1998) provide evidence that the acquisition of alphabetic writing changes people's perception of speech, enabling them to handle and to name individual sounds and to establish formal and language specific boundaries between words. However, the case of TA, as well as any case of hyperlexia, shows that the ability to translate graphic signs into sounds, or sounds into graphic signs, can develop without modifying in any crucial manner other cognitive and linguistic abilities. Encapsulated abilities, acquired automatically and independently from underlying cognitive skills, are unlikely to produce any effect on other cognitive or symbolic skills. In the case of certain pathologies, there is no reading or writing acquisition; only one component of the reading or writing process is automatically acquired and deployed. The acquisition of transcoding skills as such does not produce any effect without interpretation and cognitive permeability. It is only through the transmission of meaning that any widespread cognitive effect of literacy can occur.

In hyperlexic children, as well as in other pathological states, acquiring decoding abilities is probably little more than a possible source of personal satisfaction; these abilities are a way of demonstrating a skill appreciated at school. In contrast, for other children, acquiring the technicalities of alphabetic writing facilitates direct access to the dominant written culture of their community, which is an enriched continuation of their home culture. For these children, learning to write constitutes a direct integration into their society and reinforcement of their cultural belonging. Through literacy, they gain access to the books they already know about and have seen on grandpa's shelves. They assimilate these new skills via the interpretative schemata they already have. The case of Menocchio was also one of assimilation of newly acquired skills to preexisting cultural frames, but in his case the divergence between the dominant culture and his own culture of reference was fatal. In other cases there is no assimilation; rather, acquiring literacy causes a breakdown in the expectations of learners. Some learners will be able to tolerate and overcome this breakdown, whereas others will not.

For Jamerey-Duval, acquiring writing represented a profound turning point—a nearly complete departure from his cultural background, and an instrument of self-transformation with which, for some unknown reason, he was able to cope. Latifa, apparently, was unable to cope with a similar departure. When the meaning that was attributed to writing at home conflicted with the culture at school, she felt writing constituted too much of an alienation from her home culture. For some, the conflict between the meaning of writing in the school culture and in the family culture is difficult to resolve. The first step toward a solution seems to lie in acknowledging the existence of this internal representation of the consequences of becoming literate and in recognizing the need to stop regarding writing as a neutral technology unrelated to the context of acquisition and use.

The following are some key points in this chapter:

- Children's (and adults') implicit knowledge of the sound structure of language, the internal structure of words, and the relations between words interact with the particular features of a writing system to become more explicit, and, in the process, they became shaped by the particular features of the writing system.
- Learning to read and write affects people's way of perceiving and thinking about language. Awareness of the sound structure of words, the morphological marking of words, the notion of grammaticality, and the definition of words in a particular language, are all shaped by literacy rather than being acquired outside the written system and subsequently applied when learning to read. This revisits the claim permeating the entire book: Knowledge of a particular domain is affected by learning the notational system of that domain.
- There are then two contradictory views as to the effects of writing as well as to the many facets, processes, and factors involved in literacy. The first would claim that literacy not only influences human perception and conception of language but transforms human life itself and brings about a qualitative change in human evolution. The second view warns against generalizing to other cognitive domains the effect of learning to read.
- The evidence provided by case studies showing that learning to write has no effect on either general intelligence or specific cognitive abilities forces serious reconsideration of the role of learning to write on cognition and language.
- The consequences of becoming literate differed greatly in each of the cases reviewed. The differences among them are related to the extent to which the newly acquired technology is adapted to the ideology of the dominant culture. Sometimes, the conflict between the values

embedded in the technology of writing are perceived as dangerous for the preservation of self-identity and belonging. In these situations, literacy, and especially school literacy, is not viewed as a positive asset and is rejected by the learning subject.

- In the case of certain pathologies, only one component of the reading or writing process (decoding) is acquired automatically. This acquisition does not produce any effect on other cognitive abilities. It might be that it is through the meaning transmitted by writing and obtained from reading, and not only from the ability to decode, that any cognitive effect of literacy occurs.

7

Closing Reflections on Notational Systems, Boomerangs, and Circles

I began this book assuring you that children have their own ideas about notational systems. Then, I tried to convince you how much these ideas owe to children's interaction with the systems. Finally, in the last chapter I tried to demonstrate that, except in pathological cases, becoming literate has a tremendous impact not only on the way people perceive and conceive of language but also on their entire way of life. The impact is not always beneficial and the effects of literacy are not always perceived as positive. Becoming literate, in a sense, cost Menocchio his life. Many children and young people see in literacy a culture hostile to their family or rejected by their peers. Thus, they prefer to distance themselves from literacy rather than from their family or friends. This rejection is, however, an implicit recognition of the powerful consequences of literacy.

But, isn't there a sort of contradiction between the claim for "having one's own ideas about notations" while at the same time claiming that notations play a determining role not only in provoking ideas about notations but also in building notions about language and ways of living? The central claim is that this apparent contradiction reflects the key process of notational knowledge. This is precisely what notational knowledge is about: a constant interaction between a person's capacities, necessities, limitations, and concepts on the one hand, and the properties of notations on the other. These properties, in turn, will have a transforming effect on the person's initial capacities, necessities, limitations, and ideas about notations. Not only that, they will also affect their conceptions of the domain of reference (what notations represent), and transform every aspect of life that is affected by notations. The interaction is constant. The starting point of these mutually transforming effects cannot be defined.

Throughout this book, I have touched on this key process when referring to writing and numbers as *epistemic tools*, or *objects to think with*, always implying that notational systems are a source of the kind of knowledge that people need in order to handle notations. At the same time, notations influence people's knowledge about the domain that notations represent. I have suggested that what drives this process is something we might call the "boomerang effect." Now, imagine a boomerang that works nonstop, and the result will be a "virtuous circle." This is one of the expressions used by the British cognitive philosopher Andy Clark to refer to the kind of reciprocal influence and enhancement between notational systems, a user's conceptions about these systems, and other aspects of cognitive life. A "virtuous circle" is a circle because it is difficult to establish the starting or the end point, and it is supposedly virtuous because it leads to an improvement of both the user's capacity and the notational system's representational facilities. Clark suggested that public speech, internal repetition (to ourselves) of verbal instructions, and written and computerized texts are powerful tools that shape our mental space. We develop a language from our specific capacities; once created it returns to our mental space to facilitate ways of thinking and understanding; this in turn improves our understanding of the language we created. Moreover, with our improved way of thinking we manage to create even more sophisticated representational artifacts that increasingly facilitate work on internal representations, and so on. We were capable of developing means for gathering, recording, classifying, and organizing information. The texts created and the procedures developed for creating those texts "return" to improve procedures for gathering, recording, classifying, and organizing information.

Time and again, internal work is interchanged with cultural representations. When people see the information gathered and the procedures that have been externally represented, they are turned into objects for reflection that can be easily manipulated. Then possible mistakes can be corrected and contradictions solved.

Everyone agrees that there are many levels at which to know things: from fully concious to automatic knowledge. For example, when we reach for a cup, we perform a set of movements adapting them to the distance at which the cup lies and to its shape and size without even being aware of what we are doing. At the other extreme of knowing, we can develop a full theory about the way our nervous system controls this same set of movements. Between one extreme and the other, there are many levels at which knowledge can be represented and accessed. We live most of our day (and life) counting on the automatic level of knowledge, but there are certain problems that can only be solved if we can access less automatic and more explicit levels of knowledge. In general, most of people's biggest achievements have resulted from more reflective levels of knowledge. When a particular operation moves from one level to the other, a cognitive change is considered to have happened. In Karmiloff-Smith's model of cognitive development (chap. 5), the process of redescription helps this movement from one level to the other. Recall that redescription is a recursive psychological process that reoccurs each time the subject is involved in acquiring new knowledge. Through this process, already acquired representations are re-represented to another part of the cognitive system so that they can be analyzed, reorganized, modified, and/or adapted to new circumstances. This is exactly what we tried to elicit when we asked children to write words that do not exist, or numbers that do not exist (chap. 5). The point was to see whether children were able internally to manipulate what they knew about writing and numerals so as to adapt this knowledge to the requirements of the task. In this case, it meant doing something opposite to what they thought would be appropriate for writing. When children succeeded in producing very different things for "words that do not exist" and for "words that exist," we interpreted this to mean that they were at a different level in their knowledge of writing. They had redescribed the features of writing that were embedded in their writing or sorting procedures, and they could purposefully manipulate them to create the nonexistent word, or number. Notational systems function very much as external devices that help to redescribe knowledge for scrutiny, analysis, and manipulation. Through these processes, children move toward improvement in a constant circle.

In the next section, I would like to look at how the boomerang effect characterizes the development of notational knowledge, the effect of notations on other domains of knowledge, the historical development of notations, and at the most general level, the relation between culture and biology.

THE BOOMERANG EFFECT ON THE DEVELOPMENT OF WRITING AND NUMERALS

Children who grow up in a literate environment will not wait until the beginning of formal instruction to explore the features of writing and numerals. The graphic patterns of writing and numerals are part of their mental space from very early on—before age 3. This is evidenced in the way they single out written words and numerals among many other kinds of graphic displays. It is also indicated by what they do when asked to write their names, captions for figures, or a phrase said by the interviewer. At this initial stage, the meaning of the written pattern is determined by the place where it appears or by the child's intention as a writer, rather than by its features. Recall that similar written patterns are "read" by the child as saying very different things. (And, if there is a string of letters under a picture depicting a boat, it reads *boat*, but when the same string of letters is put under a picture depicting a duck, it will mean *duck*.) Gradually, two things happen: First, children become more selective as to what forms or combinations of forms are accepted as "readable" or "writeable." In order to be "good for reading," strings of letters must have a certain number and variety. Their writing also becomes constrained by the same self-imposed criteria of number and variety. The second thing that often happens is that children start introducing some elements into their writing that hint at the content of the words they are attempting to write. Thus, *little pigs* might be written with fewer marks than *pigs*, because the pigs are smaller. It is usually during this phase, in which writing becomes communicative, that children start looking for some correspondence between the length of words or phrases and the number of marks they put on paper. At the beginning, this correspondence is very global: If they are attempting to read, then they will start saying a sentence pointing at the beginning of what they have written and will attempt to finish saying the sentence at the same time as their finger reaches the end of the written pattern. Slowly, however, they start looking for more articulated correspondences between parts of the utterance and elements in the written string. At this third stage, children find a stable frame of reference useful for representing any word, and they realize that number and variety of letters relate to the sound patterns of words. Finally, at a fourth stage, children discover the alphabetic principle in which a letter represents each consonant and vowel in a word.

There are, then, three crucial transitions in the development of early writing: The first is from undifferentiated to formally constrained, which also entails that children start relating to the communicative functions of writing; the second is toward the phonetization of writing; and, the third is toward the alphabetic principle. There is a boomerang effect at any one of these transition points. Initially, children are not bothered by the fact that they produce very similar patterns for representing very different things. Their internal representation of writing is as an action (a set of movements) or a particular visual pattern. However, because what they write remains in front of them, and they can see what they have done when they are required to interpret, what they have produced is turned into an object of scrutiny. It is now possible for them to realize that they have produced very similar marks. This realization leads them to look for some way to differentiate among productions. The quantity (or length of the string) of marks seems to be the most salient feature to manipulate. Thus, a change in the number of marks seems like a good way to differentiate between writing patterns. As a result, first there is a reduction in the number of marks, as compared with the long strings they have been producing. At this point, children also begin to control the internal variety. After this reduction, written strings become manageable and the value of the elements can be worked out. What children say when attempting to interpret what they have just written will now be performed on a written string containing a reduced number of marks. Therefore, it will be easier for them to monitor their interpretation and use the verbal utterance they are producing (their "reading") to attribute value to the elements. It will be easier for them to look for some sort of correspondence between the spoken and the written. Initially, the correspondences are global and vague, but with successive attempts at interpretation they become more articulated and more specific until there is a term-to-term correspondence between sounds in a word and letters in a string. At the beginning, the correspondences are produced after writing, on the already produced notation. Later, however, they are anticipated and a child is able to control the selection of number and kind of letters. Throughout the development of writing there are further opportunities for interaction, but the main source of this development is the act of writing. The conventions of writing (i.e., letter–sound correspondences, word separation) cannot be learned outside the written system. There is no way to acquire the conventions of a particular system except by discovering them in the system.

In the development of numerical notation there is also a constant interplay between the information gathered from the environment and children's own imposed constraints. Children include numerals in their repertoire of notational forms very early. However, there is a delay in their use of numerals for representing quantities and in their use of the same numerals for representing various other functions. Before being able to do that, children must accept the arbitrary nature of notational elements and their compiled way of representing multiplicity. In other words, although children learn the conventional shapes and names of numerals very early on, they do not at first apply them to convey numerosity. When the purpose of the notation is to communicate a certain content, children between ages 4 and 5 prefer to reflect the quantity of elements included in a collection in a more direct and explicit way. This seems to be a necessary step before individual digits, in which multiplicity and iteration are compiled, become useful for the external representation of cardinality.

A boomerang effect is also present in this transition. Children approach the notation of quantity with the idea of making amount and graphic marks correspond in a direct way. That is why they use multiple and repeated shapes to display amount explicitly. This is the notational period in which children repeat the same numeral or the same written string many times. However, the fact that children can *see* directly the amount they are attempting to represent modifies this initial idea, and it also facilitates their acceptance of the more hermetic way in which conventional numerals represent quantities. The properties of external representation, in this case perdurability and detachment from the notator, are what enable children to examine, as external observers, the notations that they themselves have created. Then, the examination of the notations that they have created according to their own convictions paves the way to understanding the meaning of numerals and to accepting the arbitrary and compiled way in which they represent quantities.

The process being characterized also underlies one of the main features of notational development—the fact that it is domain specific. From a very early age, children attribute certain properties to writing but not to numerals, and they are aware that certain activities are performed with writing but not with numerals. It has been shown how 4-year-olds are able to sort out written texts, numerals, and drawings in accordance with the different constraints operating in each system. If a card contains repeated letters, then they will reject it as good for reading. But, if a numeral is repeated many times, then they will not reject it as good for counting. They never confound writing with numbers when they have to decide which graphic marks are used for counting and which for reading. Also, older children, when inventing numerals that do not exist and words that do not exist, violate these constraints. Words that do not exist may contain repeated letters and numerals that do not exist may look like writing. These productions are taken to mean that older children have an internal representation of the constraints they impose on each system and can manipulate them to produce invented notations; they have an explicit representation of the features that differentiate between systems. When this happens, children will no longer cross boundaries between systems by using writing for representing quantity or drawing for showing the objects they want to represent. A functional differentiation between systems is attained.

The initial source of this domain specificity lies in some inborn propensity to attend to number-relevant and language-relevant input. On the basis of this bias, children are able to map talk, gestures, and movements occurring in natural contexts of use to their corresponding notational support. This biological underpinning facilitates the creation of expectancies. However, the role of exposure and successive interaction between notational input and users is at least a necessary condition for fulfilling the initial expectancies that are created by assigning forms to certain activities. Expectancies are confirmed and differentiation is reinforced if the actions that follow after people have looked at certain marks are different from the actions that follow after people have looked at another set of marks. For example, in one case, the response to a set of marks is to push a button to get to a certain floor in a building and, in another case, it is the telling of a story.

Various factors contribute to the distinction between sets of marks and their allocation to different territories: the fact that the numerical meaning of numbers coincides with their name (*four* means 'four') and the fact that there is less graphic variation among numerals than among letters, making it easier for children to identify them. It has been demonstrated that an initial differentiation between the two systems is a comfortable way to learn in a more systematic way the properties of each. However, later on, once the features of each system are mastered, older children will have to learn that the same graphic marks can be used for many different purposes (e.g., letters for algebra or numerals for providing geographic information). This realization is enabled by an important feature of external representation in general and notations in particular: There is no obligatory unique link between form and meaning; the same form can be interpreted in many different ways. It is probably only at this point that users are tapping the deep sense of notations: A finite set of marks becomes resignified in the different functions they fulfill but can still transport messages from one context to the other.

THE BOOMERANG EFFECT ON USERS' IDEAS
OF THE DOMAINS OF KNOWLEDGE
REPRESENTED BY NOTATIONS

The writing system someone learns is a determining factor in the way that person analyzes language. As children interact with the specific characteristics of a given writing system, their implicit knowledge about the sounds in a word or the words in a sentence becomes increasingly accessible and shaped by the particular features of that system. Therefore, people who become literate in different writing systems develop different abilities for analyzing language.

Thus, interaction with notational systems not only affects children's developing ideas about the systems, but also their intuitions about the domains of reference. Writing and numerals shape children's linguistic intuitions. This sort of interaction has been witnessed at different points in development. Children's initial abilities to segment words are affected by interaction with the features of writing. The fact that written strings are formed by graphic elements makes it easier for children to monitor the sound structure of words. The presence of separated elements helps them handle the sounds. When they are attempting to write a particular word, the graphic elements provide a more tangible support for the analysis of the sounds in the word. This in turn helps children in their search for the number and type of letters they need for writing a word. That is, using letters facilitates the analysis of the spoken word, and the analysis of the spoken word, in turn, facilitates the selection of letters. But this is not all. Having used the number and type of letters required for representing a word facilitates recognition of the same word in the future. Certainly, this interplay requires an initial idea on the part of the child: the idea that writing is somehow related to speech, which probably emerges in the context of occasions in which children both participate in and witness the use of notational artifacts by "significant others." Indeed, encounters between users and notations are often mediated by other users; people act as interpreters and provide clues for interpretation through their reactions.

Every dimension of linguistic representation seems to be affected by a similar dynamic. The fact that grammatical suffixes are spelled in fixed ways helps children to consolidate their explicit recognition of these elements, which in turn improves their written morphology. The way in which writing systems represent words influences individuals' practical, intuitive definition of words, and graphic words then become their definition of words. The ideas underlying this boomerang effect are in line with those expressed by Olson (1994) in his interpretation of the consequences of literacy. It is people's capacity to create representations, including speech, that enables the emergence of writing systems. But, these systems of writing are not mere transcriptions of speech. Different writing systems select different units of speech to be represented, and not all aspects of speech are represented in writing. Syllabaries are built on syllables and alphabetic systems on subsyllabic constituents that are close, but not identical, to phonemes. Each script serves as a "model of speech," but each brings into consciousness distinct linguistic segments. This in turn affects the kind of linguistic segments of which users of different writing systems are aware. In Olson's words, "We introspect our language in terms laid down by our scripts" (Olson, 1994, p. 258). That is, although similar human capacities make possible the creation of writing systems, the particular interactions created between users and writing systems that model different units affect the users' awareness of their own languages. Because of the way writing represents language, it transforms our view of what is represented.

Writing also enables individuals to become aware of things that are not represented in writing. Despite some children's belief of the impossibility to write false statements (see Introduction), the falsity or truth of utterances is never represented in writing. A letter beginning with the words "My dear Ann" may be sincere or cruelly ironic. Olson suggested that people are in a better position to distinguish between what is being said and what is being meant thanks to the possibility offered by writing to reflect on speech. The possibility of recording and returning to what has been said for contrast and confrontation is what favors the distinction between literal meaning and intended meaning, a distinction crucial for interpersonal communication, legal issues, literary criticism, and many other human activities.

Similarly for written numeration, in more transparent languages, children find it easier to write numerals. Transparency also helps to understand the additive structure of the system. In languages where there are more spoken cues about this structure, children understand place value at an earlier age and more efficiently (Miller & Stigler, 1987). When Chinese, Japanese, or Korean children were asked to represent a multidigit number using building blocks, some of which represented tens and others represented units, they were able to combine them to build the required number better than their English counterparts. For example, for the number 43 they used four blocks representing tens and three representing units. The English-speaking children, in contrast, tended to build the number using the blocks that represented the units, that is, they used 43 blocks; English-speaking children see numbers as the grouping of counted objects. Transparent counting systems facilitate learning in a more global fashion, enabling children to understand the additive structure of the system.

THE BOOMERANG EFFECT ON THE HISTORY OF NOTATIONAL SYSTEMS

The history of writing systems highlights the role of outsiders in the development of new systems or redeployment of existent systems under different principles. Most writing systems evolved from people's attempts to translate messages written in languages different from their own. In the "translation process," the writing systems became modified and adapted to the necessities of the users. This, in turn, provided the user with a more efficient tool to fulfill the different functions that writing may serve, from the most mundane to the most sacred. This was the case with the Sumerian script, with the Phoenician alphabet, and with the Latin script, as discussed in chapter 2. No doubt the users' initial capacities were put into play to find the way in which the writing worked. They had to compare different written messages to look for similarities and differences, and they had to make inferences about the possible meaning of what was written and how best to adapt the features they were discovering to their own language. These operations affected both the system of representation and the users themselves. As in the individual history of writing, the process of interpretation, an operation performed on the notations, was crucial for triggering the modification of the script and the eventual benefits to the users. However, were it not for the intrinsic features of writing as an external system of representation, including the fact that it is permanent and enables interaction, the very process of interpretation as it was carried out could not have taken place.

A historical view of notational systems highlighted the positive role of heterogeneity in development and served as another illustration of what is considered to be the key process in notational development. There was heterogeneity between the language of the users and the language in which the written message was encoded. There was also heterogeneity between the language of the scribes and the language used by the rest of the community; this describes diglossic situations. This heterogeneity opened up new representational horizons. Extrapolating from historical development, this makes a claim for the positive effect of a multilingual environment on the development of both spoken and written language.

THE BOOMERANG EFFECT IN THE RELATIONS BETWEEN BIOLOGY AND CULTURE

The case of writing and numerals can be taken as a "paradigmatic illustration" of a more general mind-brain/culture dialectic process (Zelazo, 2000, p. 146). We humans have created our own cultural artifacts. Once created, they transform our own capabilities not only by empowering them, which they do, but also by shaping them according to many of the properties with which we endowed the artifacts.

No doubt cultural objects are born from our cognitive capabilities but also from our cognitive limitations. Chapter 2 showed how, unable to "see" beyond four in an instantaneous way, individuals were capable of discovering ways to group elements to make counting easier. This notational solution was revolutionary for the development of numeration systems: It opened new possibilities for representation in more economical ways. Recognition of quantities became more efficient. Transactions could be made more quickly and with less effort. It also created new problems. The fact that the same signs had two meanings (as units and as groups of units) made the system more ambiguous. When ambiguity was solved by the creation of different signs, one for units and another for groups, the system became even more efficient and computation was probably easier, but the user required additional information. The user had to know the different meaning of a greater number of signs that were no longer self-evident. That is, a higher degree of expertise was needed to deal with the system.

Notations were born from people's possibilities and limitations, but they were turned into cognitive tools that facilitate the handling of notions and operations and increase their cognitive power. Chapter 1 discussed the extent to which the specific properties of external representations and notational systems serve to explain why they are such potent cognitive tools. Their potency is derived from the amount and variety of cognitive work that users put into play each time they use, create, and/or interpret a notation. Notations enable both anticipation and online and offline interaction. When preparing for writing, during the act of writing, and after writing, each and every one of these moments is a potential occasion for identification, comparison, inference making, and so on.

The boomerang effect may operate indefinitely because, at each step of historical development, there can be similar processes of improvement in notational facilities leading to more effective use, which increases the required level of user expertise on the part of both the notator and the interpreter.

LOOKING FORWARD AND APPRECIATING WHAT HAS BEEN LEARNED

Throughout, this book has insisted that the study of notational development is separable but not separate from cognitive development. In this respect, it departs from the Piagetian consideration of symbolic means as a part of the figurative aspect of knowledge that is thus subordinate to operational knowledge (see Introduction). Nevertheless, future research should be devoted to clarifying the relation between cognitive development and notational development, which is still a big incognito. Cognitive processes have been mentioned that are put into play in the development of the use of notations, including categorical perception, comparison, and inference making. Obviously, these processes also operate in other domains of knowledge. People recognize "a dog" despite their different colors, shapes, and sizes: They perceive in a categorical way. They also compare dogs with other animals and nonanimal input, and make the inference concerning whether or not they belong to the "dog" category, and so forth. So far, however, nobody knows how distinct or similar these operations on notations are to operations in other domains of knowledge. Certainly, some very relevant data come from neuropsychological case studies. Chapter 4 pointed out that the relations established between letters and sounds, the encoding and decoding processes, seem to be separable from other cognitive processes. Their function is "encapsulated," or enclosed within themselves, separated from other processes. The ability to map a letter to a sound seems to be very different from the ability to map a line to a visual stimulus. That is why the child in the case analyzed was unable to copy a numeral despite his ability to decode. Neuropsychological studies are indeed fundamental in shedding light on the relations between different cognitive domains. Nevertheless, research in typically developing children is also very much needed.

When psychologists and educators had a derivative view of the relations between notations and domains of knowledge, the effort was put into understanding the development of the domains of knowledge, with the assumption that this development would subsequently be reflected in notations. If we believe that knowledge of writing is derived from knowledge of spoken language, and knowledge of numerals is derived from the conceptual notion of number, then all our efforts will be invested in understanding how these domains of knowledge develop. Now, if we think that the development of writing and the development of numerals are not simply derivative from their respective domains of reference (language and number) but are separable developments, with each following the regularities of their own system, then we will also be interested in exploring these developments as such (as in this book). Nevertheless, how these developments (of writing and numerals) interact with language and the conceptual development of number, and how they interact with general cognitive process, is still an issue to be explored. Until these relations are studied in depth, claims about domain specificity, such as those made here, are still speculative.

Despite what is still unknown, what has already been learned about early notational development has many implications. The "discovery" of the existence of knowledge of writing prior to formal instruction is a demonstration of children's precocious engagement with notational systems. Writing and numerals are for them interesting objects for exploration, as real as objects and people. Thus, based on the many studies just discussed, it is not the case that adults must "motivate" children's interest in writing and numerals so that they will be more "permeable" to formal instruction. Toddlers and preschoolers seem motivated and interested enough. The point might rather be how to preserve this motivation and interest in the context of formal instruction.

This discovery has implications for understanding child development in general. It compels psychologists and psycholinguists to take it into account when evaluating other aspects of knowledge, in particular linguistic knowledge. If the conventions of writing are part of children's knowledge from so early on, then they form a basis on which to construct future knowledge. Therefore, the influence of written language on children's initial intuitions, and on the developmental changes in phonological, morphological, or syntactic representations, cannot be disregarded. Similarly for mathematics, no account of mathematical development can disregard the role of symbolic systems in children's understanding of mathematical concepts.

Moreover, in the notational domains of writing and numerals, children have demonstrated that they are active and constructive learners. The main Piagetian epistemological tenets are once again confirmed. There is no knowledge that starts from zero: All knowledge has its own developmental history, and to incorporate information, even of a conventional kind, children make that information their own through reorganization and reconstruction processes. I believe that I have shown that keeping this constructivist stance is not contradictory with positing a domain-specific view of development under-pinned by innate propensities. Accepting that human babies come in to the world with a particular sensitivity for distinguishing human faces from other objects, language from other noises, and numerical features from color or shape does not convert them into passive receptors of environmental input. By the same token, asserting that the particular properties of the object of knowledge being worked with are fundamental in the process of learning, because it is with these properties that subjects have to work and check their ideas, does not mean that these properties are directly incorporated by the learners. It has been shown once and again that the properties of conventional systems are constantly reworked through the representational needs and ideas of the learners. Children incorporate social knowledge—the features of writing, the names and shapes of the letters, and the way written words are interpreted—as raw material on which to build their strategies for representational purposes.

Finally, consider another way in which notations act as cognitive agents. It is through their perpetuation by institutional networks that notations survive and expand. It is not accidental that notations were always linked to education. As an example, according to a recent finding, 15% of the archaic Uruk texts that were referred to at length in chapter 2 were lists of words (lexical lists) that were apparently "writing manuals." Indeed, throughout the history of writing, "there was a constant concern for the structured transmission of the system from generation to generation and the method of instruction was passed along with the practical knowledge of the script" (Cooper, 1996, p. 37). It is no exaggeration to say, in line with Halliday (1987), that school was born hand in hand with writing.

There are two reasons why the link between notational systems and institutional support is so strong. On the one hand, it is strong because writing and numerals have always been in the hands of the powerful or at least in the hands of those who serve the powerful (e.g., in the church and the palace). On the other hand, it is strong because a place was needed to train people and to keep the writing. Even today, people generally learn to write seated in a particular space. These two factors, one ideological and the other practical, created a long-standing association between writing and education that still endures.

The educational implications of the circle of constant interaction between children's own ideas and the features of the notational system, what we have called the boomerang effect, are clear. If children's interaction with notational systems is limited on the premise that understanding letter-to-sound correspondences or the positional value of written numeration must first be acquired outside the systems and then applied to them, then this will interfere with children's development. In contrast, if interactions with notational artifacts are encouraged, then conceptual understanding and notational knowledge have a bootstrapping effect. As the aphorism says, and as many teachers throughout the world know, "we learn to write by writing."

Human beings have a specific propensity to leave intentional traces and a special sensitivity to features of notations. Writing and numerals appear to be interesting objects to explore, even before (and sometimes without) formal instruction. Therefore, if notational artifacts form part of a child's environment and both spontaneous and guided activities promote a constant interaction with the notational systems of writing and numerals, children turn them into a problem space. Consequently, they observe regularities, they map talk onto the observed graphic shapes, and they make inferences about functions and functioning.

Whenever someone is asked about the function of writing, the first quality they highlight is that it is a tool for communication. And there is no doubt that both writing and numerals are useful communicative tools. But this is only one of the many facets of notational systems. They have been characterized as problem spaces, as objects to think with, as epistemic tools, as providing learning experiences as real as people or any other object. It has been demonstrated how for some people they represent the creation of new cultural referents and bring about huge improvements in the conditions of their life. For others, however, they mean alienation and even death. Thus, only by looking at the multiple facets of this complex object of knowledge—personal, social, and biological—is it possible to come to grips with the consequences its mastery has on human development.

References

Adams, M. J. (1991). *Beginning to read: Thinking and learning about print*. Cambridge, MA: MIT Press.

Adkins, L., & Adkins, R. (2000). *The keys of Egypt*. New York: Harper Collins.

Allardice, B. (1977). The development of written representation for mathematical concepts. *Journal of Children's Mathematical Behavior, 1,* 135–148.

Anderson, S. W., Damasio, A. R., & Damasio, H. (1990). Troubled letters but not numbers: Domain specific cognitive impairments following focal damage in frontal cortex. *Brain, 113,* 749–766.

Antell, A., & Keating, D. P. (1983). Perception of numerical invariance in neonates. *Child Development, 54,* 695–701.

Aronoff, M. (1985). Orthography and linguistic theory. *Language, 61,* 28–72.

Aronoff, M. (1994). Spelling as culture. In W. C. Watt (Ed.), *Writing systems and cognition* (pp. 67–88). Dordrecht: Kluwer.

Auzias, M., Casati, I., Cellier, C., Delaye, R., & Verleure, F. (1977). *Écrire à cinq ans?* [Writing at five?]. Paris: Press Universitaires de France.

Barton, D. (1994). *Literacy: An introduction to the ecology of written language*. Oxford, England: Basil Blackwell.

Bednarz, N., & Janvier, B. (1984a). La numération: Les difficultés suscités par son apprentisage [Numeration: The difficulties caused by its learning]. *N, 33,* 5–31.

Bednarz, N., & Janvier, B. (1984b). La numération: Une strategie didáctique cherchant à favoriser une meilleure compréhension [Numeration: A didactic strategy aimed at improving a better comprehension]. *N, 34,* 5–17.

Bednarz, N., & Janvier, B. (1986). Une étude des conceptions inappropriées dévelopées par les enfants dans l'apprentisage de la numération au primaire [A study of the inappropriate conceptions by children when learning the numeration system in primary school]. *Journal Europeen de Psychologie de l'Education, 1–2,* 17–33.

Bednarz, N., & Janvier, B. (1988). A constructivist approach to numeration in Primary school: Results of a three year intervention with the same group of children. *Educational Studies in Mathematics, 19,* 299–331.

Beilin, H. (1985). Dispensable and core elements in Piaget's research program. *The Genetic Epistemologist, 13,* 1–16.

Bergeron, J. C., Herscovics, N., & Sinclair, H. (1992). Contribution à la genese du nombre [A contribution to the genesis of number]. *Archives de Psychologie, 60,* 147–170.

Bergeron, A., & Herscovics, N. (1990). The kindergartners' knowledge of numerals. In G. Booker, P. Cobb, & T. N de Mendecuti (Eds.), Proceedings of the 14th Psychology of Mathematics Education Conference (vol. III, pp. 111–117). México, CD: México.

Bergeron, A., Herscovics, N., & Bergeron, J. C. (1987a). Kindergartners' knowledge of numbers: A longitudinal case study, Part I: Intuitive and procedural understanding. In J. C. Bergeron, N. Herscovics, & C. Kieran (Eds.), Proceedings of the 11th Psychology of Mathematics Education Conference (vol. II, pp. 88–97). Montreal: Canada.

Bergeron, A., Herscovics, N., & Bergeron, J. C. (1987b). Kindergartners' knowledge of numbers: A longitudinal case study, Part II: Intuitive and procedural understanding. In J. C. Bergeron, N. Herscovics, & C. Kieran (Eds.), Proceedings of the 11th Psychology of Mathematics Education Conference (vol. II, pp. 98–106). Montreal: Canada.

Berman, R. (1978). *Modern Hebrew structure.* Tel Aviv: University Publishing Projects.

Bertelson, P., Cary, L., & Alegria, J. (1986). Literacy training and speech segmentation. *Cognition, 24,* 45–64.

Berthoud-Papandropoulou, I. (1980). *La réflection métalinguistique chez l'enfant* [The metalinguistic reflection in the child]. Geneva: Imprimerie National.

Bialystok, E. (1992). Symbolic representation of letters and numbers. *Cognitive Development, 7,* 301–316.

Bickerton, D. (1990). *Language and species.* Chicago: University of Chicago Press.

Bissex, G. (1980). *GNYS AT WRK. A child learns to write and read.* Cambridge, MA: Harvard University Press.

Blanche-Benveniste, C. (1982). La escritura del lenguaje dominguero [The writing of Sunday language]. In E. Ferreiro, & M. Gómez-Palacio (Eds.), *Nuevas perspectivas sobre los procesos de lectura y escritura* (pp. 247–270). México, DF: Siglo XXI.

Blanche-Benveniste, C. (1997). The units of written and oral language. In C. Pontecorvo (Ed.), *Writing development. An interdisciplinary view* (pp. 21–46). Amsterdam: John Benjamins.

Blanche-Benveniste, C., & Chervel, A. (1970). *L'Orthographe* [The orthography]. Paris: Maspero.

Bolter, J. D. (1991). *Writing space.* Hillsdale, NJ: Lawrence Erlbaum Associates.

Bottari, P., Cipriani, P., & Chilosi, A. M. (1993/1994). Protosyntactic devices in the acquisition of Italian free morphology. *Language Acquisition, 3–4,* 327–369.

Bottero, J. (1987). *La Mésopotamie. L'écriture et les dieux.* [The Mesopotamia, writing and the gods]. Paris: Gallimard.

Brennemann, K., Massey, C., Machado, S., & Gelman, R. (1996). Notating knowledge about words and objects: Pre-schoolers' plans differ for "writing" and "drawing." *Cognitive Development, 11,* 397–419.

Bruce, D. (1964). The analysis of word sounds by young children. *British Journal of Educational Psychology, 34,* 158–170.

Brun, J., Giossi, J. M., & Henriques, A. (1984). A propos de l'ecriture décimale. [On decimal writing]. *Math-École, 23,* 2–11.

Bruner, J. (1957). On perceptual readiness. *Psychological Review, 64,* 123–152.

Bruner, J. (1966). On cognitive growth. In J. Bruner, R. Olver, & P. Greenfield (Eds.), *Studies in cognitive growth* (pp. 1–29). New York: Wiley.

Bus, A. G., & Van Ijzendorm, M. H. (1988). Mother–child interactions, attachment, and emergent literacy: A cross-sectional study. *Child Development, 59,* 1262–1273.

Bus, A. G., van Ijzendorm, M. H., & Pellegrini, A. D. (1995). Joint book reading makes for success in learning to read. A meta-analysis on intergenerational analysis of literacy. *Review of Educational Research, 65,* 1–21.

Byrne, B., & Fielding-Barnsley, R. (1989). Phonemic awareness and letter knowledge in the child's acquisition of the alphabetic principle. *Journal of Educational Psychology, 81,* 313–321.

Cajori, F. (1993). *A history of mathematical notation.* New York: Dover. (Original work published 1928)

Camean Gorrias, C. (1990). *Las diferencias cualitativas en los periodos previos a la fonetización de la escritura* [Qualitative differences during the periods prior to the phonetization of writing]. Unpublished master's dissertation, Centro de Estudios Avanzados del Instituto Politécnico Nacional, México.

Cardona, G. (1994). *Antropología de la escritura* [The anthropology of writing]. Barcelona: Gedisa.

Carey, S. (1985). *Conceptual change in childhood.* Cambridge, MA: MIT Press.

Carruthers, M. J. (1990). *The book of memory: A study of memory in medieval culture.* Cambridge, England: Cambridge University Press.

Cassirer, E. (1944). *An essay on man: An introduction to a philosophy of human culture.* New Haven, CT: Yale University Press.

Cassirer, E. (1972). *La philosopie des formes symboliques,* I. *Le langage* [The philosophy of symbolic forms, Vol. I. Language]. (Original work published in 1923)

Catach, N. (1989). *Les délires de l'orthographe* [Orthographic delirium]. Paris: Plon.

Chan, L. (1990). *Pre-school children's understanding of Chinese writing.* Unpublished master's thesis, University of London, London, England.

Chan, L., & Nunes, T. (1998). Children's understanding of the formal and functional characteristics of written Chinese. *Applied Psycholinguistics, 19,* 115–1311.

Chomsky, C. (1979). Approaching reading through invented spelling. In L. B. Resnick & P. A. Weaver (Eds.), *Theory and practice of early reading* (vol. 2, pp. 43–65). Hillsdale, NJ: Lawrence Erlbaum Associates.

Chomsky, N. (1957). *Syntactic structures.* The Hague: Mouton.

Chomsky, N., & Halle, M. (1968). *The sound pattern of English.* New York: Harper & Row.

Churchland, P. M. (1988). *Matter and consciousness* (rev. ed.). Cambridge, MA: MIT Press.

Cipolotti, L., Warrington, E. K., & Butterworth, B. (1995). Selective impairment in manipulating Arabic numerals. *Cortex, 31,* 73–86.

Cipolotti, L. (1993). *Acquired disorders of numerical processing.* Unpublished doctoral dissertation. University of London.

Clark, A. (1997). *Being there: Putting brain, body, and world together.* Cambridge, MA: MIT Press.

Clark, E.V. (1978). Awareness of language: Some evidence from what children say and do. In A. Sinclair, R. J. Jarvella, & W. Levelt (Eds.), *The child's conceptions of language* (pp. 2–43). New York: Springer-Verlag.

Clay, M. (1982). *What did I write? Beginning writing behavior.* Portsmouth, NH: Heinemann.

Clemente, A. R. (1984). La segmentación de textos. El comportamiento evolutivo [The segmentation of texts. A developmental behavior]. *Infancia y Aprendizaje, 26,* 77–86.

Cohen, S. (1983). *The development of notational skills in children.* Unpublished dissertation, Stanford University.

Cohen, S. (1985). The development of constraints on symbol-meaning: Evidence from production, interpretation and forced-choiced judgements. *Child Development, 56,* 177–195.

Cole, M., & Griffin, P. (1981). A socio-cultural approach to remediation. In S. Castell, A. Luke, & K. Egan (Eds.), *Literacy, society and schooling* (pp. 110–131). Cambridge England: Cambridge University Press.

Cooper, J. (1996). Sumerian and Akkadian. In P. T. Daniels & W. Bright (Eds.), *The world's writing systems* (pp. 37–40). New York: Oxford University Press.

Cooper, R. G., Jr. (1984). Early number development: Discovering number space with addition and subtraction. In C. Sophian (Ed.), *Origins of cognitive skills* (pp. 157–192). Hillsdale, NJ: Lawrence Erlbaum Associates.

Cossu, G. (1997). Domain-specificity and fractionability of neuropsychological processes in literacy acquisition. In C. Pontecorvo (Ed.), *Writing development: An interdisciplinary view* (pp. 243–258). Amsterdam: John Benjamins.

Cossu, G., & Marshall, J. C. (1990). Are cognitive skills a prerequisite for learning to Read and write? *Cognitive Neuropsychology, 7,* 21–40.

Cossu, G., Shankweiler, D., Liberman, I., Katz, L., & Tola, G. (1988). Awareness of phonological segments and reading ability in Italian children. *Applied Psycholinguistics, 9,* 1–16.

Coulmas, F. (1990). *The writing systems of the world.* Oxford, England: Basil Blackwell.

Cowan, R., Rogers-Ewers, J., & Chiu, W. (1997, August). *Much ado about nothing.* Paper presented at the EARLI Conference, Athens, Greece.

Cromer, R. (1988). The Cognition Hypothesis revisited. In F. Kessel (Ed.), *The development of language and language researchers: Essays in honor of Roger Brown* (pp. 223–248). Hillsdale, NJ: Lawrence Erlbaum Associates.

Crump, T. (1990). *The anthropology of numbers.* Cambridge, England: Cambridge University Press.

Cutler, A., Mehler, J., & Segui, J. (1986). The syllable's differing role in the segmentation of French and English. *Journal of Memory and Language, 25,* 385–400.

D'Andrade, R. (1981). The cultural part of cognition. *Cognitive Science, 5,* 179–195.

Damasio, A. R. (1994) *Descartes Error.* New York: Grosset/Putman.

Danesi, M. (1996). Introduction to *Signos: Una introducción a la semiótica.* Barcelona: Paidos.

DeCasper, A., & Fifer, W. P. (1980, June 6). On human bonding. Newborns prefer their mothers' voice. *Science, 208,* 1174–1176.

Dehaene, S. (1992). Varieties of numerical knowledge. *Cognition, 44,* 1–42.

Dehaene, S. (1997). *Number sense.* London: Allen Lane.

Dehaene, S., & Cohen, L. (1991). Two mental calculation systems: A case study of severe acalculia with preserved approximation. *Neuropsychologia, 29,* 1045–1074.

Déjerine, J. (1892). Contribution à l'étude anatomoclinique et clinique des differentes variétés de cécité verbale [Contribution to the anatomic-clinical and clinic study of different variables of verbal blindness]. *Memoires de la Société de Biologie, 4,* 61–90.

, A., Orsolini, M., & Pace, C. (1990). Consapevolezza linguistica nei bambini in età prescolare [Linguistic knowledge in preschool age children]. *Rassegna di Linguistica Applicata, 5,* 153–177.

Diringer, D. (1962). *Writing.* London: Thames & Hudson.

Donald, M. (1991). *Origins of the modern mind: Three stages in the evolution of culture and cognition.* Cambridge, MA: Harvard University Press.

Durking, D. (1966). *Children who read early: Two longitudinal studies.* New York: Teacher's College Press

Eco, U. (1988) *Sémiotique et philosophie du langage* [Semiotics and the philosophy of language]. Paris: Presses Universitaires de France.

Ehri, L. C. (1984). How orthography alters spoken language competencies in children learning to read and spell. In J. Downing & R. Valtin (Eds.), *Language awareness and leaning to read* (pp. 119–147). New York: Springer-Verlag.

Ehri, L. C. (1993). English orthography and phonological knowledge. In R. Scholes (Ed.), *Literacy and language analysis* (pp. 21–43). Hillsdale, NJ: Lawrence Erlbaum Associates.

Eimas, P. H., Siqueland, E. R., Jusczyk, P., & Vigorito, J. (1971, January 22). Speech perception in infants. *Science, 171,* 303–306.

Ewers-Rogers, J., & Cowan, R. (1996). Children as apprentices to number. *Early Child Development and Care, 25,* 15–25.

Ferreiro, E. (1983). Los adultos no—alfabetizados y sus conceptualizaciones del sistema de escritura [Illiterate adults and their conceptualization of the system of writing].

Cuadernos de Investigación Educativa, 10 Departamento de Investigaciones Educativas, Cento de Investigación y de Estudios avanzados del I.P. N, México.

Ferreiro, E. (1984). The underlying logic of literacy development. In H. Goelman, A. Oberg, & F. Smith (Eds.), *Awakening to literacy* (pp. 154–173). Portsmouth, NH: Heineman.

Ferreiro, E. (1985). Literacy development: A psychogenetic perspective. In D. R. Olson, N. Torrance, & A. Hildyard (Eds.), *Literacy, language and learning* (pp. 217–228). Cambridge, England: Cambridge University Press.

Ferreiro, E. (1986). The interplay between information and assimilation in beginning literacy. In W. Teale & E. Sulzby (Eds.), *Emergent literacy: Writing and reading* (pp. 15–49). Norwood, NJ: Ablex.

Ferreiro, E. (1988). L'écriture avant la lettre. In H. Sinclair (Ed.), *La production de notations chez le jeune enfant: Langage, nombre, rythmes et melodies* [The production of notations in young children: Language, number, rhythms, and melodies] (pp. 17–70). Paris: Press Universitaires de France.

Ferreiro, E., Pontecorvo, C., Ribeiro Moreira, N., & García Hidalgo, I. (1996). *Chapeuzinho vermelho aprende a escrever* [Little Red Ridinghood learns how to write]. Sao Paulo: Atica.

Ferreiro, E., & Teberosky, A. (1979). *Los sistemas de escritura en el desarrollo del niño* [Literacy before schooling]. México: Siglo XXI.

Fevrier, J. (1971). Los semitas y el alfabeto. Escrituras concretas y escrituras abstractas [The Semitic people and the alphabet. Concrete writing and abstract writing]. In M. Cohen, & J. S. Fare Granot (Eds.), *La escritura y la psicología de los pueblos* (pp 115–128). Buenos Aires: Siglo XXI.

Filliozat, J. (1971). Las escrituras indias. El mundo hindú y su sistema gráfico [Indic writing of the Indian world and its graphic system]. In M. Cohen & J. S. Fare Granot (Eds.), *La escritura y la psicología de los pueblos* (pp. 145–166). [Writing and the psychology of peoples]. Buenos Aires: Siglo XXI.

Fordham, S., & Ogbu, J. U. (1986). Black students' school success: Coping with the burden of "acting white." *The Urban Review: Issues and Ideas in Public Education, 18,* 176–206.

Fox, B., & Routh, D. K. (1975). Analyzing spoken language into words, syllables and phonemes: A developmental study. *Journal of Psycholinguistic Research, 4,* 331– 342.

Fraenkel, B. (1992). *La signature* [The signature]. Paris: Gallimard.

Freeman, N. H. (1980). *Strategies of representation in young children: Analysis of spatial skills and drawing processes.* New York: Academic Press.

Frith, U. (1980). Unexpected spelling problems. In U. Frith (Ed.), *Cognitive processes in spelling* (pp. 495–516). London: Academic Press.

Frith, U. (1989, April). *Aspectos psicolingüísticos de la lectura y la ortografía. Evolución y trastorno.* [Psycholinguistic aspects in reading and spelling: Development and disorders]. Paper presented at the V Simposio Escuelas de Logopedia y Psicología del Lenguaje, Salamanca, Spain.

Fuson, K. (1990). Issues in place value and multidigit addition and substraction learning and teaching. *Journal of Research in Mathematical Education, 21,* 273–280.

Gallistel, C. R., & Gelman, R. (1991). The preverbal counting process. In W. E. Kessen, A. Ortony, & F. I. M. Craik (Eds.), *Thoughts, memory and emotions: Essays in honor of George Mandler* (pp. 65–81). Hillsdale, NJ: Lawrence Erlbaum Associates.

Gallistel, C. R., & Gelman, R. (1992). Preverbal and verbal counting and computation. *Cognition, 44,* 43–74.

Gelb, I. J. (1963). *A study of writing* (2nd ed.). Chicago: University of Chicago Press.

Gelb, I. J. (1980). Principles of writing systems within the frame of visual communication. In P. A. Kolers, M. E. Wrolstad, & H. Bouma (Eds.), *Processing of visible language* (Vol. 2, pp. 7–25). New York: Plenum.

Gelman, R. (1982). Accessing one to one correspondence: Still another paper on conservation. *British Journal of Psychology, 73,* 209–220.

Gelman, R. (1990). Structural constraints on cognitive development: Introduction to a special issue of cognitive science. *Cognitive Science, 14,* 3–9.

Gelman, R. (1998). Domain specificity in cognitive development: Universals and non-universals. In M. Sabourin, F. Craik, & M. Robert (Eds.), *Advances in psychological science volume 2: Biological and cognitive aspects* (pp. 557–579) Hove, UK: Psychology Press, Ltd., Publishers.

Gelman, R., & Gallistel, C. R. (1978). *The child's understanding of number.* Cambridge, MA: Harvard University Press.

Gelman, R., & Meck, E. (1986). The notion of principle: The case of counting. In J. Hiebert (Ed.), *The relationship between procedural and conceptual competence* (pp. 72–96). Hillsdale, NJ: Lawrence Erlbaum Associates.

Gibson, E., & Levin, H. (1975). *The psychology of reading.* Cambridge, MA: MIT Press.

Gil, R., & Tolchinsky, L. (1997, August). *Small children's notation of big numbers.* Paper presented at the EARLI Conference, Athens.

Ginzburg, C. (1982). *The cheese and the worms. The cosmos of a sixteenth-century miller.* London: Penguin.

Gleitman, L. R., & Gleitman, H. (1979). Language use and language judgement. In C. J. Fillmore, D. Kempler, W., & S.-Y Wang (Eds.), *Individual differences in language ability and language behavior* (pp. 103–123). New York: Academic Press.

Gombrich, E. H. (1960). *Art and illusion: A study in the psychology of pictorial representation.* New York: Bollingen/Pantheon.

Goodman, N. (1976). *Languages of art.* Indianapolis: Hacket.

Goodman, Y. (1982). El desarrollo de la escritura en niños muy pequeños [The development of writing in very small children]. In E. Ferreiro, & M. Gómez Palacio (Eds.), *Nuevas perspectivas sobre los procesos de lectura y escritura* (pp. 107–128). México, DF: Siglo XXI.

Goody, J. (1977). *The domestication of the savage mind.* Cambridge, England: Cambridge University Press.

Goody, J., & Watt, Y. (1968). The consequences of literacy. In J. Goody (Ed.), *Literacy in traditional societies* (pp. 27–68). Cambridge, England: Cambridge University Press.

Goswami, U., & Bryant, P. (1990). *Phonological skills and learning to read.* Hove, UK: Lawrence Erlbaum Associates.

Gould, S. J. (1989). *Wonderful life: The Burgess shale and the nature of history.* New York: W. W. Norton.

Grau i Franch, X. (1988). La serie numérica: reconstruir para generalizar [The number series: Reconstructing for generalizing]. In M. Moreno (Ed.), *Ciencia, aprendizaje y comunicación* (pp. 187–199). Barcelona: Laia.

Greco, P. (1963). Le progrés des inférences itératives et des notions arithmétiques chez l'enfant et l'adolescent [The progress of iterative inferences and arithmetic notions in the child and the adolescent]. In P. Greco, B. Inhelder, B. Matalon, & J. Piaget (Eds.), *La formation des raisonnements recurrentiels* (pp. 134–152). Paris: Press Universitaires de France.

Green, J. N. (1990). Spanish. In M. Harris & N. Vincent (Eds.), *The Romance languages* (pp. 79–130). London: Routledge & Kegan Paul.

Greeno, J. (1991). Number sense as situated knowing in a conceptual domain. *Journal for Research in Mathematics Education, 22,* 170–218.

Gruber, H. E., & Vonechè, J. (1977). *The essential Piaget.* London: Routledge & Kegan Paul.

Halliday, M. K. S. (1987). Language and the natural order. In N. Fabb, D. Attridge, A. Durant, & C. MacCabe (Eds.), *The linguistics of writing* (pp. 147–164). Manchester, England: Manchester University Press.

Harris, R. (1986). *The origin of writing.* London: Duckworth.

Harris, R. (1987). *Reading Saussure: A critical commentary on the Cours de linguistique générale.* London: Duckworth.

Harris, R. (1992). Écriture et notation [Writing and notation]. *Proceedings of the Workshop on Orality versus Literacy: Concepts, Methods and Data.* Siena, Italy: ESF.

Harris, R. (1995). *Signs of writing.* London: Routledge & Kegan Paul.

Harste, J. C., Woodward, V. A., & Burke, C. L. (1984). *Language stories and literacy lessons.* Portsmouth, NH: Heinemann.

Hass, W. (1990). On the writing of numbers. In N. Catach (Ed.), *Pour une theorie de la langue écrite* [For a theory of written language] (pp. 203– 212).Paris: Editions du CNRS.

Havelock, E. (1996). *La musa aprende a escribir* [The muse learns to write]. Barcelona: Paidos.

Heath, S. B. (1983). *Ways with words: Language, life and work in communities and classrooms.* Cambridge, MA: Harvard University Press.

Hébrard, J. (1993). L'autodidaxie exemplaire: Comment Valentin Jamerey-Duval apprit-il á lire? [The exemplar self-teaching: How did Valentin Jamerey-Duval learn to read?]. In R. Chartier (Ed.), *Pratiques de la lecture* (pp.29–78). Paris: Rivage.

Hildreth, G. (1936). Developmental sequences in name writing. *Child Development, 7,* 291–303.

Hodge, C. (1975). Ritual and writing: An inquiry into the origin of Egyptian script. In M. D. Kinkade, K. L. Hale, & O. Werner (Eds.), *Linguistics and anthropology* (pp. 123–157). Lisse: Peter de Ridder.

Hughes, M. (1986). *Children and number difficulties in learning mathematics.* Oxford, England: Basil Blackwell.

Hurford, J. (1987). *Language and number. The emergence of a cognitive system.* Oxford, England: Basil Blackwell.

Ifrah, G. (1981). *From one to zero: A universal history of numbers.* Harmondsworth, UK: Penguin.

Ifrah, G. (1997). *Historia universal de las cifras* [Universal history of ciphers]. Madrid: Espasa Calpe.

Inhelder, B., & Cellérier, G. (1996). *Los senderos de los descubrimientos del niño* [Children's ways of discovery]. Barcelona: Paidos.

Jakubowicz, C. (1997). L'acquisition des clitiques nominatifs en français [The acquisition of nominative clitics]. In A. Zribi-Hertz (Ed.), *Les pronoms: morphologie, syntaxe et typologie* (pp. 57–99). Paris: Presses Universitaires de Vincennes.

Jusczyk, P. W. (1997). *The discovery of spoken language.* Cambridge, MA: MIT Press.

Kamii, C. (1986). Place value: An explanation of its difficulty and educational implications for the primary grades. *Journal of Research in Childhood Education, 1,* 75–85.

Kamii, C., & De Clark, G. (1985). *Young children reinvent arithmetic.* New York: Teacher's College Press.

Kamii, C., Long, R., Manning, G., & Manning, M. (1993). Les conceptualisations du système alphabétique chez les jeunes enfants anglophones [The conceptualization of the alphabetic system in small English speaking children]. *Etudes de Lingüistique Appliquée, 91,* 34–47.

Karanth, P., & Suchitra, M. G. (1993). Literacy acquisition and grammaticality judgments. In R. Scholes (Ed.), *Literacy and language analysis* (pp. 143–156). Hillsdale, NJ: Lawrence Erlbaum Associates.

Karmiloff-Smith, A. (1986). Stage/structure versus phase/process in modeling linguistic and cognitive development. In I. Levin (Ed.), *Stage and structure: Reopening the debate* (pp. 164–190). Norwood, NJ: Ablex.

Karmiloff-Smith, A. (1990). Constraints on representational change: Evidence from children's drawing. *Cognition, 34,* 57–83.

Karmiloff-Smith, A. (1992). *Beyond modularity: A developmental perspective on cognitive science.* Cambridge, MA: MIT Press.

Karmiloff-Smith, A., Grant, J., Sims, K., Jones, M-C., & Cuckle, P. (1996). Rethinking metalinguistic awareness: Representing and accessing knowledge about what counts as a word. *Cognition, 58*, 197–219.

Karpova, S. N. (1955). Abstracts of Soviet studies of child language. In F. Smith & G. A. Miller (Eds.), *The genesis of language* (pp. 363–386). Cambridge, MA: MIT Press.

Kipling, R. (1989) *Just so stories.* London: Penguin (Original work published 1902)

Lahire, B. (1995). *Tableaux de famille* [Family Pictures]. Paris: Seuil/Gallimard.

Lavine, L. (1972). *The development of perception of writing in pre-reading children: A cross-cultural study.* Unpublished doctoral dissertation. Department of Human Development, Cornell University.

Lavine, L. (1977). Differentiation of letterlike forms in prereading children. *Developmental Psychology, 23*, 89–94.

Lee, K., & Karmiloff-Smith, A. (1996). The development of cognitive constraints on notations. *Archives de Psychologie, 64*, 3–26.

Lee, K., & Karmiloff-Smith, A. (1997). Notational development: The use of symbols. In E. C. Carterette & M. P. Friedman (Eds.), *Handbook of perception, 13: Perceptual and cognitive development* (pp. 185–211). New York: Academic Press.

Lerner, D., & Sadovsky, P. (1994). El sistema de numeración: Un problema didáctico [The system of numeration: A didactic problem]. In C. Parra & I. Saiz (Eds.), *Didáctica de las matemáticas* (pp. 95–184). Buenos Aires: Paidos.

Levin, I., & Korat, O. (1993). Sensitivity to phonological, morphological and semantic cues in early reading and writing in Hebrew. *Merrill-Palmer Quarterly, 392*, 233–251.

Levin, I., Ravid, D., & Rapaport, S. (1997, March). *Developing awareness and learning to write: A two-way street.* Paper presented at the international symposium Integrating Research and Practice in Literacy, Institute of Education, University of London.

Levin, I., & Tolchinsky-Landsmann, L. (1990). Becoming literate: Referential and phonetic strategies in early reading and writing. *European Journal of Behavioural Development, 12*, 369–384.

Lévi-Strauss, C. (1973). *Tristes tropiques* [Sad Tropics]. London: Cape.

Luria, A. R. (1978). The development of writing in the child. In M. Cole (Ed.), *The selected writings of A. R. Luria* (pp. 146–194). New York: M.E. Sharpe. (Original work published 1929)

Lyon, J. (1971). *Theoretical linguistics.* London: Cambridge University Press.

Mandler, G., & Shebo, B. J. (1982). Subitizing: An analysis of its components processes. *Journal of Experimental Psychology: General, 111*, 1–22.

Mann, V. A. (1986). Phonological awareness: The role of reading experience. *Cognition, 24*, 65–92.

Markman, E. M., Horton, M. S., & McLanahan, A. G. (1980). Classes and collections. Principles of organization in the learning of hierarchical relations. *Cognition, 8*, 227–241.

Mattingly, I. G. (1972). Reading, the linguistic process and linguistic awareness. In J. F. Kavanagh & I. G. Mattingly (Eds.), *Language by ear and by eye* (pp. 133–147). Cambridge, MA: MIT Press.

McGarrigle, J., & Donaldson, M. (1975). Conservation accidents. *Cognition, 3*, 341–350.

McLane, J. B., & McNamee, G. D. (1990). *Early literacy.* Cambridge, MA: Harvard University Press.

McLuhan, M. (1962). *The Gutenberg galaxy.* Toronto: Toronto University Press.

McNeill, D., & Lindig, K. (1973). The perceptual reality of phonemes, syllables, words, and sentences. *Journal of Verbal Learning and Verbal Behavior, 12*, 419–430.

Mehler, J., Dommergues, J., Frauenfelder, V., & Segui, J. (1984). The syllable's role in speech segmentation. *Journal of Verbal Learning and Verbal Behavior, 20*, 298–305.

Mehler, J., & Dupoux, E. (1990). *Naitre Humain* [To be born human]. Paris: Odile Jacob.

Merlo de Rivas, S., Scheuer, N., & Criado, N. (1993). *Caminos: Modalidades en la representacion de la cantidad* [Ways: Modalities in the representation of quantity]. Paper presented at the Jornadas Interinstitucionales sobre Psicopedagogía Clínica y Problemas de Aprendizaje, Universidad de Buenos Aires.

Métraux, A. (1971). Los primitivos. Señales y símbolos, pictogramas y protoescritura [The primitives. Signals and symbols, pictograms and protowriting]. In M. Cohen, & F. Garnot (Eds.), *La escritura y la psicología de los pueblos* (pp. 1–22). Buenos Aires: Siglo XXI.

Michalowski, P. (1996). Mesopotamian Cuneiform. In P. Daniels, & W. Bright (Eds.), *The world's writing systems* (pp. 33–36). New York: Oxford University Press.

Miller, K. (1996). Origins of quantitative competence. In R. Gelman & T. Kit-Fong Au (Eds.), *Perceptual and cognitive development* (pp. 213–243). San Diego, CA: Academic Press.

Miller, K., & Stigler, J. W. (1987). Counting in Chinese: Cultural variation in a basic cognitive skill. *Cognitive Development, 2,* 279–305.

Miura, I., Okamoto, Y., Kim, Ch., Steere, M., & Fayol, M. (1993–1994). First grader's cognitive representation of number and understanding of place value: Cross-national comparisons: France, Japan, Korea, Sweden and the United States. *Journal of Educational Psychology, 85,* 21–30.

Moore, D., Benenson, J., Reznick, J. S., Peterson, P., & Kagan, J. (1987). Effect of auditory numerical information on infant's looking behavior: Contradictory evidence. *Developmental Psychology, 23,* 665–670.

Morais, J. (1991). *L'art de lire* [The art of reading]. Paris: Odile Jacob.

Morais, J., Cary, L., Alegría, J., & Bertelson, P. (1979). Does awareness of speech as a sequence of phones arise spontaneously? *Cognition, 7,* 323–331.

Morris, C. (1964). *Signification and significance: A study of the relations of signs and values.* Cambridge, MA: MIT Press.

Moyer, R. S., & Landauer, T. K. (1967, September, 30). The time required for judgement of numerical inequality. *Nature, 215,* 1519–1520.

Munn, P. (1994). The early development of literacy and numeracy skills. *European Early Childhood Education Research Journal, 2,* 2–18.

Munn, P., & Schaffer, H. R. (1993). Literacy and numeracy events in social interactive contexts. *International Journal of Early Years Education, 1,* 61–80.

Nemirovky, M. (1995). Leer no es lo inverso de escribir ni escribir lo inverso de leer [Neither reading is the inverse of writing nor writing is the inverse of reading]. In A. Teberosky & L. Tolchinsky (Eds.), *Mas allá de la alfabetización* [Beyond Literacy] (pp. 243–284). Buenos Aires: Santillana.

Nespor, M., & Vogel, I. (1986). *Prosodic phonology.* Dordrecht: Foris.

Ninio, A., & Bruner, J. (1978). The achievement and antecedents of labeling. *Journal of Child Language, 5,* 1–15.

Nunberg, G. (1990). *The linguistics of punctuation.* Stanford, CA: Center for the Study of Language.

Nunes, T., & Bryant, P. (1996). *Children doing mathematics.* Cambridge, MA: Basil Blackwell.

Nunes, T., Bryant, P., & Bidman, M. (1997). *Morphological spelling strategies: Developmental stages and processes.* London: University of London Press.

Nunes, T., Schlieman, A. L., & Carraher, D. (1983). *Street mathematics and school mathematics.* New York: Cambridge University Press.

Ogbu, J. V. (1990). Cultural models, identity and literacy. In J. W. Stigler, R. A. Shweder, & G. Herdt (Eds.), *Cultural psychology* (pp. 520–541). Cambridge, MA: Harvard University Press.

Olson, D. (1994). *The world on paper. The conceptual and cognitive implications of writing and reading.* Cambridge, England: Cambridge University Press.

Pettersson, J. S. (1996). Numerical notation. In P. Daniels & W. Bright (Eds.), *The world's writing systems* (pp. 794–806). New York: Oxford University Press.

Parkes, M. B. (1992). *Pause and effect: An introduction to the history of punctuation in the West.* Hats, UK: Scholar Press.

Paulos, J. A. (1995). *El hombre anumérico.* Barcelona: Tusquets. [Original: *Innumeracy: Mathematical illiteracy and its consequences*, 1988.]

Perfetti, C. (1985). *Reading ability.* New York: Oxford University Press.

Piaget, J. (1951). *Play, dreams and imitation in childhood.* London: Routledge & Kegan Paul.

Piaget, J., & Inhelder, B. (1966). *L'image mentale chez l'enfant* [The child's mental image]. Paris: Press Universitaires de France.

Piaget, J., & Szeminska, A. (1967). *La génesis del número en el niño* [The child's conception of number]. Buenos Aires: Guadalupe. (Original work published 1941)

Pick, A., Unze, M. G., Brownell, C. A. , Drodzal, J. G., & Hopman, M. (1978). Young children's knowledge of word structure. *Child Development, 49*, 669–680.

Pierce, C. S. (1966). *Collected papers.* In C. Hartshorne, P. Weiss, & A. W. Burks (Eds.). (Original work published 1935)

Pinker, S. (1995). *The language instinct.* New York: Harper Perennial.

Pontecorvo, C. (1985). Figure, scritture, numeri: Un problema di simbolizazione [Pictures, writing, and numbers: A problem of symbolization]. *Età Evolutiva, 22*, 5–33.

Pontecorvo, C., & Rossi, F. (2001). Absence, negation, impossibility and falsity in children's first writing. In L. Tolchinsky (Ed.), *Developmental aspects in learning to write* (pp. 13–32). Dordrecht: Kluwer Academic.

Power, R., & Del Martello, M. (1990). The dictation of Italian numerals. *Language and Cognitive Processes, 5*, 237–254.

Prakash, P., Rekha, D., Nigam, R., & Karanth, P. (1993). Phonological awareness, orthography and literacy. In R. J. Scholes (Ed.), *Literacy and language analysis* (pp. 55–70). Hillsdale, NJ: Lawrence Erlbaum Associates.

Ravid, D., & Tolchinsky, L. (2002). Developing linguistic literacy: A comprehensive model. *Journal of Child Language, 29*, 417–447.

Read, C. (1971). Pre-school children's knowledge of English phonology. *Harvard Educational Review, 41*, 1–34.

Read, C. (1973). Children's judgement of phonetic similarities in relation to English spelling. *Language Learning, 23*, 17–38.

Read, C. (1986). *Children's creative spelling.* London: Routledge & Kegan Paul.

Read, C., Zhang, Y., Nie, H., & Ding, B. (1986). The ability to manipulate speech sounds depends on knowing alphabetic writing. *Cognition, 24*, 31–44.

Resnick, L. B. (1983). A development theory of number understanding. In P. Ginsburg (Ed.), *The development of mathematical thinking* (pp. 109–151). New York: Academic Press.

Richards, J., & Carter, R. (1982, March). *The numeration system.* Paper presented at the annual meeting of the American Education Research Association, New York, USA.

Ross, S. H. (1986, April). *The development of children's place value. Numeration concepts in grades 2 through 5.* Paper presented at the annual meeting of the American Education Research Association, San Francisco.

Sampson, G. (1985). *Writing systems.* Stanford, CA: Stanford University Press.

Saussure, F. de (1987). *Curso de lingüística general* [Course in general linguistics]. Madrid: Alianza Editorial. (Original work published 1916)

Savage-Rumbaugh, E. S. (1990). Language acquisition in non-human species. Implications for the innateness debate. *Developmental Psychobiology, 23*, 599–620.

Savage-Rumbaugh, S., Shanker, S., & Taylor, T. (1998). *Apes, language, and the human mind.* Oxford, England: Oxford University Press.

Scheuer, N. (1996). La construction du système de notation numérique chez l'enfant [The child's construction of the number notation system]. Unpublished dissertation, University of Geneve.

Schmandt-Besserat, D. (1978). An archaic recording system and the origin of writing. *Syro-Mesopotamian Studies*, ½, 2–32

Schmandt-Besserat, D. (1990). Symbols in the prehistoric Middle East: Developmental features preceding written communication. In R. Enos (Ed.), *Oral and written communication: Historical approaches* (pp. 16–31). London: Sage.

Schmandt-Besserat, D. (1996). *How writing came about.* Austin: University of Texas Press.

Scholes, R. (1993). In search of phonemic consciousness. In R. Scholes (Ed.), *Literacy and language analysis* (pp. 45–54). Hillsdale, NJ: Lawrence Erlbaum Associates.

Scinto, L. (1986). *Written language and psychological development.* London: Academic Press.

Scollon, R., & Scollon, S. B. K. (1981). *Narrative, literacy and face in interethnic communication.* Norwood, NJ: Ablex.

Scribner, S. (1985). Vygotsky's uses of history. In J. V. Wertsch (Ed.), *Culture, communication, and cognition: Vygotskian perspectives* (pp. 119–145). Cambridge, England: Cambridge University Press.

Scribner, S., & Cole, M. (1983). *The psychology of literacy.* Cambridge, MA: Harvard University Press.

Sebeok, T. (1996). *Signos: Una introducción a la semiótica* [Signs: An introduction to semiotics]. Barcelona: Paidos.

Serpell, R. (1993). *The significance of schooling: Life journeys in African society.* Cambridge, UK: Cambridge University Press.

Serra, M., Serrat, E., Sole, R., Bel, A., & Aparici, M. (2000). *La adquisición del lenguaje* [The acquisition of language]. Barcelona: Ariel.

Shimron, J. (1993). The role of vowels in reading: A review of studies of English and Hebrew. *Psychological Bulletin, 114*, 52–67.

Shipley, E. F., Smith, C. S., & Gleitman, R. S. (1969). A study in the acquisition of language: Free responses to commands. *Language, 45*, 322–342.

Siegler, R. (1981). Developmental sequences within and between concepts. *Monographs of the Society for Research in Child Development, 46* (2, Serial No. 189).

Sinclair, A. (1997, August). *To two, to three, to minus one, to five: Numbers, numerals, fingers and things at age three.* Paper presented at the EARLI Conference, Athens, Greece.

Sinclair, A., Mello, D., & Siegrist, F. (1988). La notation numérique chez l'enfant [The child's notation of number]. In H. Sinclair (Ed.), *La production de notations chez le jeune enfant: langage, nombre, rythmes et melodies* [The production of notations in children: language, number, rhythms and melodies] (pp. 71–99). Paris: Press Universitaires de France.

Sinclair, A., & Scheuer, N. (1993). Understanding the written number system: 6 year-olds in Argentina and Switzerland. *Educational Studies in Mathematics, 24*, 199–221.

Sinclair, A., Siegrist, F., & Sinclair, H. (1983). Young children's ideas about the written number systems. In D. Rogers & J. Sloboda (Eds.), *The acquisition of symbolic skills* (pp. 535–542). New York: Plenum.

Sinclair, A., & Sinclair, H. (1984). Pre-schooler interpretation of written numerals. *Human Learning, 3*, 173–184.

Sinclair, A., Tieche Christinat, C., & Garin, A. (1992). L'interpretation des nombres écrits chez l'enfant de cinq à sept ans [The interpretation of written numbers by 5- to 7-year olds.]. *Archives de Psychologie, 61*, 75–93.

Sinclair, H. (1988). Introduction to H. Sinclair (Ed.), *La production de notations chez le jeune enfant: langage, nombre, rythmes et melodies* [The production of notations in children: language, number, rhythms and melodies] (pp. 9–16). Paris: Press Universitaires de France.

Sirat, C. (1994). Handwriting and the writing hand. In W. C. Watt (Ed.), *Writing systems and cognition* (pp. 375–461). Dordrecht: Kluwer.

Skemp, R. (1986). *The psychology of learning mathematics.* London: Penguin.

Snow, C. E. , & Ninio, A. (1986). The contracts of literacy: What children learn from learning to read books. In W. Teale & E. Sulzby (Eds.), *Emergent literacy: Writing and reading* (pp. 116–139). Norwood, NJ: Ablex.

Spencer, A. (1996). *Phonology.* Cambridge, MA: Blackwell.

Stanovich, K. E. (1986). Matthew effects in reading. Some consequences of individual differences in the acquisition of literacy. *Reading Research Quarterly, 21,* 360–406.

Starkey, P., & Cooper, R. G., Jr. (1980). Perception of number by human infants. *Science, 200,* 1033–1035.

Starkey, P., Spelke, E., & Gelman, R. (1983). Detection of intermodal correspondences by human infants. *Science, 222,* 179–181.

Strauss, M. S., & Curtiss, L. E. (1981). Infants' perception of numerosity. *Child Development, 52,* 1146–1152.

Strauss, M. S., & Curtiss, L. E. (1984). Development of numerical concepts in infancy. In C. Sophian (Ed.), *Origins of cognitive skills* (pp. 131–155). Hillsdale, NJ: Lawrence Erlbaum Associates.

Starkey, P., Spelke, E., & Gelman, R. (1983, October). Detection of intermodal correspondences by human infants. *Science, 222,* 179–181.

Street, B. V. (1984). *Literacy in theory and practice.* Cambridge, England: Cambridge University Press.

Sulzby, E. (1994). Children's emergent reading of favorite storybooks with postscript. In R. B. Rudell, M. R. Rudell, & H. Singer (Eds.) *Theoretical models and processes of reading* (4th. ed., pp. 244–280). Newark, DE: International Reading Association.

Teale, W., & Sulzby, E. (Eds.). (1986). *Emergent literacy: Writing and reading,* Norwood, NJ: Ablex.

Teberosky, A. (1990). Re-escribiendo noticias: Una aproximación a los textos de niños y adultos en proceso de alfabetización [Rewriting news: Approaching children and adults' texts in the process of becoming literate]. *Anuario de Psicología, 47,* 11–28.

Terrigi, F. (1991). *Psicogénesis del sistema de numeración* [The psychogenesis of the numeration system]. Unpublished student report, University of Buenos Aires.

Teubal, E., & Dockrell, J. (1997, August). *The relation between the nature of the stimulus input and children's notations with numbers.* Paper presented at the EARLI Conference, Athens, Greece.

Tolchinsky, L. (1995). Dibujar, escribir, hacer numeros [Drawing, writing and making numbers]. In A. Teberosky & L. Tolchinsky (Eds.), *Mas allá de la alfabetización* (pp. 215–242). Buenos Aires: Santillana.

Tolchinsky, L., & Teberosky, A. (1997). Explicit word segmentation and writing in Hebrew and Spanish. In C. Pontecorvo (Ed.), *Writing development. An interdisciplinary view* (pp. 77–98). Amsterdam: John Benjamins.

Tolchinsky, L., & Teberosky, A. (1998). The development of word segmentation and writing in two scripts. *Cognitive Development, 13,* 1–21.

Tolchinsky-Landsmann, L. (1989). Form and meaning in the development of written representation. *European Journal of Educational Psychology, 3,* 385–398.

Tolchinsky-Landsmann, L. (1990). Early writing development: Evidencies from different orthographic systems. In M. Spoelders (Ed.), *Literacy acquisition* (pp. 222–234). Lier, Belgium: Van In and C & C.

Tolchinsky-Landsmann, L. (1991). The conceptualization of writing in the confluence of interactive models of development. In L. Tolchinsky-Landsmann (Ed.), *Culture, schooling, and psychological development* (pp. 87–111). Norwood, NJ: Ablex.

Tolchinsky-Landsmann, L. (1993). *El aprendizaje del lenguaje escrito* [Learning written language]. Barcelona, Spain: Anthropos.

Tolchinsky-Landsmann, L., & Karmiloff-Smith, A. (1992). Children's understanding of notations as domains of knowledge versus referential-communicative tools. *Cognitive Development, 7,* 287–300.

Tolchinsky-Landsmann, L., & Karmiloff-Smith, A. (1993). Las restricciones del conocimiento notacional [Constraints on notational knowledge]. *Infancia y Aprendizaje, 62–63,* 19–51.

Tolchinsky-Landsmann, L., & Levin, I. (1985). Writing in preschoolers: An age related analysis. *Applied Psycholinguistics, 6,* 319–339.

Tolchinsky-Landsmann, L., & Levin, I. (1987). Writing in four-to six-year olds: Representation of semantic and phonetic similarities and differences. *Journal of Child Language, 14,* 127–144.

Treiman, R. (1985). Onsets and times as units of spoken syllables: Evidence from children. *Journal of Experimental Child Psychology, 39,* 161–181.

Treiman, R. (1992). The role of intrasyllabic units in learning to read and spell. In P. Gough, L. Erhri, & R. Treiman (Eds.), *Reading acquisition* (pp. 65–106), Hillsdale, NJ: Lawrence Erlbaum Associates.

Treiman, R. (1993). *Beginning to spell.* New York: Oxford University Press.

Treiman, R., & Baron, J. (1981). Segmental analysis ability: Development and relation to reading ability. In G. E. Mackinnon & T. G. Waller (Eds.), *Reading research: Advances in theory and practice* (Vol. 3, pp. 159–177). New York: Academic Press.

Treiman, R., Tincoff, R., & Richmond-Welty, D. (1996). Letters' names help children to connect print and speech. *Developmental Psychology, 32,* 505–514.

Treiman, R., & Zukowski, A. (1988). Units in reading and spelling. *Journal of Memory and Language, 27,* 66–85.

Trick, L. M., & Pylyshyn, Z. W. (1993). What enumeration studies can show us about spatial attention: Evidence for limited capacity preattentive processing. *Journal of Experimental Psychology: Human Perception and Performance, 19,* 331–351.

Tubb, J. (1998). *Canaanites.* London: British Museum Press.

Tunmer, W. E., Bowey, J. A., & Grieve, R. (1983). The development of young children's awareness of the word as a unit of spoken language. *Journal of Psycholonguistic Research, 12,* 567–594.

Tunmer, W. E., Pratt, C., & Harriman, M. L. (Eds.). (1984). *Metalinguistic awareness in children.* Berlin: Springer-Verlag.

Tusón, J. (1999) *El llenguatge* [Language]. Barcelona: Ampúries.

Tversky, B., Kugelmass, S., & Winter, A. (1991). Cross-cultural and developmental trends in graphic productions. *Cognitive Psychology, 23,* 551–557.

Vacheck, J. (1989). *Written language revisited.* Amsterdam: John Benjamins. (Original work published 1932)

Van Bon, M. H. J., & Duighuisen, H. C. M. (1995). Sometimes spelling is easier than phonemic segmentation. *Scandinavian Journal of Psychology, 36,* 82–94.

Van Loosbroek, E., & Smitsman, A. W. (1990). Visual perception of numerosity in infancy. *Developmental Psychology, 26,* 916–922

Von Glaserfeld, E. (1982). Subitizing: The role of figural patterns in the development of numerical concepts. *Archives de Psychologie, 50,* 191–218.

Vygotsky, L. S. (1978). *Mind in society.* Cambridge, MA: Harvard University Press.

Vygotsky, L. S. (1986). *Thought and language.* Cambridge, MA: MIT Press.

Walkerdine, V. (1988). *The mastery of reason.* London: Routledge.

Wells, G. (1999). From action to writing: Modes of representing and knowing. In J. W. Astington (Ed.), *Minds in the making* (pp. 115–140). Oxford, England: Basil Blackwell.

Willats, J. (1977). How children learn to draw realistic pictures. *Quarterly Journal of Experimental Psychology, 29,* 367–382.

Willats, J. (1985). Drawing systems revisited: The role of denotation systems in children's figure drawings. In N. H Freeman & M. V. Cox (Eds.), *Visual order: The nature and development of pictorial representation* (pp. 78–100). Cambridge, England: Cambridge University
Press.

Wittgenstein, L. (1958). *Philosophical investigations* (3rd ed., G. E. M. Anscombe, Trans.).
New York: Macmillan.

Wolf, D., & Gardner, H. (1983). Waves and streams of symbolization. In D. R. Rogers & J. A.
Sloboda (Eds.), *The acquisition of symbolic skills* (pp. 19–42). London: Plenum.

Wright, R. (1982). *Late Latin and Early Romance in Spain and Carolingian France.* Liverpool:
Francis Cairns.

Wynn, K. (1992a, August 27). Addition and subtraction by human infants. *Nature, 358,*
749–750.

Wynn, K. (1992b). Children's acquisition of the number words and the counting system.
Cognitive Psychology, 24, 22–251.

Zebroski, J. (1982). Soviet psycholinguistics: Implications for the teaching of writing. In W.
Frawley (Ed.), *Linguistics and literacy* (pp. 51–74). New York: Plenum.

Zelazo, P. D. (2000). Minds in the (re)making: Imitation and the dialectic of representation.
In J. W. Astington (Ed.), *Minds in the making* (pp. 143–164). Oxford, England: Basil
Blackwell.

Glossary

This glossary lists simple definitions of the technical terms that appear in the book. It should be taken into account that some of these terms are linguistic or mathematical constructs. That is, they are notions that linguists and mathematicians have worked out within particular theoretical frameworks following the methodologies of linguistic and mathematical research. As such, some notions are still the subject of controversy and elaboration.

Abjad: a writing system that denotes only consonants.

Additive systems: numeration systems in which the value of a compound number is obtained by adding the elements. For example, the numeral 12 in an additive system would mean 3.

Alphabet: a writing system that denotes consonants and vowels.

Allograph: variant of a character within a writing system. For example, the different forms of B/b/ b/B. Some allographs have a defined function in the system, as for example, the use of capitals in English to indicate the start of a sentence, proper names, or titles. Another example is the use of a different shape for the same letter when it appears at the end of a word, as in the Hebrew alphabet.

Consonant: the kind of phonemes in which obstruction of the air stream is created in the vocal tract (e.g., /t/, /f/). It is also the character (e.g., T, F) designating such a category of sound.

Core syllable: syllables formed by one consonant and one vowel (CV). There are no languages in which the CV type of syllable is not found. When children are acquiring the phonological system of their language, they go through a phase in which almost all the syllables they use are of this type.

Character: a general term for the elements in any type of writing system. N. Goodman (1976) used this term for referring to categories of marks. It also has a more specific meaning when referring to the units of the Chinese writing system.

Decoding: refers to different things in reading research. This book uses it to mean the transformation of a letter or a string of letters into sounds. The strings of letters can be words or nonwords. Decoding does not mean saying the word or the nonword aloud but just providing an interpretation for the string of letters in terms of its sounds, a phonetic interpretation (Perfetti, 1985).

Determinative: signs that serve to indicate how a sign should be read (usually a logogram) when the latter has different readings (usually a reading for meaning and another reading for sound).

Diacritic: a mark added to a character to indicate a modification in the pronunciation.

Digit: numerals from 1 to 9, from *digitus:* finger. Bidigits are numerals containing two digits (e.g., 54, 76) and *multidigits* are numerals containing more than two digits (e.g., 538, 1279). A digit can also be called a numeral. For example, it could be said that the numeral 324 has three numerals 3, 2, and 4. But, in order to avoid repetition, it is more usual to say, "the numeral 324 has three digits." Note that the term *digital* derives from this word. A digital watch, for example, is a watch that shows time using numerals (digits) instead of using the typical quadrant with hands.

Explicit: fully expressed.

Explicitation: process by which something implied (or implicit) becomes expressed and can thus be observed.

Genetic epistemology: a particular approach to the study of knowledge and scientific thought. It is an interdisciplinary endeavor whose aim is to address central issues of scientific thought (e.g., the notion of causality) by studying how they develop in the child and in the social history of science and thus to provide empirical support to the philosophy of science. The center of Genetic Epistemology was founded by Jean Piaget in Geneva in 1955 and is still active.

Glottographic system: (see Phonographic systems)

Graph: the general term for any unit of any script.

Grapheme: suggested as a technical term to refer to units of writing systems in the same way that morphemes or phonemes are units of language. This book avoids the use of this term, preferring to use the more direct, *letter.*

Ideography: characteristic use of ideograms (or ideographs), or signs representing an idea or a message as a whole (e.g., trademarks).

Logography: characteristic use of logograms (or logographs), or signs that indicate words but that give no indication as to how to pronounce them.

Logographic systems (or lexical systems): systems in which each sign roughly represents what would be called a word.

Morpheme: the minimal unit of grammatical analysis that has a meaning. The meaning can be either grammatical like (-s) in *boys,* which means plural, or lexical, like *boy.* Sometimes it coincides with a word, so the word *boy* has one morpheme, *boys* has two morphemes, and *unacceptable* has three—*un accept able.*

Morphological features: features related to morphology. It includes both the grammatical process resulting in the different forms of a single word that are called *inflections (friends* is an inflected form of *friend, replies* an inflected form of *reply),* and the grammatical process called *derivation,* the result of the movement of a word from one category to another, as when an adjective (*doable*) is obtained from a verb (*to do*).

Morphology: denotes both the part of linguistics that concerns morphemes or the morphemic structure of language and the speaker's internal representation of this structure. Orthographies in which the spelling of words is related to the morphology of a word and not to its pronunciation are sometimes called *morphophonemic.* English is a morphophonemic orthography because the spelling of words remains constant when a morpheme undergoes changes in pronunciation. For example, *medicine* and *medical* are spelled with the same letter *c* despite the different pronunciation because they derive from the same morpheme.

Morphosyntactic: level of language including both morphology and syntax. At this level both word internal structure and the relation between words are considered. Some linguists consider that morphology has such consequences on the relation between words that they should speak about *morphosyntaxis* rather than about morphology and syntax separately.

Multiplicative systems: to arrive at the value of a numeral, the elements should be multiplied. The numeral 12 in a multiplicative system means 2.

Number: a unit belonging to an abstract mathematical system, subject to laws of succession, addition, and multiplication (Pettersson, 1996).

Numerals: symbols for the name of a number '5,' 'five,' 'V,' '101' (in binary), regardless of the medium (written or oral) or the system (decimal, Roman, binary).

Orthography: conventional spelling in a particular language.

Phoneme: the minimal unit of sound that makes a difference in meaning, the segment that makes the difference between *fuss* and *bus* or between *thing* and *sing.* Phonemes are neither pronounceable nor perceived as such in isolation. It is impossible to hear the individual phonemes in a word because the attributes of each phoneme blend (or spill over) into that which precedes and that which follows. A phoneme can be considered as a speaker internal representation of a category of speech sound. This representation disregards the variations that are produced when phonemes are pronounced in words. Almost all the words in every language are formed by more that one phoneme.

Phonetic writing: writing that represents phones, which are units of sound in any language. Within any given language, not all the differences between phones are significant or 'distinctive.' Consider, for example, the English /t/. Although /t/ heard in the word *tear* is physically different from /t/ heard in the word *stair,* the two phones are not significantly distinct. The two phones are allophones of a single phoneme.

Phonetization: process by which writing systems become phonographic.

Phonographic systems: systems in which the individual signs evoke pronunciation. The individual signs are called *phonograms* (or phonographs). A letter is a phonogram. In syllabic systems, they are the signs that indicate a syllable. Phonographic systems have also been called *glottographic* or *cenemic* by various authors. What all these systems have in common is that the signs are related to the sound pattern of words. They differ, however, in accordance with what each sign represents. In *syllabic systems,* individual signs represent syllables. In *alphabetic systems,* individual signs roughly represent phonemes. For example, take the word "egg." To write this word in a strictly syllabic system would require one phonogram. A strictly alphabetic system would need two. The reason it is written with three letters in English is orthographic. It relates to the conventions of spelling in English, but it has no bearing on pronunciation.

Phonological: related to phonology. Denotes both the part of linguistics that concerns the sounds or sound patterns of language and the speaker's internal representation of these sounds. To describe the sound patterns, linguists find it useful to distinguish between levels of abstraction from deep to more superficial. The *phonetic* level is more superficial, more related to details of pronunciation, and includes the inventory of speech sounds used in a language. These sounds are called the phones of a language. The phonetic level is studied by phoneticians, who are concerned with the physical aspect of speech. It concerns the actual articulation of sounds in speech production and such things as height or frequency of the sound wave in speech perception. At the deeper, more abstract level, "we distinguish a set of sound types. These are the phonemes and they do not necessarily correspond in a direct way to any particular physical (phonetic) sound" (Spencer, 1996, p. 8).

Pictography: characteristic use of *pictograms* (or pictographs), or signs that take the form of a simplified picture of what they represent.

Positional system: a system that utilizes the concept of place value. A number notation is said to obey the place value system when the quantity that a digit represents varies depending on the place it occupies in the number (Dehaene, 1997, p. 98). To illustrate, if someone rewrites XXXVI using a positional system, it would look like this: III I I, where the first position from right to left denotes ones, the second five and the third tens. In a place-value notation, there is a privileged number called the base. Base-2 systems are called binary, base-10 systems are called decimal, base-16 hexadecimal, base-20 vigesimal, and base-60 sexagesimal. Successive places in the numeral represent successive powers of the base.

The Mayan system was vigesimal, but to conform to their 360-day calendar it was modified so that successive positions had the following values: $20^0 = 1$, $20^1 = 20$, $18 = 20^1 = 360$, $18 = 20^2 = 7,200$, and so on, rather than strict powers of 20 ($20^0 = 1$, $20^1 = 20$, $20^2 = 400$, $20^3 = 8,000$, etc). Our system of numeration is decimal involving units of different orders, each being a power of ten: $10^0 = $ one, $10^1 = $ ten, $10^2 = $ hundred, $10^3 = $ thousand, and so on. The notational elements are the nine digits (one, two, three ... nine) that are smaller than the base. It is a hybrid multiplicative-additive system and it is positional. The position of each digit in the numeral determines the power of the base by which it must be multiplied (e.g., $45 = [4 \times 10] + 5$; $453 = [4 \times 100] + [5 \times 10] + 3$).

Principles in writing systems: No writing system is strictly phonographic (or strictly logographic, or strictly just any one form); writing systems are regulated by more than one principle. For any literate English speaker, a written word contains not only clues to its pronunciation but also to its grammar: The last letter in 'girls' does not merely represent a sound, but also the plural morpheme. In the texts that are composed every day, people include ideographic signs such as & or %. Even Chinese writing, traditionally considered to be ideographic, is another example of the use of mixed principles in one writing system. The ideographic principle is only one of the principles by which characters can be formed. There are five more principles among which the most common, the one on which 90% of the characters are based, is the semantic-phonetic compound principle. In this class, each character consists of an element indicating meaning and another indicating sound. Moreover, the Chinese writer must observe explicit rules in the order of strokes for each character; otherwise the cursive writing is not legible. This means that Chinese characters can be analyzed as configurations of individual strokes. Many of these configurations recur as the building blocks of more complex characters. Thus, like other scripts, Chinese characters form a system based on double articulation where a number of signs serve a double function.

Script: equivalent to writing system.

Semasiographic systems: contain ideograms or pictograms. These two terms refer to signs unrelated to pronunciation. For example, the ideogram '%' is pronounced very differently in Portuguese, English, or French, but it refers to the same idea. Similarly, pictograms are unrelated to pronunciation and are usually defined as symbols that resemble the object they represent.

Subtraction Principle: to arrive at the value of a numeral, one element is subtracted from another. When a smaller sign appears to the left of a larger sign, the smaller is subtracted from the larger (e.g., in the Roman system IV equals 4, MCMXCIX is 1999) (Petersson, 1996).

Syllabary: a type of writing system whose characters denote syllables, with no deliberate graphic similarity between characters denoting phonetically similar syllables.

Syllables: distinguishable linguistic units. People recognize intuitively the number of syllables in a word: *tea* has one syllable, *table* two. Nevertheless, there is some disagreement among linguists as to the way words should be divided into syllables. One of the issues they discuss is whether certain consonants should be considered as the end of one syllable or the beginning of the next. English, like many other languages, has a system of poetry based on the final part of the syllable. Even very young children recognize that words like *bat*, *cat*, *gnat*, and *sat*, rhyme with each other. It is typically the last part that makes a pair of words rhyme; more specifically, it is the vowel plus its following consonants. Thus, a word like *cat* can be split into two parts /k/ + /aet/. The second can be called the rhyme and the first the onset (see Spencer, 1996, p. 38).

Syntactic: related to syntax. Denotes both the part of linguistics that studies the relation between words used to form sentences and the speaker's internal representations of these relations. For example, being-a-subject-of and being-subordinate-to are syntactic relations between words or groups of words.

Utterance: any stretch of talk by one person, before and after which there is a silence. This is a unit of language use. Utterances may correspond to words or sentences, but they need not correspond exactly to any unit of grammatical analysis (see Harris quoted in Lyon, 1968, p. 172).

Vowel: the kind of phoneme in which no obstruction to the air stream is created through the vocal tract (e.g., /a/, /e/); also, a character designating such a sound (e.g., A, E).

Written words: strings of one or more letters with blanks on both sides. But, the notion of written words is language dependent. In Eskimo, no element except proper names appears isolated; in English, prepositions and articles are written with blanks on both sides; in Hebrew, most of the prepositions and the only existing article are written as prefixes bound to the content word. Even in languages from the same family, like Spanish and Italian (both Romance languages), the same elements "to" and "the" would be written separately in Spanish, *a la playa* 'to the beach,' but together in Italian, *alla spiaggia*.

Author Index

Subject Index

A

Abstraction, 100
Accounting systems, 31
Additive notations, 37, 40
Additive systems see additive notations
Adults' ideas on writing, xxviii–xxx
Adults' perception of speech, 83
Adults as interpreters, 72
Akkadian, 47
Alienation, 205–206
Alphabethic principle, 84–89, 216
Alphabetic correspondences see Alphabetic principle
Alphabetic mapping see Alphabetic principle
Alphabetic writing, xxii
    and numerals, 147–151
    child's path to, 55–89
    developmental view, xxiii–xxv,
Autodicdactic process, 203
Aztec, 43

B

Babylonian, 37, 39
Biology and culture, 222–223
Book –reading, 72
Borrowing, 42, 51 see also adaptation processes
Botocudos, 35
Brahamani script, 28
Bullae, 31–32, 33

C

Cannanites, 48
Cardinality, 100, 120
Cognitive change, model 166–168
Cognitive flexibility, 4
Communicative writing, 69–71
Conceptual environment see domain of knowledge
Consonantal writing, 48
Consonants, 49, 66, 84,192
Constraints, formal 19, 62–69, 145, 216
    on legibility, 62–65, 216
    on writability, 65–69, 216
    on numerals, 145
Constructivist perspective, xxv–xxvii, 95
Conventionalists,14
Core syllables see syllabic hypothesis
Cuneiform, 2, 25, 44–48 see also Sumerian

D

Derivative view, xviii, 98
Diglossia, 50, 202
Domain of development see domain
Domain of inquiry see domain of
Domain specificity see Domain–specific view
Domain, xvi–xviii, 53
Domain–specific view, xvi. 217

E

Education see Schooling
Egypt, 43–44
Elamite, 47